The Silents

The Silents

Charlotte Abrams

Gallaudet University Press
Washington, D.C.

Gallaudet University Press
Washington, DC 20002

Library of Congress Cataloging-in-Publication Data

Abrams, Charlotte, 1929–
    The silents / Charlotte Abrams.
      p.   cm.
    ISBN 1–56368–055–6 (alk. paper)
      1. Abrams, Charlotte, 1929–   .   2. Children of
    handicapped parents—Illinois—Chicago—Biography.
    3. Handicapped parents—Illinois—Chicago—Biography.
    4 Deaf—Illinois—Chicago— Biography.
    5. Chicago (Illinois)—Biography.   6. Deaf—Illinois—
    Chicago—Family Relationships.   I. Title
    HQ759.912.A27   1996
    306.874—dc20   96–19638
                                                       CIP

∞ The paper used in this publication meets the minimum
requirements of American National Standard for Information
Sciences—Permanence of Paper for Printed Library Materials,
ANSI Z39.48-1984

IN 1962, when I was thirty-three years old, my husband Al drove alone to Los Angeles to start a new job with Hughes Aircraft Company. Some months later, my three children and I boarded the Super Chief train to join him. My father had suggested we go first class, just as he used to. At that time, every aerospace company in the West was hungry for engineering talent, and Hughes Aircraft was willing to pay all our moving expenses. It was an offer we couldn't refuse, so it was easy to oblige my father.

The whole family had come to see us off: aunts, uncles, friends, my sister Adelaide, my mother, and my father, who stood stoically with his arm around my mother, his ever present wad of chewing tobacco like a ping pong ball in his right cheek. He took my hand and kissed me. Then my mother gave me a small peck on the mouth (she wasn't big on kissing). Instead, it was my father who would fill with emotion at the slightest provocation. But this time, he stood bravely by.

They would come next year, he promised, for my oldest son's bar mitzvah. Who knows, if they liked the weather, they might leave the snow in Chicago every winter and come to see me. I needn't worry about them. Adelaide would be there to talk for them. And Adelaide would call long distance to let me know how things were.

There were no tears; I would learn later that they had saved them for the ride home. My tears were saved for the ride across the Mississippi the next day, for I had never been more than a bus ride away from their deaf talk or more than a week away from touching my mother's hand.

I wondered how it would feel to keep my hands still for long periods of time. Sometimes I would sign to myself to clear my thoughts as my father did. Now I supposed I would do more of it to keep me remembering. My favorite place to sign alone was in the bathtub before going to bed, when the house was quiet and I could sink into my thoughts.

It was strange to live where nobody knew my parents were deaf. I would find an excuse to tell people and turn ordinary conversation into a personal revelation. Then, of course, the questions would pour out: How did you . . . ? When did they . . . ? Why did they . . . ? Yet, as much as I wanted to enlighten these new acquaintances, I resented their intrusive questioning. They are my parents. How much more do you need to know? They are my past. This is my new life. But, just in case you stumble into some foolish remark about deafness, I think you should know. . . .

But my past was always with me. I would stop deaf people in the street, butting into their business with my fingers to tell them "My parents. . . ." Then I would say good-bye and mentally kick myself for my impertinence.

Years later, my friends—who didn't know how bad my signing was—urged me to become an interpreter for the deaf. I enrolled in a night class to improve my signing skills. Although I was an accomplished fingerspeller (using the deaf alphabet to form words), my limited vocabulary did not include many of the signs that now comprise American Sign Language.

I dropped out of the class three weeks later, asking myself why I had bothered. I was not altruistic, hoping to do good things for the deaf, nor was I in it for the money. Besides, signing had become a complex, visual language with many features that were beyond my grasp. I would come home tired, my brain unwilling to absorb new signs. I told myself that my deaf past should stay where it belonged—buried deep with my childhood.

Then, when my youngest son, Larry, and his wife made me a grandmother, I asked how it had felt to have deaf grandparents. He had never wondered about it, he said. It was as natural to him as breathing. But, as he grew older, he realized that *my* growing up was different from his, and he had wondered about *that*.

So I decided to write this book for him and the others who have wanted to know more about my growing up. But it is not my story—it is my parents' story, for they are the ones I would like you to know. They were ordinary people who lived extraordinary lives.

Mama and Papa, wherever you are, I hope this brings laughter to your eyes and a chuckle to your bellies.

PART

CHAPTER

1

WHEN I was seven, when I had learned to read and write in school, I finally got into my father's head. Until then, he poked me to get my attention, then pointed to things and moved his arms to convey his meanings in signs, leaving me to wonder whether I'd understood all he wanted to tell me.

He had had his problems, too. When I stomped my foot on the floor or squeezed his hand tight to show him I was afraid, he had his doubts, and, in desperation, he'd turn to my mother—who could read my lips—to find the true meanings of my tantrums or fears. My father never learned to speak words as my mother did, and he couldn't read anyone's lips, but he was an excellent fingerspeller and signer. So was my mother, but she saved those skills for my father, complaining once in a while that he was less than a man for not anticipating that one day he'd have to "speak" to his daughters.

But Dick, Jane, and Spot changed everything for me. Printed words on the page began to make sense, and my spelling blossomed. When I could spell enough to learn the deaf alphabet, a new world opened up for me with my father: We could communicate. We could sit at the kitchen table where my father—his fingers flying—told me of Indians and Pancho Villa and the days when he hoboed through America in search of adventure.

He had seen Indians in person, he explained, dramatically fingerspelling each letter and punctuating his tales with a smack of tobacco to the side of his cheek and a slap of his hand on the table. He drew me pictures of Indians—only the heads, never the bodies—with fierce looking eyes, square jaws, and graceful feathers. I would save these drawings in the corner of my dresser drawer and then take them out on rainy days to color. One day—on Independence Day in the summer of 1936—when my finger-spelling had progressed to meaningful dialogue, my father explained his fondness for Indians. "Indians fine people," he spelled, leaving out the little words; deaf language could be understood without them. I spelled back to him in the same way.

"Why Indians fine people?" I asked.

"Quiet, strong, brave," he answered, packing a fresh plug of Mail Pouch tobacco into his cheek. But, at that moment, he changed his mind about his abbreviated language, determined to instill in me the "proper" way to speak. He kept the little words in, and we spoke as if we were writing in English. As I grew older and for the rest of his life, we spoke deaf because he was satisfied by then that I had learned my language—English.

"I saw them out West," he continued. "I saw cowboys, too. I've seen the whole country. I've been everywhere."

I'd never been anywhere. My world was limited to a small part of Chicago—the northwest side and Washtenaw Avenue, to be exact, plus an occasional walk to Humboldt Park, a streetcar ride to Lake Michigan, and exciting trips to the Loop.

My sister Adelaide, my mother and father, and I had just returned from the Loop that afternoon after watching the Independence Day parade on State Street. We lit sparklers in front of our apartment building, and, when it started to rain, Mama made cucumbers, tomatoes, green onions, and sour cream for lunch. We all sat around the kitchen table, eating and trembling with every thunderclap. Adelaide and I heard it with our ears, Mama and Papa felt it through their feet, but we all shook with each rumble. Mama's eyes glinted with annoyance (it was no fun to have the quiet of your body disturbed) and Papa jiggled with laughter at our fright.

4

Papa's laugh came out as a *hmn, hmn*. When he was really convulsed with amusement, the sound came out as a *cough, cough*. Mama always laughed with her mouth closed, her eyes squinted, and her hand to her lips, so the sound came out like Papa's *hmns,* but much quieter and more lilting.

He finished a large Indian head and presented it to me, his *hmns* mingling with the chewing of his tobacco. "I was born in Indianapolis," he said. "You know where Indianapolis is?"

"No, Papa."

"Not far. Near Chicago. I'll buy a map, show you where it is. I'll buy another map and show you where Germany is."

"Why do I need to know where Germany is?"

"Because your grandma and grandpa Herzberg, my parents, came from Germany. Lucky for me I was not born there." Then he put his fingers to his nose to say Germany stinks. I understood the sign. Long before I'd learned to fingerspell, he'd been putting his fingers to his nose to say "you've got something in your diaper" as he marched me to the bathroom, or "why did you get yourself all dirty in the backyard? Don't you know how to behave like a lady?"

I pinched my nose, gave him a questioning look, and crossed my lips with my index finger. "Really, Papa? Is that the truth?"

"Yes, Joe, why would you say Germany stinks?" my mother signed from her chair across the kitchen table, sarcasm spilling from her fingers, her eyes blinking with fatigue from the long streetcar ride home. "You were never there, so how would you know Germany stinks?" Her fingers could poke a hole through my father's talk like a surgeon's scalpel. Sometimes it took only one finger—straight up in the air.

He blinked, a sign that he was wounded by the attack; bending his head so his jaw took on its own sharpness, he spelled, "Listen, Ruthie," followed by a storm of words that I couldn't follow. After telling her off, he turned to me and said, "America is the only place to live. I love America."

"I know, Papa, you told me before."

"The land of the free," he said.

"And the home of the brave," my mother spelled to him. She *hmned* quietly, then smiled. He coughed and smiled at her.

"Did you see the way Mayor Cermak waved to me at the parade today, Ruthie?" he asked, heartened by her smile.

"Don't be silly, Joe. He waved to everyone."

But that didn't stop him. He told me proudly that he had shaken the mayor's hand once, then rattled off the names of aldermen and other Chicago "pols" whose hands he had touched in greeting. I was impressed. My mother stuck her finger in the air.

Her eyes told me that she was tired of his stories. She hummed a couple of times, which was different from *hmning*. You could tell by the tone—it was way down low. And she didn't have her fingers across her mouth. This was the sound of irritation. She hummed as if the vibration in her mouth would keep her awake. But as she nodded, her hands dropped to her lap, and soon her muted, monotonous voice became a whispered breathing.

There was no radio or phonograph or telephone to add noise to our second-floor apartment, only the murmur of my sister's conversations with her dolls—a Shirley Temple, a mama doll, and a "Baby Wet." In the alley, the neighbor's dog howled whenever the peddlar's wagon rumbled past. And in my parents' bedroom off the kitchen, where boredom with Papa's talk had finally driven her to nap, my mother's alarm clock—snug under the pillow beneath her head—ticked rhythmically away.

My father's disappointment at her leaving colored his cheeks and filled his watery blue eyes with unhappiness; his mouth bit down hard on his tobacco. He sat very still.

I played with my fingers on the table, making slight noises while Papa tapped his fingers, drum, drum, drum. The ice box knocked. My sister chattered. Papa was lost in thought. I wished he'd spell; instead, he thought some more and drummed some more, so I drummed along with him. Abruptly his mood changed as if all this thinking were a waste of time. He got up, made me a glass of Ovaltine, and sat down again.

"You know how far Germany is?"

"Very far, Papa. Right?" I asked, plying my fingers through imaginary waters.

"Yes. Right. Did you learn that in school?"

"No, I just figured."

"You figured right. Do you read good in school?"

"Teacher says I learn perfect."

"Good," he smiled, making the OK sign.

I think he smiled more about my fingerspelling than about my progress in school. I tripped over my P, mistaking it for K; Papa's eyes flickered with impatience but he listened, his cheeks bulging with tobacco. The pink flesh around his eyes crinkled when he smiled. "It's important you read. To read newspapers every day. To learn all about America."

"I try."

"I know you try. Do you say your ABCs good? Do you speak clearly for the teacher?"

"Definitely, Papa," but I gave up on that word and changed it to "sure."

"When you were a baby, I worried you wouldn't hear sound right, so everybody hearing came to the house to talk to you and your sister. Everybody! My father, my mother. . . ." He ticked off the names, spelling and saving them on his fingers to remember: first his parents, Grandma and Grandpa Herzberg, on his pinky, then Helen, the neighbor, on his ring finger, and so on until he ran out of fingers. Then he started over to include Mama's family, Grandma and Grandpa Rubenstein and all the aunts until he ran out of fingers once more.

I could see his hands were tired. He rested his elbows on the table to support them. If I had been a better signer, he would have given up on the fingerspelling and finished his recollections in signs, which would have taken half the time.

"When you were a baby, I was rich. We had a fancy apartment and a nurse for you. I smoked expensive cigars. You know how much they cost?"

"Lots of money, I bet."

"And we had a woman to clean the house. Mama liked that." He sat quiet for a while, his eyes taking in the scratched linoleum, the cracks in the ceiling, and the broken oven door.

"Babe Ruth is the greatest ballplayer of all time," he said, changing the subject. "I saw him homer out of Sox Park." He swung his arms across his chest. "And Jimmy P . . . sky."

"Who?"

He spelled it, but it made no sense to me. As I grew older, I would learn that he was a terrible speller, especially with the long names of the Polish players. But at the time I blamed my poor understanding of his fingerspelling, so I pretended to know what he had spelled. His knowledge of stats was perfect, however: Who had earned the most runs. Who had won the league in what year. He kept notes on these facts, followed the papers, and talked about baseball with his friends in front of Charlie Mandel's candy store at the corner of Washtenaw and Potomac. If they weren't around, he collared a hearing neighbor and took his pen and paper out of his shirt pocket.

I could always spot him from our living room window by the way his fedora tilted back on his head and the way he politely turned his head aside to spit out his tobacco juice.

Papa began talking about his father. He said something that escaped me and opened his hand in a "what do you think about that?" motion, but the peddlar was leaving the alley just then, and I—tuned in to the sounds my parents couldn't hear—interrupted his storytelling.

"Peddlar's selling oranges. You want?"

"In the rain? Silly man. He should stay home. It's not fair to

8

the horse to get him all wet. He treats the horse like dirt. No, you drink your Ovaltine. Don't go. Tomorrow we'll walk to Mr. Laykin's store to buy oranges."

"So what about Grandfather Herzberg?"

"Grandfather Herzberg died when you were a baby," he said, slitting his throat and pointing his finger down to indicate six feet under. "Very sad!"

Adelaide took her dolls into the living room. Papa watched her go, blinking his eyes in disappointment. I was the only one left to listen, so I asked, "Are you sorry he's dead?"

"Sorry for him—that he lost all his money. He should never have taken the chance and bought a candy store. He threw his money down the toilet." His fingers turned down again.

"Mistake, huh?"

"Big mistake!"

"Too bad."

"Yes," he sighed. "I lost money, too. In the stock market crash of '29, the same year you were born."

I thought if Mama were sitting next to us, she'd say, "why does Sha (she called me 'Sha' because 'Charlotte' was too hard for her to say) need to know this? Don't talk to her about dying and money. You fill her head with foolish talk." She would slap her head with her hand and circle her finger around her ear.

But Mama was still asleep, and Papa was free of her admonitions. "I went to a deaf school," he said, changing the subject as if he had decided this talk was indeed too sad.

"I know. I saw pictures in your album. You wore a fancy uniform."

"I didn't like it there."

"Why? It must be fun to wear a uniform in school. I wish I could wear one."

"Silly. The uniform was only for that picture, to send to the family."

"Which is your family?"

"You don't remember!?" He asked astonished. "Well, sure, you don't remember Grandma Herzberg. She's dead, too. But you know the uncles: Jerry, Sam, Dave, Lou, Jake," he counted on his fingers.

"That's right, I forgot. And Flora, too," I touched a finger.

Sometimes I forgot Papa's brothers because they lived on the other side of town, so I hardly ever saw them, but I always remembered Aunt Flora because she was a carbon copy of him—blonde, blue-eyed, and deaf. And because he always complained to Mama about something stupid Aunt Flora had done.

"Did Aunt Flora go to deaf school like you?"

"She was still a baby when I went to school. She went to deaf school after I ran away. Flora's a spoiled brat."

I nodded my head in acknowledgment that baby sisters could be stupid and troublesome. I understood his running away because sometimes I had the same feelings. "Were you happy you ran away?"

"Oh yes. I got to see exciting things. I got to see America. I had a good life on the road," he smiled, moving his arms wide to show me that he'd been everywhere.

"Just like a hobo, huh?"

"How do you know about hobos?" he laughed.

"I saw it in the movies. Did you hop boxcars?"

"P-l-e-n-t-y," he spelled with great exaggeration.

We had been talking for most of the afternoon, and he had been drawing Indian heads all the while. He got up to fill his coffee cup and drank quietly. When Mama's alarm clock rang, I stared off into their bedroom. He saw me and poked me to get my attention. As he turned and saw her standing behind him, he held his hands out palms up. "What?"

"Where is Addle?" she asked. That was the name she used for my sister because "Adelaide" was filled with sound traps. My father reduced it to an "A," just as he reduced my name to a "C."

He pointed to the living room. She walked to the stove, turned on the gas, and started dinner.

Papa's eyes followed her movement to the stove. Her back was turned to him, but he smiled anyway. She must have felt it because she curved her hips in that secret way she had of sending him messages that made him smile or wink or blush or puff up his tobaccoed cheeks. He got up, folded his newspaper under his arm, and poked me again. "I don't need adventure now," he laughed. "I have Mama and you and Addle." He left everything out of her name but the A. Then he walked up to my mother, patted her on the shoulder, and left the kitchen to sit at the dining room table until dinner was ready. She *sighed* a tired sigh— her hand still on the soup spoon—and straightened her hips.

By the time dinner was served, I'd forgotten the uncles' names and Germany and dead Grandfather Herzberg and remembered only Aunt Flora because she was deaf and his hobo days and boxcars and running away from school. And *I* sighed, wondering how it was that these two people, whom I loved so much, came to be mine.

CHAPTER

2

SOMETIMES, WHEN my parents' fingerspelling
and lipreading made me feel too different, I pretended I belonged to someone else. Lying sleepless in my bed
next to Adelaide, I willed the bed to rise and lift me into the air,
through the ceiling and out the hard brick of our apartment
building and across the dark sky, like a magic carpet, until it
landed in a pink-and-white bedroom. A gentle voice would come
through the white painted door. "Honey, will you look in on the
girls and see if they're finally asleep?" said the mother. The father
replied, "Don't fret, dear, they're as snug as a bug in a rug."
Then he'd say, "Goodnight, my honeys," or something equally
enchanting. I filled in the details with scenes from whatever
movie I had last seen.

I usually included Adelaide in my magic carpet rides, but when
her personality aggravated me too much, I abandoned her in my
dreams—left her hanging onto the edge of the bed, hoping she
would fall into the great darkness below. But morning would
come, and I'd know that Adelaide—her face a mirror image of
mine with her straight black hair and dark eyes—belonged to me
and we belonged to this family who walked down Washtenaw
Avenue, listening to people say, "Here come the Silents."
Sometimes their Yiddish would come tumbling out, and they'd
call us the "Shtimmers," which was Yiddish for "silents," but for
a long time I didn't know that and thought they were calling us
some awful name.

I suppose it was just their way of identifying us, but it was always on the tip of my tongue to say, "I'm not deaf and neither is my sister." But the truth was, we were all deaf in a sense because that's the way it is when you live with deaf people. You talk like them and open your eyes wide to take in their fingers, and you stand straight and tall because you know everyone's looking. Every shrug, every flick of your hand, every bat of your eye takes on meaning. Nothing goes to waste. And everything's got to show.

We showed everything. Adelaide and I pretended we didn't care. We waved, grinned, and pulled our faces up and down and sideways. When we ventured outside that world, riding the streetcar where nobody knew us, we played our deaf game, pretending to be deaf until, finally, the lady (there was always some lady hanging onto the strap) turned to another passenger and said, "Will you look at those adorable girls? Pity they're deaf!" Then we'd giggle and speak real words, and Mama would yank my hair so hard I thought I would faint. She didn't like our fooling other people. But Papa would grin, get up, and offer his seat to the embarrassed lady, *hmning* all the while. The lady would smile back in thanks, puzzled by his little noises.

Papa's gentlemanly ways made Mama puff up like the queen on a playing card. So impressed was she with my father's manners that she would forget our impudence, stick her nose three inches higher in the air, and move her primly gloved fingers delicately as she spoke to Papa. She kept her mouth shut because it would have spoiled the mood for strangers to hear her monotonous drone.

Sometimes we would ride past the Loop, transferring to the South Side streetcar, to visit Mr. and Mrs. Epstein and their son, Bobby. We ate fried chicken and cole slaw and lifted our fingers in talk, stopped to eat, and lifted our fingers again. And when our stint with the grownups was finished, we'd rush to Bobby's bedroom, cross our legs Indian fashion, and talk a blue streak as if all normal talking had been stored up for ages.

13

I felt sorry for Bobby because he was an only child. I wanted to ask him, "Doesn't it drive you crazy not to have anyone to talk to or hear you?" but we never discussed our deaf mothers and fathers. It was an unspoken bond between us, and, although I knew from the way Bobby stared at me that he was baffled, too, we never said, "So why do you think this happened to us?"

We'd go home late at night, leaving Bobby all alone in his tiny bedroom with nobody to giggle with or tell scary stories to. Our legs heavy with fatigue, Adelaide and I would be too tired to play the deaf game. We'd tug at Papa's arms until he finally looked down and saw our begging fingers; then he'd hoist us up and lay our heads on his shoulders. All the talking would stop because Papa's arms were busy, and all the staring would stop, too.

The next thing I'd know it would be morning, and Mama would slam the icebox door after taking out the milk and clop her two-inch Cuban heels across the wooden floor, through the dining room and living room and into our bedroom to wake us up. "Sha, Addle, wake up. Time for school," she'd shout, unaware of how loud her voice sounded in the privacy of our home. Or if she was aware of it, she didn't care.

The South Side was as far as we ever went except for Brookfield Zoo, where Yiddish talk disappeared amid the flat, twangy Midwestern voices. We would meet our parents' friends with their hearing children and play the deaf game, which was a lot more exciting with a dozen kids pretending to be deaf. Like seals stuck to the sides of a rock in the ocean, whooping and flapping our fingers, we pretended it wasn't necessary to explore with each other what it meant to have deaf parents.

Mama was too intimidated by our numbers to protest, so she'd fluff her blanket out, anchor her shoes on the corners, and greet her friends Rosie and Sarah, who spoke in a monotonous voice just as she did.

Papa would be off with the other men who never spoke. (Strange that the men never spoke, never used their voices or read lips like the women. Why? I wondered.) They played baseball and whooped and hollered noises that made no sense.

Navy Pier was closer than Brookfield Zoo—only one streetcar trip away. While Mama and Papa talked with their deaf friends, Adelaide and I tapped our toes to the honky-tonk music sung by a man in a candy-striped jacket and straw hat. He bellowed out "I met a million-dollar baby in the five-and-ten cents store." It was glorious to hear, and I didn't care if Mama and Papa couldn't hear it. This was for Adelaide and me. And as long as I stayed far enough away from the deaf talkers and rode the carnival rides, I was just like all the rest of the talking crowd.

In school, I was not deaf. I blended in with my classmates until one day, when I was nine, my mother came to school at recess, her dark eyes searching for me in the crowd, straightforward and intense because they worked harder to take in everything around her. I waved my hands above the crowd so she could see me. She caught my wave, held her nose high, opened her mouth, and said, "You forgot your notebook," only it came out "you fogot your nobuk." When she left, everything changed.

Carol, my classmate, looked at Mama's back and grinned, her Shirley Temple curls bobbing up and down as she laughed. She opened her mouth and said something as I jumped over the hopscotch lines. Then she said it louder, and it finally struck me. Black spots formed in front of my eyes. I turned to Carol and said, "My mother is not crazy. She's just deaf!" But Carol wouldn't shut up. She kept chanting it, so I hopped back to number one box and in an instant was on top of her, pulling her golden curls until her blood-curdling screams jolted the other girls. Somebody yelled, "Get the teacher!"

I left her there—my sensation of victory turning to fear of punishment—and ran out of the schoolyard, heading for home. The black spots wouldn't go away. One of them blotted out my vision as I crossed Evergreen Avenue. A driver slammed on his brakes and opened his mouth; his lips moved, but I couldn't make out the words. Mr. Laykin ran out of his grocery store, yelling, "Vat's da matter mit you? Didn't you see the car?!" Embarrassed at my close call, I smiled painfully at him and ran until I reached our apartment building. Slamming the door of the vestibule behind me, I sat down on the marble steps.

"Now what?" I thought. "I can't go upstairs. Mama will punish me for fighting. She'd know. She'd take one look at me and see I was a mess." The ribbon she had pinned to the side of my head that morning had slipped down to my cheek and was filthy with schoolyard dirt. Rivulets of blood trickled down my skinned knees to my ankles.

What if she was crazy? What did I really know about being deaf and dumb? People sometimes used that expression when we walked in the park, and, because it had hurt my feelings to hear someone call her dumb, I had never wanted to injure *her* by asking for an explanation.

While I planned on running away or stretching out on the marble to die—I hadn't decided which yet—her Cuban heels came clopping down the steps. True to her punctual, ordered life, she had looked at her watch as she did every morning, seen that it was ten-thirty, and was coming down for the mail. A small voice inside me said, "This isn't too clever of you, Charlotte. If you really didn't want Mama to know, you wouldn't be here." I made a move as if to run, but my legs stayed locked together in pain. She stopped two steps above me, looking as I had imagined a crazy person would look—her black hair coming loose from the bun on the back of her head, her dress disheveled and smelling of furniture polish, her cheekbones protruding sharply.

"You're not in school," she said.

"What a crazy thing to say," I thought. "Doesn't she see me sitting here all shriveled up and scared?" I didn't answer her.

"Why aren't you in school?" she demanded. Before I could come up with an excuse, she screamed, "My God, something's happened to you!"

She hauled me up the stairs like a pile of wet wash and sat me in the kitchen chair, got out the iodine, and poured hot liquid fire over my legs.

"Ow, ow," I pulled at her hands.

"Never mind ow, ow. Did you fall?"

"No."

"Did someone hit you?"

"No."

"Then *you* hit someone. Why were you fighting? Why do you make me nervous?" meaning that I was driving her nuts.

"Ow, ow."

"Hum, hum," she muttered. She walked away from me as if I weren't there and made Ovaltine, still humming. That's what she did when people made her nervous. She didn't hmn. She hummed. When genuinely aggravated or terrified, she made sounds like a coyote. She poured a cup of Ovaltine and shoved it in front of me. "Drink," she ordered, drumming her fingers on the table.

I obeyed her, but it tasted awful. Brown bits of undissolved Ovaltine lay on top of the milk, and the inside of my mouth was gritty with dirt; the mixture tasted like baby powder.

She kept drumming and humming, her face pinched with anger. I could hear the clock ticking under her pillow, and the ice box made knocking noises until I thought my ears would explode. I opened my mouth and formed the words, "Carol said you're crazy. It isn't true, is it?"

She opened her eyes wide and made noises so quiet I thought I'd gone deaf myself. Then she started laughing so hard her body shook all over. I thought she had missed what I said. Maybe I hadn't formed my lips properly.

"Crazy? Crazy?" she shouted. "Don't be silly. Carol is wrong. Deaf people are not crazy. Well, maybe some are. How do I know? Just like hearing people can be crazy. Like the janitor who lives in the basement. I told you he was crazy. Something wrong with his head. Gassed in the war. Do you understand now?"

I started to cry. Having been reassured that she wasn't crazy, I should have been laughing, but tears dribbled down my face, so I pretended my knees were still smarting from the iodine. I pointed to them. "Ow, ow."

"Never mind ow, ow," she said softly. "Change your clothes. I'll take you back to school."

"No. Teacher will punish me for fighting."

"Teacher won't punish you. Listen, if I tell you a story, will you go back?"

"I'm never going back to school! And I'm not interested in your fairy tales," I said, waving my arms in signs.

"Silly. Of course, you're going back to school. This is a good story. A true story. So you listen," she continued. "When I was a little girl, I could hear."

"When?!"

"Three, four years old. Can't remember for sure." She threw her arm over her shoulder to show it was a long time ago.

"What happened to you, Mama?"

"I got sick with typhoid fever, and it made me deaf. I remember hearing the cows moo on the farm in Russia, but by the time I came to this country, it all disappeared," she said, waving her arms dramatically.

"True story?"

"Yes. True story," she said, tucking her hair back into her bun. "And if you think my ears will come back, they won't."

I did think it. And I wondered what it would be like to sit across the table and hear her perfect voice. I also wondered what it would be like to wake up one morning and not hear a thing.

"I'll always be deaf," she continued. "But I learned my lessons in a school just like yours, except I learned in a special class. That's where I learned to speak all over again and read lips. So you see. . . ."

18

But I wasn't listening anymore. I was thinking of stupid Carol and what I'd like to do to her and the other ignorant people who stared at us when this was nobody's fault. A sickness. That's all! Then Mama got up and said, "So that's the end of the story. Let's go back to school."

She put the dirty cups in the sink, walked me to my bedroom, and pulled a dress from my closet.

"What about Papa?" I asked, pulling her face in front of me.

"Same thing," she answered with a bobbypin in her mouth, making the words even flatter. She took the bobbypin out and stuck it in the bow and onto my hair. "When he was a baby, he got sick and lost his hearing."

"Is this really the truth?"

"Yes, yes. Now we're going!"

She took my hand and dug her nails into it as if I'd escape. Her own hands were trembling as we walked down the steps and out the vestibule. By the time we reached Evergreen Avenue, her trembling had stopped.

With a grocer's apron tied around him and a pencil behind his ear, Mr. Laykin came running out of his store again. He was about to say something to Mama, probably to rat on me for my carelessness. I began to shake. He opened his lips wide so she would be able to understand, but, on looking at me, he changed his mind and merely tipped his finger to his forehead to say hello. In that moment, Mr. Laykin earned my undying gratitude for not spilling the beans.

Mama nodded her head, hello, and we resumed walking, only her grip on my hand was tighter now. "Ow, ow," I yelled, but she never saw my mouth.

When we reached the schoolyard, she said, "Wait," almost in a whisper, and walked into the building herself. When she returned and took my hand again, we walked through the quiet corridors. All the law-abiding, decent children were sitting in their seats in their classrooms. I felt like a criminal walking to my doom. Passing the principal's office, I tugged at Mama's sleeve.

"What?" she asked.

"Here," I pointed to the principal's door.

"Don't be silly," she responded, pulling me along until we reached my classroom. Mrs. Miller, my teacher, opened the door a crack, stuck her head out, and whispered, "Everything will be fine, Charlotte." Then she spoke right in front of Mama's face: "I'll speak to Carol, Mrs. Herzberg. Thank you for telling me."

Mama let go of my hand, turned, and, without another word, walked down the hall and out of the building. I sat down at my desk and put my fingers on my reader, but my eyes began to blur with tears. My best friends, Shirley and Hannah, smiled at me from their desks, assuring me with a shake of their heads and a deaf "OK" that, no matter what had happened, I was not to blame.

Hannah herself had weathered the bewilderment of my mother's voice when she first rang our doorbell, triggering the dining room light that alerted Mama and Papa to visitors. She would tell me many years later that it had frightened her to hear my mother say, "Who is it?" It made no sense to her that Mama would even bother to say it since she couldn't hear Hannah's answer. But she told me, "I got used to it."

And Shirley loved my father's magic tricks so much that strange voices and sounds could never keep her away.

CHAPTER

3

M AMA'S NERVES could be shaken by the slight-est display of disobedience or the breakdown of her ordered days. If she expected to cook trout for Thursday's dinner and Mr. Solomon, who owned the fish store on Division Street, told her he had no trout, she would stare at his lips with disbelief. Then she'd turn to me and ask, "What did he say?" as if she didn't know, and I'd have to fingerspell to confirm Mr. Solomon's disappointing news. She'd say "He makes me nervous" and walk out in a huff. Having to change her menu threw the whole day off schedule and put her into a blue funk.

It amused Papa that she would put such stock in the promises of tradesmen, for he never did. He'd cast a shadowy eye at anyone who rang our bell light, whether they were selling insurance or a magazine subscription.

"Ruthie," he said one morning, when she complained that the drugstore ran out of her favorite hand lotion. "That's the way life is. You can't trust anybody."

I suspected his mistrust was aimed especially at hearing people because he once commented to Mama that "a hearing man had done him dirt." I never heard him say that about a deaf man.

Aware that I had thrown Mama's nerves out of whack on a grand scale, I walked home with Adelaide that afternoon, carefully this time, because I was in charge of her between home and school. Mama's rules. This was in accordance with her interpretation of the *Bible*. It was her answer to Cain's question. Besides, my knees were stiff as boards by then.

"What happened to your knees?" Adelaide asked as we crossed Evergreen Avenue and reached Mr. Laykin's store.

"Nothin'."

Mr. Laykin was behind the counter, putting cans in a brown paper bag. I tried to walk casually past his window in case he looked up, but my knees wouldn't cooperate. I hopped on the one leg that didn't hurt as much until we were out of his sight. Adelaide jumped over the cracks in the sidewalk until we reached our building, and we walked up the stairs to the second floor landing. I reached for my key, but it was gone.

"Knock on the door, Adelaide."

"*You* knock on the door," she demanded. "You're the one who forgot the key."

"I can't," I answered, "I have to pee." I closed my legs tight in a scissorlock and sat down on the steps.

Adelaide pounded. She started to cry because she knew it would take Mama forever to figure out that the pounding that rumbled through the door and to her feet was not a truck going by. Or somebody hauling furniture up the stairs. Even if Adelaide ran down the stairs and rang the bell, Mama wouldn't see the light because she'd be reading a book, her nose stuck between the pages. "Doo doo pants," she shrieked. The same words she used to shame me out of our double bed when heavy sleep kept me from the bathroom. She pounded until the skin on her knuckles turned red. Every time she pounded, her dress rose to reveal her underpants. They were still dry. Mine were already soggy.

Mrs. Goldberg, who lived on the third floor, shouted down from her apartment. "Vy do you do dis to Mama? Poor dear. So come up and have milk and cookies. Leave Mama alone."

"I can't, Mrs. Goldberg."

"Vy?"

"Just can't." I knew if I unlocked my legs, everything would come dripping down.

Adelaide yelled, "I'm going!" She crossed over me and climbed the steps to Mrs. Goldberg's milk and cookies and bathroom. When Mama finally opened the door, my legs were wet. She peered into the darkness. "Where is your key? Where is Addle?"

I pointed upstairs, ran to the bathroom, and slammed the door. Mama was shouting through the door, "You forget your key every time."

That wasn't true. I was conscientious about carrying my key, fiddling with it in my pocket to be sure it was there, for I knew the consequences of forgetting it. I was sure the neighbors heard her screeching at me; the whole world didn't need to know I wet my pants. I may have forgotten the key once a month, even twice. Not always, like she was shouting.

Looking at the wall next to the toilet, I discovered that Papa had made pretty designs with his tobacco spit. His aim was less than perfect when he bent over the toilet to get rid of the stuff. Brown cat, brown flower, brown elephant. I dropped my underpants on the floor and shoved them into the corner, where I hoped they would be invisible, and opened the door, ready for more scolding, but Mama merely stood there, a fresh pair of underpants and my play pants in her hand.

"Sorry," she said, standing tall and determined to weather my latest "make her nervous." No matter how hard I tried her patience, she never hit me. The closest she ever came to a slap was to raise her hand to my cheek, then turn her palm back to her breast in shame.

"Take them," she offered, handing me the clean clothes. "Call your friends. Play Monopoly. You had a bad morning, and I'm truly sorry." Her hand rubbed a circle on her chest in the sorry sign.

Getting nothing more than a single shriek was a miracle. I tried to think of words to make her feel better, but nothing came out. "Okay, Mama," I said and left her standing in the bathroom doorway.

SHIRLEY, HANNAH, and our friend Timmy came up the back stairs, and together we played a ferocious game of Monopoly. The way we played it was far from expert. Our knowledge of real estate and finances was limited, but we improvised, emulating the older children in the building with mock deliberation, acquiring utilities, and going to jail as if we had real understanding. The board was kept on our back porch except when it rained or when Mama demanded space to hang out the laundry.

I was glad that Mama had suggested we play a game. It gave me a feeling of normalcy, even if my stiff knees distracted me from astute negotiations. Shirley smiled, signaling that everything was all right, that she hadn't abandoned me and gone over to visit Miss Curly Locks and talk behind my back. Timmy stared at my knees and asked, "What happened?"

"Nothin'."

Shirley smiled even wider and winked. Timmy won so much property that afternoon that money kept falling out of his socks, where his bank was stashed. We girls closed up the board in despair. Timmy was a born property owner. It had been months since anyone else had won anything except a small property here and there.

Mama brought us some lemonade. Later she came out with Papa's wet underwear and hung it on the lines above us. She looked truly sorry, smiling at Shirley and Hannah, and teasing Timmy with a pull of his red hair. She seemed to be trying to forget, to go back to a time when nothing made her nervous. Yet, her eyes could transform worry into a smile in an instant. They were faster than her mouth or her hands. She had passed this trait on to both Adelaide and me. It came with the territory. It was deaf talk.

Because there were no more vacant chairs, Mama sat on the steps to Mrs. Goldberg's porch. She hugged her knees. "Did you play a good game?"

"I won," Timmy said, pointing to himself and spelling "won."

She smiled. "You save the spelling for Mr. Herzberg," she said, only it came out Mushter Hushbug. "I can understand you. How is your mother?"

"Fine," Timmy mouthed.

"Did Sha teach you the alphabet, too?" she asked the girls.

"A, B, C . . ." Shirley and Hannah spelled.

Mama watched patiently until they finished. "Very good," she applauded.

Yes, it was very good. Better than a poke in her daughter's heart by an unfeeling child, her eyes said. It was good they drank her lemonade, and it was good they smiled and played on her back porch.

She searched for more words to make them feel at home but settled for another smile. Then she lifted her head and shouted up the stairs, "Mushes Gobug, send Addle down." She clasped her knees and waited a moment. "Maybe she didn't hear me."

"I'll call her," I said.

"No, I'll go. You stay. You play."

PAPA CAME home from work at dinnertime with his shirt hanging out of his pants and his hands grimy from moving rental chairs all day. Mama announced, "Go home, everybody," while Papa went into the bathroom to wash and spit his tobacco out, but they hung around until he came out again. His shirt was now tucked back into his pants, and his hands and face were still damp from washing.

He looked at my knees and spelled, "Hurt?" I spelled, "Not any more." Then he waved hello to my friends and said, "Ome" and shooed them away. It was the only word he knew how to say except "coffee," which came out "awfee."

They smiled at him and shook their heads no. So he played every magic trick he knew. He had a knack for it, like the circus clown at Navy Pier, animated, a show person, hands moving nimbly. He pulled a penny from Hannah's ear, wrote a riddle on my slate for Shirley, and arm wrestled with Timmy. But it wasn't enough. It never was, so they waved their hands, begging for more, until Timmy's mother called him with her own shrill noises from her back porch. Then they all walked down the back steps to their own apartments.

At dinner, Papa tired of being interrupted by Adelaide, who insisted he watch her talk, grunted a warning, his mouth full of roast beef. She pulled her fingers down to her fork and started eating slowly, picking at peas and surreptitiously dropping them into her lap and onto the floor. She was a finicky eater, skinny, half my size, but only twenty months younger. She had my knock knees, but hers were more pronounced since there was less flesh to hide them.

"I learned a new song in school," she persisted. "Listen," and she opened her mouth again. But Papa grunted a final warning and—his fork waving menacingly—fingerspelled, "No talking while eating. A (he slapped an A on his cheek) needs her food."

"She wants to sing me new song she learned," I boldly interrupted. He relented and smiled, and Mama smiled, too.

"Which song?" my mother asked.

"Red Sails in the Sunset," Adelaide spelled so Papa could see.

"Very nice," said Mama, as if she were familiar with the melody.

After the song, Adelaide and I talked with clenched teeth between mouthfuls, watching to be sure that Papa did not realize we were conversing. Our words came out mumbled. Finally, when Papa was engrossed in his dinner, forgetting to look up, we carried on a normal conversation. Eventually, Adelaide was through with her meal, at least as through as she wanted to be since half of it was discarded in a pile under her chair. Mama would know, of course, but it would be our secret because, no matter what was said, Adelaide would remain skinny.

Because Papa was known to strike anyone who hurt us, accidentally or not, I worried that Mama had told him about the incident at school. I was convinced Carol would have her head smashed against a brick wall if he knew. Well, perhaps not Carol, but certainly her father, man to man. Papa did not take the time to write his anger away. It rose too quickly for him to reach for a pen. The magician could turn deadly if he felt wronged. "He talks with his hands," my mother always said, meaning he punched, which seemed funny to me because it was the only way he talked.

Mama cleared the table and began washing the dishes. I went out to the porch to sit and think. I was confused about so many things—human beings, their behavior, my own shameful dreaming that I belonged in another family, and thoughts about murdering Carol.

Black clouds began to form in the sky. I called to Adelaide, "Tell Mama it's going to rain."

Mama came out, pulled the clothes off the line, and handed them to Papa, who sat in a chair, making his lap wide so he could lay the clothes flat in a pile. Adelaide sat on the steps leading to Mrs. Goldberg's back porch.

"That one is an elephant," Adelaide spelled to Papa.

"Which cloud is that?" he asked.

"The one over the pepper tree in Mrs. Kaplan's backyard."

"Never," Papa said. "It's a giraffe."

"It's a hippo!" my mother declared. "You're all wrong."

"You're absolutely right, Ruthie," Papa grinned.

I searched the clouds but could find no hippo. Why did Papa give in so easily? I poked him to tell him that, but by then the rain had started to come down and turned the sky all to black.

Mrs. Goldberg's voice thundered down the stairs. "Tell Mama I heard vat happened in school today. Tell her I think that brat should be in reform school."

"I'll tell her what you said, Mrs. Goldberg."

"What happened in school today?" Adelaide asked.

"I told you, nuthin'!"

Mama inquired, "Who are you talking to?"

"Mrs. Goldberg."

"Nice lady. Does she talk good, without an accent?"

"She talks like Grandpa Sam."

"Just like Zadie?" she asked, using the Yiddish word for "grandpa."

"Yes. Did you talk like that before. . . ." I looked at Adelaide and stopped, but I was thinking, when Mama could hear, she must have talked like him, with a Jewish accent. So if she could talk now, she'd sound like Mrs. Goldberg. I mean if she could really talk. Not like a deaf person talks with flat "mushes" for "Mrs." So did she get rid of this accent in school? Did she speak Russian, too? First Yiddish, then Russian, then English? She must have been a genius.

I hadn't told Adelaide about the incident at school. Apparently, Mama hadn't told Papa, either. He looked too content with the laundry in his lap and a cigar in his mouth. He puffed a big smoke ring and poked Mama, and his fingers flew fast.

Mama signed, "No, Joe. Not tonight. It's too late. The children have school in the morning. Maybe tomorrow. What's playing?"

"A western," Papa signed. "Easy to follow the action."

No need to read lips, I knew. A horse across the screen, with Hoppy on it and his sidekick close by, and the rustlers hiding behind the bushes; then a shootout right before the ending. Forget about words on the bottom in the silent movies. There weren't that many around anymore.

Once in a while Rudolph Valentino appeared on a special matinee, and Mama made pleasing noises at the screen. Occasionally, while Hoppy searched for the outlaw, Mama made loud whispers that echoed through the theater. Somebody

28

always asked, "What was that?" It was Mama telling us and *everybody* who the murderer was because she was bored. Adelaide and I would have to poke her in the ribs to be quiet.

AFTER PAPA patted the blanket around us, shook his finger at me, and said, "No peeing" and I answered, "I promise," Mama switched off the bedroom light. I rolled over to Adelaide's side of the bed and whispered, "When Mama was a little girl, she could hear. Just like us, and by the time she was almost your age, before five, she couldn't hear anymore. She had a horrible sickness. Typhoid fever. And she probably spoke Russian!"

Adelaide sat up and pulled the blanket around her like she was shivering, but it was warm in the bedroom. "You're lying," she protested. Pulling my part of the blanket with her, she lay back down and pretended to sleep.

"I am not. If you don't believe me, ask her yourself."

"I will not," she whispered.

CHAPTER

4

MAMA DID not get nervous again until I was eleven. This time it had nothing to do with me; it happened because Adelaide got locked in the basement. Mama, after getting the spring clothing from our storage bin, had locked the door behind her, thinking Adelaide was with me. When she carried the clothes up the stairs and saw me sitting alone, she started yelling "Addle," but Adelaide didn't come.

I heard my sister yelling "Help, help!"—as if she were in a tunnel far away—and followed the sound to the other side of the basement door. I shouted, "Wait, Adelaide," and ran for Mama, who was already searching the streets, her hand shading her eyes from the sunlight so she could see into all the nooks and crannies of the neighborhood—in the alley, behind Laykin's store, everywhere. She turned and saw me, and it registered instantly that I knew where Adelaide was.

"In the basement," I mouthed and spelled at the same time. She was too far down the street to see my mouth, so I spelled in wide movements.

She came running back, put her key in the door, and practically fell on top of Adelaide.

My sister had many nightmares over this episode, bolting upright in bed like a zombie, yelling "Mama, Mama," in her sleep. When I got tired of walking to Mama's bedroom in the middle of the night to tell her Adelaide was crying, I would put my arms around her to quiet her. She doesn't remember any of it now.

This incident prompted my mother to keep us in her protective sights at all times. We were not allowed to play in the street or on the front sidewalk so we played kick-the-can in the backyard. I stowed my skates in the closet, hoping that Mama would soon come to her senses. In the meantime, I learned to jump rope with Shirley and Hannah under the poplar trees along the back fence.

We were not permitted to go to the movies alone, so Mama accompanied us to showings of Hoppy, Roy Rogers, and Flash Gordon that summer. We made a day of it. First, we walked through Humboldt Park to see the rose garden, Mama's hat brim shading her eyes and her good hand holding Adelaide's; her bad one—the one that was kicked by a horse when she was little—held mine. It would be truer to say I held hers because I had to grab on to two of her fingers. She had no feeling in that hand, and the two fingers were as icy as snowballs. From there we meandered along the lagoon, watching the rowboats, and out of the park and on to Division Street, where the Vision Theater was.

I began to question Mama's intentions when the Vision announced an evening give-away: one dish for every ticket purchased. Lured by the prospect, she changed our attendance from afternoons to evenings, altering her daily routine, leaving Papa to fend for himself when he came home late from an extended work shift.

Occasionally, Papa came with us. On those evenings, our bounty would swell to four dishes. She hurried us through dinner, washed and dried the dishes, and left a film of kitchen cleanser in the sink to soak up food stains until we returned. By the end of the summer, she had collected a set of company dishes, a set for Passover, and a set of silverware. She served the ladies of her bridge club a lovely luncheon on rose-rimmed plates with elegant matching flatware. Having filled out her collection of dinnerware, she finally loosened her grip on us, allowing us the pleasure of visiting Hoppy alone and without her whispered intrusions.

Then, without warning, Mama's euphoria over her glamorous dishes turned into a fit of nervousness, the kind that made her hum all day. It happened soon after her luncheon for the bridge club.

Mr. Trask, the landlord, a decent man, my father called him, who had a kind face and always a pleasant nod for Papa, strode onto the lawn one afternoon and found us jumping rope. There must have been six girls lined up near the fence, pounding together, right foot, left foot, with chorus line perfection. His jaw opened wide and emitted a loud wail. It was a pitiful sight. Our ropes fell to the ground in one combined silent glide. But it was too late. A summer of dedicated rope jumping and bike riding had turned the grass into a thatch of brown clumps. Mr. Trask left in a huff.

Rumors flew through the building. Mrs. Goldberg told Mama that at least three sources had reported that Mr. Trask was going to cement the yard in: the neighbor in the next hallway, the one over Mr. Laykin's store, and the old lady who came out of her apartment only to take in her milk bottles and who spent most of the day listening to gossip on her back porch.

"Over my dead body," my mother grumbled to Mrs. Goldberg.

Despite my mother's willingness to die over the issue, three men in overalls appeared one day with cement, water, and wheelbarrows. Mr. Trask trailed behind them, hands in pockets, looking triumphant while everybody in the building hung over their railings to watch the excitement. Except Mama. She hung over the railing and told him it was a dirty shame the way he treated us. What kind of man was he to take away a lawn? Her shrieking provoked a wave of murmurs along the back porches, causing Mrs. Goldberg to shout down from her landing, "Tell Mama it's no use."

I told her.

"Why would Mrs. Goldberg say that?" demanded Mama.

"Why would you say that, Mrs. Goldberg?" I shouted.

"Because it's no use, tell her. Already it's too late!"

I told her. Dejected, she sat on the steps and hummed. Then, with renewed fervor, she rose and hung over the railing and shouted again. Mr. Trask looked up at her and said, "You don't understand, Mrs. Herzberg."

Then Mama blinked her eyes at him like Carole Lombard. I couldn't believe it. Did she really think she could persuade him to order the wheelbarrow off the property with a bat of her eyelashes? I pulled at her sleeve.

"What?"

"He's not looking any more, Mama."

"I know that!"

"Then why are you blinking?"

"I'm doing no such thing."

But she was. And I believe she knew exactly how it affected Mr. Trask, even if the wheelbarrow stayed firmly in place. I'd seen her blink her eyes at the butcher once. It had worked: She got a fresh chicken. This time, however, cement poured onto the soft earth and hardened before she ever had a chance to complain to Papa.

PAPA DIDN'T care. He came home from work that day tired and out of sorts. He spit a big hunk of tobacco into the toilet as I washed my hands for dinner. Another animal blossomed into existence on the wall. Then he left the bathroom, pulled out his *Tribune*, and waited for dinner. Between stirring the soup and checking the oven to make sure the roast hadn't burned, Mama stood over him and poured out the whole story of her crushing failure to save our grass. All Papa did was bob his head up and down in sympathy and gnaw on a fresh plug of tobacco.

I knew he didn't mean to be callous. He simply didn't have time for this sort of sadness. Every morning he left for work at the Roosevelt Chair Company before I got out of bed. I'd hear him walk down the steps, slam the hall door, and go out into the street, frequently while the street lamps were still lit.

33

On Saturdays when he didn't have to work, he'd be off to a ball game. He'd put on his straw hat to protect the bald spot on his head and walk out the door, promising to be back in time to take us to Pierce's Deli on Division Street. If he didn't make it back on time, Mama prepared a cold supper—salami, dill pickles, tomatoes, and macaroni salad—and left his in the ice box.

Mama didn't care if he went to a ball game. But she did care that his teeth were permanently stained from Mail Pouch tobacco and that he stained the bathroom wall.

Having lost the battle of the backyard, having nowhere to go with the anger still churning in her belly, she turned all her energy into winning the battle of the brown wall. For days—even weeks—after the backyard fiasco, she lifted insistent fingers in front of Papa to get him to quit chewing. Ignoring her, he stuck his head in the *Tribune*.

One day, when he had had enough of her nagging, he signed, "Get the hell off my back, Ruthie." At least, that's what I thought he signed. Mesmerized by the look of his anger, the way his face turned wine red and his cheeks got hard like walnuts, I missed most of the signs.

Taken aback at his display of emotions, Mama quietly turned to her reading, and, as far as I know, never mentioned it to him again. As long as we lived on Washtenaw Avenue, the wall next to the toilet stayed brown, even when it was painted green one year and pink the next. And Mama muttered under her breath every time she scrubbed the toilet bowl.

When winter's snow arrived and turned our backyard into a fairy land, my mother looked longingly at its beauty. I wished that it could stay that way forever, but I knew that, come spring, my mother's sensibilities would be assaulted once more by the ugly concrete. As the snows melted, my mother's humming grew louder while she hung the clothes on the line.

Mama had lost two battles that year, but Passover was coming, and she set her mind to the task before her.

CHAPTER

5

MAMA ASKED the crazy janitor to bring up the Passover dishes from the basement. She wrote her request on a piece of paper in her dainty penmanship, crossing her *t*'s perfectly and writing "Mrs. Herzberg" so ornately that the *H* curled under the rest of her name in a big swirl. The janitor lugged the dishes up the stairs, one carton at a time, while Adelaide and I were sitting on the landing. He got as far as the step below us and smiled. I shivered, but he smiled again, and I let him pass. Mama gave him a tip, smiled at him, and shooed us into the apartment. "Poor man," she said to herself. She unwrapped the dishes, put them in the sink, and started washing them.

The light went on in the dining room, and, before Adelaide opened the door, I knew it would be Zadie. He lived only two blocks away on Fairfield Avenue, so he visited every Tuesday and sometimes Wednesday. When he was really worried about something, he would show up every day dressed in a three-piece suit— even in the hottest weather—because he would be on his way home from the synagogue. His face was permanently red from the heat stored up in his clothing, and his gray mustache with its little red hairs drooped from the sweat.

Zadie, or Grandpa Sam, was Mama's father. He and Mama had almost the same conversation each time he came to see us. Zadie, staring straight at her, nose to nose, so she could read his lips, would say "Nu?" "So? Everything fine?"

"Sure, Pa, fine, fine."

"Joe is working?"

"Yes, Pa. Joe is working. Don't you worry."

"You have money?"

"Yes, Pa."

"Nu. Good-bye."

"Good-bye, Pa."

He'd turn to Adelaide and me and ask, "Nu, everything is fine?"

"Sure, Zadie, everything is fine," although we really didn't know if everything was fine, trusting that my grandfather's and mother's eye-to-eye contact had told Zadie more than we would ever know.

I loved Zadie. He was the spitting image of Maurice Chevalier, the good-looking French singer who had charmed me from the screen of a darkened movie house. He and my mother shared the same high cheekbones, dark eyes, and intense look when speaking. Because his English was poor and I knew only a few words in Yiddish, our conversations limped along. But all he had to do was smile, say "Nu," tweak me under the chin, and I was a goner.

Zadie asked, "Is Papa coming to shul?"

"No, Zadie. He can't go to synagogue." Then I changed *synagogue* to *shul* so he would understand. "He has to work, but he'll come to your house after work."

He didn't look happy when I told him, but I knew that if Papa had gone to shul, he would have lost what he called a decent day's pay. I was never sure if it was a decent living. The Roosevelt Chair Company had plenty of rental chairs to deliver, and sometimes Papa worked both Saturdays and Sundays, but many nights, when I went to the bathroom, I found Papa sitting at the dining room table, writing numbers on pieces of paper, throwing his hands up in the air, scrunching the papers, and throwing them on the floor. Sometimes, he'd fingerspell to himself with his hand down his side, the way he did when he didn't want anyone to see him thinking out loud.

36

"Rent, gas, lights. . . ." That's all I ever saw, but it clearly worried him, and taking off a day would only mean more paper scrunching.

"But Mama and Adelaide and I are coming to shul," I assured Zadie.

"Nu. You coming to shul?"

"Yes, Zadie."

"Goot." And then he left.

Mama got down on her knees and searched the floor for bread crumbs—the biggest taboo for Passover. It was the last of her rituals. She had cleaned, scoured the stove, wiped out the ice box, and thrown out every piece of bread except the loaf that Papa insisted on eating. He told her he wasn't about to change his ways. He'd been doing it for years, even in his mother's house, so she carried the bread by the tips of her fingers like it was poison to the farthest corner of the pantry and stuck it on a shelf so high that the rest of us wouldn't be tempted.

She spotted a couple of crumbs under a kitchen chair—Adelaide's no doubt, the remnants of last night's dinner—and triumphantly hauled them off to the back porch. Then she wiped the dishes and put them in a special place in the pantry.

When Passover came, I got up later than on a school day, opened the back door, stood on the porch in my bathrobe, and watched the Polish kids walking down the alley to school. They constituted less than ten percent of Von Humboldt's school enrollment. My Polish friend, Dolores Bankowsky, confided that Jewish holidays were a treat for her because Mrs. Miller couldn't put in a decent day's teaching with most of the students gone. In our absence they read stories and discussed the Jewish holidays.

One day Dolores wondered out loud why the Jewish kids got to take off on their holidays as well as Christmas. I couldn't give her a reasonable answer except to say it wasn't our doing. The school just closed on Christmas. Figuring there had to be another answer, I had questioned Mama about it.

37

"We didn't ask for it," she said. "Tell Dolores that this is a Christian country. Everyone else just tries to fit in."

Mama had matzo and jelly on the kitchen table for breakfast. I hated matzo. It tasted like cardboard to me, but Adelaide—in the strange ways of finicky eaters—ate it like she was eating chocolate eclairs. Mama soaked mine in milk. I managed to work it down my throat, but it still tasted like cardboard except it was soggy now.

"Get used to it. We've got eight days of this," Mama sighed.

When a deaf person sighs, you know there's true unhappiness behind it. It's a dead giveaway, just as Papa's grunt is a sure sign of anger. It was then I realized Mama hated matzo, too.

I went into the bedroom to get my new clothes. Adelaide was already dressed and prancing around like a princess. She wore a powder blue creation with a matching beanie hat.

"You look very pretty," I said.

"Thank you," she bowed.

Mine was navy blue with a sailor collar and a three-pointed navy hat with white trimming. I pulled the dress over my shoulders and let it slide down. It felt like silk. I knew it wasn't, but it felt just the way Aunt Marian's dress did when she let me touch it one New Year's Eve. She had come to show Mama her fancy dress, and we all went into appropriate rapture over the fineness of the material.

Mama was an expert on material. She had sewn hats for a living until she met Papa. Her specialty was to sew a rose or comparable froufrou on the hat brim. I was in awe of her abilities. To be able to sew with one cold, lifeless hand stuck under a hat while she plied her needle on the top seemed a remarkable feat.

She could do other wonders with that lifeless hand. She could hold a dinner plate on top of it while spooning food into it with her good hand and never drop it. And when she wasn't using it, she kept it quiet in her lap.

But this year she didn't sew our dresses. She had complained to Mrs. Luft, her very close friend, that she couldn't handle the eyestrain, so Mrs. Luft obliged Mama with her handiwork.

"You look very pretty," Adelaide returned the compliment.

"Thank you," I bowed.

But Mama was the prettiest. She came out of her bedroom dressed in a dark blue shirtwaist with pale gray flowers all over it. Her hair was swooped up off her forehead, and a dark blue hat covered her head. In the shadow of the hat brim, the sharpness of her cheekbones was quite pronounced. The hat had a rose on it, and I recognized it as one of the hats she had made when she worked at the hat factory. I kept looking at the dress, thinking I'd seen it before, but I couldn't remember where.

"Is it new, Mama?"

"What difference is it?" she said.

And then I remembered. It was Aunt Marian's. She had worn it one afternoon while visiting. I was ashamed to think that Mama spent all that money to have Mrs. Luft make us new clothes.

"It's very pretty, Mama."

"Thank you," she bowed.

TOGETHER WE walked down Washtenaw Avenue across Evergreen, then to Hirsch.

The neighbors, also dressed in their holiday clothes, filled the sidewalk. Some said hello; some waved their hands and nodded. Mama nodded and walked tall. Papa always said she was beautiful, showing his feelings through his fingers and flashing eyes, but this time I knew it. The blue dress with the pale flowers made her elegant.

We held hands because Mama occasionally zigzagged when she walked alone. Something to do with signals from ear to brain, Zadie had told me. Mama held Adelaide's hand, and I held on to Mama's two right fingers. Sometimes we didn't hold on tightly enough, and the three of us would zigzag down the street, mimicking the drunks that staggered out of the tavern on North Avenue late at night.

WE WERE the only family I knew that went to two "shuls." Because Grandma Bessie, whom I called Bubbi— Yiddish for "grandma"—didn't like Zadie's shul, she went to her own on Talman Avenue. That meant we had to visit Bubbi first, spend some time with her in the ladies' section upstairs, then leave quietly and walk to Zadie's shul on Maplewood. It was only a block away.

The Talman Avenue shul was boring, but Mama preferred it because her mother was there. Bubbi always saved her a seat. Adelaide and I had to hustle to find a place to sit because Bubbi didn't appreciate our bad manners; she'd just as soon we didn't show up. She never forgave me for bringing candy on Yom Kippur, the holiest of holy days, when everyone fasted and was dying of hunger. Impertinently, I sucked loudly on a peppermint with no regard for their misery. One of Bubbi's neighbors leaned over and whispered something in Yiddish to her. I knew she was criticizing me because she kept pointing to me and clucking her tongue.

Bubbi retorted sharply with all the energy her fat little body could muster, her Yiddish spilling out like BB gun pellets. I didn't understand a word of it but figured that, whatever sin I had committed, Bubbi was nevertheless solidly in my corner. But then, as if it were her duty to upbraid me, she turned to me and scolded, "On a fast day, you bring candy to shul?"

"But Bubbi," I said, "Mama says I'm too young to fast."

"Still, you don't bring candy to shul."

Then the neighbor turned to whisper something to another lady, but all I heard was the word "shtimmer." I think that's what Bubbi was really angry about. I had embarrassed her in front of the congregation when I should have been a model child of Bubbi's shtimmer. It was my obligation to show them that, despite Mama's "unfortunate handicap," Bubbi could be proud of us. I had disgraced my mother's family. I had brought shame to the Rubensteins.

I SPENT an uncomfortable ten minutes in the ladies' section, remembering my previous sins and trying to be good. Meanwhile, Mama opened her prayer book, repeated some Hebrew words she had memorized, and skimmed her fingers over the pages as if she knew what she was reading. It always sounded like "zzzzz," just the way she intoned over the Sabbath candles on Friday night. On Friday nights, however, she draped a shawl over her head and fell into a sort of trance, the light from the candles shining on her face, as if she were in another world.

Nobody looked at me this time. I knew candy was also forbidden on Passover, and I had promised myself not to embarrass Bubbi again. I sat as long as I could at the Talman Avenue shul out of respect for Mama and Bubbi; finally, I poked Adelaide. We slipped down the stairs and out of the shul into the bright sunlight. Shirley, Hannah, and Timmy were cracking walnuts on the side of the building. I thought, how stupid of me. I could have brought walnuts and sucked on the insides and never have brought shame to Bubbi. I resolved to get clarification on what one could eat in a synagogue and on what holy days one could do it. After a quick hello, Adelaide and I dashed to the Maplewood shul.

I LOVED Maplewood. It was small, dark, and crowded, and nobody ever gave us a dirty look or made us go upstairs to the ladies' section. We walked down the carpeted aisle, smiling back at the men who peeked through their shawls to smile at us. Zadie stood in the third pew, all wrapped up in his prayer shawl, turning his head every so often, waiting for us to come into view. Seeing us, he smiled and spread his prayer shawl wide, and we tucked inside its dark folds and inhaled the odor of his mothballed suit. He zzzed for a long time, bobbing back and forth, and then he let us go, pointing to two empty seats across the aisle and motioning for us to sit down. It made me feel very important, especially in our new clothes. I could hear Zadie whisper to his brethren, "Yes, mine." And he smiled across the aisle at us.

Even Adelaide—who couldn't sit still in a seat for more than two minutes—enjoyed Maplewood. We loved the bobbing back and forth, with everyone in their dark suits and hats and white shawls with fringes. Once in a while someone boomed loudly; at other times, someone almost sang the words. Although we didn't understand their prayers—we had just begun our Hebrew lessons—we enjoyed the singsong of the words and bobbed our bodies forward and backward, keeping time with the mood.

Each man seemed to proceed at his own pace, flipping pages in the prayer book from time to time. Sometimes they'd wait for the others to catch up. At other times they just kept zzzing until they were finished.

When the Rabbi began to preach to the congregants about money, everybody looked around to see who would lift a finger to pledge a dollar. At that point, Adelaide and I left. It wasn't fun anymore.

6

W E PASSED the big Catholic church on Washtenaw and Hirsch. It was scary, although I didn't let on to Adelaide. Mama had cautioned us a dozen times never to go into the church. It was all right to smile at the nuns, she informed us, because they were people just like us under their fancy wimples. Adelaide refused to believe Mama's reasoning, however, and trembled whenever she passed them. I never put one foot on the steps that led to the large double doors of the church. Nevertheless, I wanted to see inside and find out how those people prayed. Were they allowed to bring food to church? If so, what kind?

A couple of nuns walked by, smiling at us. Adelaide grabbed my hand tight.

BUBBI AND Mama had already come home from shul, and everybody except Zadie and Papa were at Zadie's house. Aunt Selma was ordering everyone around. She and her husband, Eddie, lived with Bubbi and Zadie and, I suspected, ruled the house. Aunt Marian and Mama's third sister, Nettie, from Janesville, Wisconsin, were busy preparing the Seder food. The uncles were lolling around the parlor, talking, immune to Aunt Selma's dictatorship. Men had special privileges on holidays, apparently. Their duties were to pray, eat, talk, and rest.

When Papa knocked on the door and Uncle Leon—Aunt Marian's husband—let him in, they all waved and went back to their talking. Papa, looking quite handsome, had changed into his suit and wore his hat in the house because that was the holiday custom. The fedora covered his bald spot, so only the thin strands of hair around the bottom of his head showed. The other men wore the traditional skullcap, the yarmulke, but Papa didn't approve of yarmulkes. I don't think he approved of shul or Passover, either. In fact, I'm not sure I ever saw him in shul.

For all I knew, his own brothers also shunned the yarmulke, but then we had never spent a Jewish holiday or set foot in a synagogue with them. I suspected that one or two of the uncles even had a Christmas tree on Christmas. When I asked Mama once about my suspicions, she darted a look at Papa and whispered, "Well, when your Bubbi Herzberg died. . . ." Then she spied his eyes on her, and, even though he couldn't make out her words, she declared, "Don't be silly!"

Aunt Selma propped two pillows in the dining room chair reserved for Zadie, waved hello to Papa, and scurried back to the kitchen for more serving dishes. Papa sat down next to the rubber trees in the parlor. He smiled, waiting for someone to take out a piece of paper and start up a conversation with him. When nobody did, he pulled out the *Chicago Tribune* and checked the baseball scores. He looked terribly lonely, so I went over to him to chat about the rubber trees that stood like a forest behind the sofa. They were so big, they reached the ceiling. I'd seen Zadie climb a ladder just to trim the top. But Papa wasn't interested in rubber trees. He kept looking over at Uncle Eddie, who was half Papa's size and wore a pointed beard on his chin. Uncle Eddie didn't look up, so Papa signed to me, "Babe Ruth hit another homer."

"That's wonderful," I answered.

"If I'm not working next Saturday, I'll take you to a ball game," he offered.

"Okay," I accepted.

He kept looking at the uncles, and, when nobody glanced back, he stuck his head back in the sports page. Finally, Uncle Eddie looked up. Papa waved, and Eddie came over and sat down next to him. They wrote back and forth. Papa was very animated, his voice *hmning* in obvious agreement, but I wasn't privy to their discussion because all the talking was on paper. Eventually Uncle Eddie remarked out loud that the Depression was lifting and wrote it at the same time. Apparently, they were talking about Papa's work. Uncle Eddie, like Zadie, was always worried about whether Papa was making a decent living.

When Zadie arrived, everybody took their seats. The table was filled with Seder books, wine, and empty plates. On a platter in the middle of the table loomed a huge pile of matzos. Zadie settled into his pillows and stuck his nose in the Seder book. Papa began sipping his wine, causing the top of his head to redden. The more he sipped, the more he smiled. Mama, sitting between Papa and me, threw him several dirty looks but to no avail. Papa was bored. Unable to read Hebrew, or talk, or interrupt anybody with paper writing, there wasn't much else he could do.

Everyone else appeared bored, too. Zadie was the only one who was *zzzing* away. The others were carrying on private conversations quietly so they wouldn't interfere with Zadie's concentration. Straining my ears to listen, I caught snippets of gossip about second cousins I didn't know and Tante Freda and Uncle Moishe, who must have been very old, because Aunt Selma related that he had to use a cane now.

My cousins, imprisoned between their parents, were picking away at the matzos and spreading the crumbs in circles around their plates. The grownups continued their gossip, paying no mind to the impromptu table decorating. Little cousin Paulie was sneezing and wheezing because of his chronic allergies. Uncle Morrie—Mama's only brother—and his wife, Ethel, both pulled out handkerchiefs to wipe Paulie's nose. As Paulie honked into the handkerchief, Zadie looked up, prompting Paulie to stop blowing. Everybody stopped talking at once as the service screeched to a halt. Then, as if on cue, everyone picked up their Seder books and started reading aloud.

Mama looked at the pages and pretended to read, but she knew the story of Moses and the exodus of the Jews, so she softly intoned the story to herself.

I was getting hungry, but there was only matzo to eat. When I tried sipping the Manischewitz, Mama slapped my hand, so I played face games with the cousins. I tried hard to cross my eyes but without much success. Cousin Albert laughed. Aunt Nettie pinched him, and he stopped laughing.

Uncle Eddie said to no one in particular, "We'd better get the show on the road before Joe gets into his cups."

I couldn't fathom why Mama asked me to tell her what Eddie said just then, but she must have had a sixth sense about it. I fingerspelled Eddie's words to her instead of saying them in order not to disturb anyone. Mama's eyes opened wide, and she spelled something fast to Papa. He just kept smiling and waved his hand, "Whatya worried about?" Then his eyes got steely cold, and Mama spelled, "Don't make a scene."

After what seemed like hours of interminable *zzzing*, Zadie put down the book and said, "Goot," and all the aunts and Mama got up and went to the kitchen to carry in the food. While we ate, Zadie walked around, stretching his back, stopping to tweak a cousin's nose and plant a kiss behind their ears. He stopped next to me and asked, "Mama is fine?"

"Sure, Zadie, she's fine." He tweaked my nose and slobbered a big kiss on my neck. When he stopped at Papa's seat, he poked him and held his hands palms up, asking the same thing. He used no words. He just stood palms up, but the question was clear. Papa nodded two strong nods, which meant "fine." Zadie patted him on the shoulder, pleased with the answer.

THE MEN, including Papa, went back into the parlor to talk, but, when I peeked out the kitchen door where we ladies were cleaning up, they were all fast asleep, their belt buckles

46

opened and their stomachs hanging over their pants tops. When I told Mama, she *hmned* a laugh and pronounced, "Lazy." Aunt Selma and Aunt Marian laughed, too.

Bubbi seemed exhausted, so she went to her bedroom to rest. I noticed that she had rolled her stockings down to her ankles, and her feet were swollen and red. When Mama saw her leave, her face turned anxious, and she said something quick to Aunt Selma. I didn't hear her words because she whispered, but Aunt Selma did. She responded, "Ruthie, it's getting worse. I don't know what we're gonna do." Then she changed the subject, and the women launched into a heated debate about the duck. Was it too fatty or was it just right?

Aunt Nettie had brought the duck from Janesville. I'd seen it alive on Zadie's porch a couple of days before, but it was mysteriously dead by the time Bubbi had to cook it. Nettie defended her choice. "I thought it was perfect," she said, fingering a gold locket that nestled in the curve of her chest. "What do you think, Marian?"

Mama swerved her head back and forth to see their lips. "What did Marian say?" she asked, drying a dish.

"She said the duck was too fatty," Selma said in front of Mama's face. "Whaddya think, Ruthie?"

"I think it was a little fatty."

Swerve, watch, bend upward, downward, and around, when all I had to do was sit in the middle and be bombarded with the chatter. Mama missed a lot of it.

Aunt Nettie wasn't much bigger than the duck and, in fact, always reminded me of a bird with bright eyes and arms that flapped while she talked. "*Hmph*," she grumbled, and went into the dining room, still fingering the gold locket. Mama missed that, too, but I didn't think it was important to tell her.

"Selma, do you still play the piano?" Mama asked, flexing her fingers as if she were about to play "Chopsticks" on the spinet. Of course, I knew she couldn't. Well, maybe she could. It wasn't difficult. Adelaide and I had learned to do it, but what was the point of Mama even asking?

"Of course," Aunt Selma said, pursing her lips, which she shouldn't have done if she really wanted Mama to get her words. "I don't play often. But when I come home from work, I like to play a little. Why are you asking?"

"I thought maybe you didn't need it anymore."

"Of course, I need it. Well, I don't *need* it. I *want* it."

"That's fine," my mother said as if she'd been holding a hot potato.

I was sitting in the middle of this exchange, too, but not understanding any of it. What was the significance of Aunt Selma's red face, Aunt Marian's and Aunt Nettie's nervous twitches, or Mama's questions? Abruptly, they dropped the subject and moved on to another topic.

By the time the dishes were done, the men had roused from their sleep, and it was time to go home. Just then, however, Bubbi started wheezing so loud that everyone ran into her bedroom. "Call the doctor," Aunt Selma commanded. "She's having another attack."

Uncle Eddie started haranguing Aunt Selma. "Listen, Selma, one day, by the time the doctor comes, it'll be too late. You have to learn to give her the needle."

"I can't do it," she moaned.

"I'll teach you. We'll practice with an orange first. You'll get the hang of it."

"Never," she cried, plopping down into the bedroom chair, her plump hips oozing over the sides.

Bubbi's wheezing diminished, and her body grew quiet under the covers. Aunt Marian poked Aunt Nettie; Aunt Nettie poked Mama; Mama poked Aunt Selma; and we all tiptoed out into the kitchen.

"Listen, Selma, . . . " began Aunt Marian, white faced and shaking as she leaned against the sink.

48

"Listen, Selma, . . ." repeated Aunt Nettie, fluttering her hands while the locket swung back and forth.

Listen, Aunt Selma, I thought, if it's going to make Bubbi better, do it. I don't want it to be too late.

By then the doctor had arrived and was surrounded by shrieking bystanders. He set his medical bag on the kitchen table and took out a stethoscope and needle. Aunt Selma groaned and wiped her hands on her apron. The doctor walked quietly into Bubbi's bedroom and shut the door.

Selma, Marian, Nettie, Mama, and I sat tight at the kitchen table. Nobody spoke. Nettie's mouth looked like a fish's puckered mouth instead of a bird's beak. Uncle Eddie paced the kitchen floor and stroked his beard, muttering, "In an orange, we'll try," but nobody listened, and I didn't explain his words to Mama. She sat too rigid and unseeing for me to even get her attention.

Uncle Morrie's round face began to sweat. "We should listen to Eddie," he advised, "or else it will be too late next time." But the aunts sat like stones.

The doctor must have injected Bubbi with something magic because she stopped wheezing and fell peacefully asleep. Zadie's ashen face relaxed and he waved his hands. "Leave Ma sleep," he said, pointing to the front door. "We'll talk more tomorrow. You should all go home."

So the exodus began. Only Aunt Selma and Uncle Eddie remained to discuss oranges and syringes. We could hear them arguing as we walked down the front steps.

Mama was so unnerved that she didn't say a word on the way home. She hung on to Papa with her bad hand and held Adelaide with the other, never paying me any mind. I lagged behind until it got too dark to walk alone, and then I grabbed Papa's other hand. We took up the whole sidewalk until two women approaching us from the opposite direction created a standoff. We split up to let them pass, then grabbed hands again. I heard one of the women mutter, "They're shtimmers. They don't know any better."

THE NEXT morning we went back to Zadie's. Bubbi was still in bed.

"Better?" Mama asked Zadie.

"Same."

Mama hummed her frightened sounds.

"She'll be fine," Zadie said. "Don't worry."

Mama walked into the living room and ran her hands over the top of the piano, still humming. Aunt Selma was sitting in a dining room chair, listening to Uncle Eddie still haranguing her about oranges and syringes. Mama just kept stroking the piano and humming.

For six days we came back to see Bubbi, and every day the doctor stuck her with something magic. On the seventh day, Aunt Selma had mastered the orange. Now it was time to try it on Bubbi, Uncle Eddie persuaded her.

"I can't do it, Eddie. I can't. In the orange is one thing, but not in Ma." She burst out crying.

Mama walked away, wringing her hands. Zadie wrapped his fingers around mine, and we walked into the parlor where the window faced the street. He pulled his phylacteries out of their velvet pouch, put them on his forehead and arm, took his prayer book, and started praying, his eyes taking in the traffic below. I stood next to him and stared at the traffic, too. I could hear Aunt Selma's crying and Uncle Eddie's encouraging words and Mama's humming.

"Do you want to pray?" he asked, looking down at me.

"Do I have to have those things on me?"

"No. Only boys do."

"What do I say?"

"Say anything you want."

"Please, God, teach Aunt Selma to use the needle."

50

"That was a very good prayer," Zadie said, slobbering a kiss on me.

Aunt Selma mastered her needle technique the day after my prayers. She stuck it directly into Bubbi's arm. I wasn't there to see it, but I felt powerful, knowing I'd contributed to her courage.

THAT PASSOVER, I asked Mama while we sat on a bench in the park across from Zadie's house. "What's wrong with Bubbi?"

"Bubbi has asthma," she answered, her hat brim resting on the upper ridge of her cheekbones. Sometimes she couldn't say her esses right, but this time it was perfect.

"Will she die?"

"Everybody dies one day. Don't drop your matzo on the ground."

"It's for the bird," I responded, pointing to a robin who had pushed his way through an army of pigeons. Smart looking and red breasted, he seemed courageous, having none of Aunt Nettie's flighty ways.

"Well, all right," she laughed.

The robin wouldn't touch the matzo. He lifted his beak and waddled away. I poked Mama, who turned to face me. "See, he doesn't like it either."

"Is it singing?" she asked, luring the bird toward her with her own matzo crumbs.

"Just a little chirp."

"I remember," she said softly.

"You remember the sound of a bird?"

"I remember Bubbi's voice."

"Like you remembered the cows?"

"Yes," she murmured.

"How about chickens? Did you hear them?"

"Don't be silly. If I heard cows, I certainly heard chickens."

"But do you remember how they sound?"

"They have a funny sound, don't they?"

"I guess so. I guess it's funny."

"I think," she mused, "I remember them on the boat. Somebody on the boat had chickens, I think."

"What boat? What boat?"

"The boat I came on to America when I was five."

"But you said you stopped hearing when you were three, maybe four. You must have heard it on the farm."

"Yes, I must have. I remember now. Aunt Nettie said I couldn't hear a thing on the boat. We had to lie. Pretend we were both scared of the inspectors, so we didn't talk. That way they'd think I was just shy. They didn't let deaf people off the boat, you see."

"Why?"

"Why are you asking me all these questions? Get your sister from the swings. The sun is too bright. Let's finish our walk."

"How about getting an ice cream?"

"No ice cream until after Passover. You were good this Passover. You didn't break any rules. I'm proud of you."

TWO MONTHS later, when the matzos were gone from our pantry and the Passover dishes had been stored back in the basement, when I had had my fill of ice cream, Bubbi died. I was standing on the sidewalk drawing hopscotch lines when I saw Uncle Eddie walking down Washtenaw. I knew something was wrong because if he needed to tell us something trivial, he called Charlie Mandel's store, and Charlie sent someone with the message. If it was important, he came in person. Hands in his pockets and head bent to his chest, he walked slowly past the drugstore and Mr. Laykin's. He didn't notice me watching him until he was in front of 1309; then he straightened up and walked quickly to 1315. He took me by the arm and led me into the vestibule. "Listen, honey, your Bubbi is dead, and I need you to tell Mama, okay? It's not something you write on a piece of paper."

I wanted to cry but had no time to think about it. I walked up the stairs with Uncle Eddie and found Mama in the kitchen reading the newspaper. I poked her on the shoulder. She turned to look at us, surprise oh her face at seeing Uncle Eddie. I could have used the short way—put my finger across my throat and point my fingers down, but it didn't seem right to assault her with the harshness of the sign, and I didn't want her misreading my lips. Nor did I want to be the one to tell her, but Uncle Eddie couldn't fingerspell or sign. Nobody in the Rubenstein family could fingerspell. They didn't have to, they always told me. Mama could understand them, they said.

"Uncle Eddie says that Bubbi . . ." I fingerspelled.

She smiled at first, then realized before I could finish why he was there. The house filled with her screams. I shivered. All that practicing in an orange hadn't helped. Neither had my prayers or Mama's humming.

WE ALL congregated at Zadie's house to comfort him and wait for news of the funeral arrangements. Uncle Eddie was put in charge. Returning from the funeral parlor, he told us, "She's stone cold, resting on a slab of ice, so there's plenty of time for Nettie to get here." Aunt Selma's plump body crashed to the kitchen floor in a heap. If Mama had heard Uncle Eddie's words, she, too, would have fainted, but I didn't repeat them.

PAPA TOOK the day off to go to Bubbi's funeral. He put on his good suit, reached into a drawer, pulled out a yarmulke, and set it on his head before he left the house. I'd never seen the yarmulke before and wondered how long he had had it. I put my hands palms up in a question. He giggled—actually coughed a big laugh—which I thought was inappropriate at such a time. He made the same questioning sign to me, shrugged his shoulders, then took my mother's arm, leaving me to ponder his meaning.

CHAPTER

7

For years I had aggravated Bubbi by pulling chicken livers and hard-boiled eggs out of the wooden bowl in her lap while she chopped and diced them into a fine paté, bouncing on her bed and begging for stories while she lay pale under the covers, creating a small inferno on her kitchen table when I got too close to the Sabbath candles and knocked them over. On every occasion, Aunt Selma and Mama had asked in exasperation, "Why must you aggravate Bubbi?"

The last straw—peppermint sucking on Yom Kippur—did her in, I was sure. I had nightmares about it. One morning I woke up, prepared to tell Mama it was all my fault, but she was smiling while putting out the jelly donuts. "I had a dream about Bubbi," she said, "I talked to her, and she talked to me. It was wonderful."

I knew she meant talking, real talking the way I had dreamed that Mama and I talked, sitting across the kitchen table, gossiping about hopes and dreams, songs and noises we heard from the street and what the peddlar was shouting as he wheeled down the alley, yelling "oranges" or "old rags and iron." Just talking.

I took a jelly donut, ate the yellow custard first, then finished the sides and drank my Ovaltine. I decided there was no point in telling her about my nightmares. She seemed happy even though Bubbi was dead.

Sensing that something was troubling me, Papa invited me to walk with him. That pleased me because walking with him was an adventure. Although he couldn't say a word to anybody, he attracted a lot of attention. Hearing men would wave to him and thump him on the back, shouting words as hearing people do to the deaf. But Papa would take out his notepad and pencil and write words, and then the talk would be quiet. At last the hearing men would shake his hand firmly, smile, and walk away.

Walking with Mama was quite different. She insisted on talking to merchants in the neighborhood, which made poor Mr. Laykin roll his eyes in helplessness. Until I intervened, he couldn't understand that the box of "toodles" she asked for was noodles. She was too stubborn to write out anything except to the janitor, who, she believed, couldn't be expected to grasp her words because he had been gassed in the war.

It was one of those lovely spring Sundays. The four o'clocks planted in the dirt alongside our apartment building had already sprouted flowers, but it wasn't four o'clock yet, so the buds stayed closed. Papa gripped my hand, saluted a neighbor sitting on a bench, and, after polite hand-waving formalities, we headed for Charlie Mandel's, where his friends would be congregating.

Before we reached the store, a skinny man came running across the street and shook Papa's hand. "Well, you old sonofagun. Howya been? Haven't seen you in a long time. You used to come to Puddie's. What's happened to you? Given up on the guys, huh?"

Papa didn't understand a word, of course, but it was as if he was expecting all this fuss, so he took out his notepad to write. The man started talking again, only this time he talked to me.

"Listen, little girl. I remember when your Daddy fought Silent Martin in Cincinnati."

Papa looked at me for translation. I looked up at him and spelled "He remembers the time. . . ."

Papa smiled, a courtesy to the stranger's words.

"Your Daddy was quite a guy. Boy, he was strong! He could fight an army of men. You tell him I remember the time he kept the cops out of Puddie's."

"He remembers the time you. . . ."

Papa quickly tipped his hat. This time he seemed embarrassed. He shook the man's hand, and we walked away.

"Who was that man?" I asked, stopping our walk so we could talk.

"I don't know, but everybody knows me. I was a big man once. I was a prizefighter." He made a fist and brushed it against my cheek.

"You're foolin'," I said, stunned.

"True," he signed. It was like flicking a piece of food off your lips.

"Who's Silent Martin?"

"Deaf fighter. Fought him a long time ago. See my nose? It's been broken many times. See my ears. C-a-u-l-i-f-l-o-w-e-r," he spelled carefully.

I'd never heard of such a word, but it was obvious his ears didn't look normal. I had always thought it had something to do with his being deaf. "How did that happen?"

"Got hit too many times," he laughed.

I stared at him as though I'd never seen him before. His nose lay flat against his face. Big pouches of flesh covered his knuckles. Until that moment, it had never seemed at all out of the ordinary.

"Did you fight with the cops?" I asked.

"Not for you to know."

"Did you ever have a gun?"

"Never had a gun," he said shaking his finger at me.

"But the man said. . . ."

"Never mind. Little girls shouldn't know."

We resumed walking. His face was turned away from me, so I couldn't observe his mood, but I had the feeling that, even though he shook his finger at me, he was pleased with my questions. We walked to Charlie Mandel's. His deaf friends were there, but I was unable to utter a greeting—I was still dumbfounded by Papa's news. A prizefighter! My father! I couldn't wait to tell Shirley and Hannah!

Papa's friend Tyrone (his name wasn't really Tyrone; he just looked like Tyrone Power. Adelaide got all starry-eyed every time he came to the house) kept trying to fingerspell to me, but I couldn't stand still long enough to pay attention to him. I ran into Charlie's store and bought three bubble gums, bursting with the desire to shout, "My father was a prizefighter once!" On second thought, however, I decided it could have been a joke. Papa could twist words around, leaving me to imagine heroic scenes when all he meant was he hit a guy in the nose once for beating up some hapless neighbor.

I walked out of the store, unwrapped the bubble gum, stuck all three in my mouth, and chomped while Papa talked to Tyrone and Little Joe (so named because he was shorter than Papa). I waited until Papa got tired of making his points, of poking Little Joe in the chest, and of Tyrone poking him. He took my hand, and we walked home. The four o'clocks had opened up.

Later, all puffed up with excitement, he pulled a box down from the closet shelf. After spilling the contents onto the kitchen table, he fished out a faded newspaper clipping and spread it before me. "Read," he insisted. I read. "Mike Fusco, the Spring Street Taxi Baron, boxed Dummy Jordan in Cincinnati on January 24, 1916. . . ."

"This is me," he said, proudly.

"This isn't your name!"

"They called deaf fighters 'Dummy.' "

"Who's Jordan?"

"Me, silly. That's what they called me. 'Dummy Jordan.' They gave me a different last name. It's all part of the act."

Then he pulled out a picture I'd never seen before. It was Papa when he was very young and slim with powerful muscles straining at his shirtsleeves. He posed in a fighting stance, arms aimed at the camera. It was a handsome picture. He even had hair on his head.

Now I believed him, and excitement overtook me. I couldn't

sit still. I was halfway over the top of the table, trying to pull more stuff out of the pile when Papa put everything back in the box. "That's enough," he said.

"But I want to see more newspaper stories."

"There aren't any more."

"Then what's all that stuff in there?"

"Things I've saved."

"What kind of things?"

He closed the box without answering, got up, and put it back on the closet shelf. I was disappointed, slightly miffed with his teasing. Why would he regale me with news that had transformed him in my eyes? A prizefighter! My God! And not want to share the rest of his glory?

"Why aren't you a prizefighter now?" I asked.

"It's too dangerous. I saw a deaf fighter get hurt in the eyes. It would be bad to be blind, too."

It sure would. I didn't want to think about it.

"Thank God," Mama interrupted. "I never want to see him fight!"

She was standing at the sink, watching our conversation while she dried the dishes. "He was a bum, that's what he was."

I was the only one who heard it. Mama said it instead of signing, and Papa asked me what she said. I told him. Papa waved wildly to Mama, and she waved wildly back. A lot of the words escaped me even though I tried hard to keep up with their furious flailing.

"What do you know?" he charged. "You've never been anywhere. I've been all over this country."

"A hobo? Hah. Box cars," she grumbled in signs. "Is that so wonderful?"

"Jealous," he smirked. "I had adventures."

"Look at you. You never learned to read lips."

He almost choked on his tobacco at that remark. Mama started laughing mysteriously, *hmning* and covering her mouth.

58

Throwing her dishtowel over her shoulder, she held her sides as if they would burst with all the laughter stored up in her. Papa couldn't hold on to his chew and made a quick run to the bathroom. I could hear him spit it out in the toilet, the spray probably making several new designs on the wall.

"You know what he's doing, don't you?" she asked.

"Yes. He spit out his tobacco."

"Just like a bum," she laughed again.

I wasn't sure this was a fight. It sounded like a fight, but they were so busy laughing at each other that I couldn't tell. I'd seen plenty of their fights. In the middle of the night when we were supposed to be asleep, chairs would get pushed around in the kitchen, and Mama's screeching, coyote sounds would wake us up. Papa would make angry grunting noises. One night Adelaide and I got up to see what the fuss was about. We sneaked into the dining room and stood near the kitchen doorway. The lights were out in the dining room, so they never knew we were standing there. When Papa didn't want to listen to Mama, he turned his back to her. That made her angry. She stamped her foot hard on the floor. When Papa finally looked her way, she spelled so fast, we couldn't make out any of the words.

"Do you think they're gonna get a divorce?" Adelaide asked me that horrible night.

"Jewish people don't get divorces."

"How do you know that?"

"Shirley said her mother told her."

"Her mother doesn't know everything."

"Yes, she does. She went to college."

That seemed to satisfy Adelaide, but I was beginning to have doubts. When we got up that next morning, Mama barely looked at Papa, but, by evening, they were smiling and friendly with each other.

But this fight was different. Despite their laughter, she had said some mean things about him, calling him a bum, blaming him because he couldn't read lips. When Papa came out of the bathroom, I pulled at his sleeve. "Why *can't* you read lips and talk like Mama?"

He started to sign something when Mama interrupted.

"Because they sent him to the wrong school, where he only learned to sign. It was a big mistake, I tell you."

"But, Mama, you sign a lot."

"Of course. How would I talk to Papa if I didn't sign?"

"So what's the difference?"

Papa kept hitting the top of the table and poking me. "What did she say?" but Mama wouldn't stop talking. "Plenty!" she said. "Your Zadie knew if I didn't learn to speak, I couldn't take care of myself. You have to learn to get along in the world." With this, she crossed her arms over her chest and stopped. Her cheeks were fiery red. I finally got a chance to tell him, but I wondered if it was wise to do so. He stared straight at me and waited while I spelled. It took so long my hand started hurting, and I rested my elbow in order to finish the sentence. Sputtering tiny bits of fresh tobacco along his lips, Papa looked at Mama, then turned to me and spelled carefully that his schooling was fine, thank you. Then he faced Mama. "Nothing wrong with the state school. I learned my lessons just like you did. Besides, what good is it if you can talk? Nobody gives a deaf person a decent job anyway." Only he said it in short deaf talk, so it went pretty fast.

Apparently worn out from all the accusations, he sat back in his chair and chewed hard. His eyes were a little wet, but he blinked it back so fast I wasn't sure I'd seen it. He pulled his face back together again and laughed, only it came out more like a hiccup.

"You're just a greenhorn from the old country with your old-fashioned ways, praying like you know what you're doing," he spelled angrily at Mama. This last remark flattened her. Nobody spoke. The silence was unnerving. They stared silently at each other, Mama's hands in her apron pocket and Papa chewing away, his blue eyes fixed on his quiet hands. I banged the table, sending vibrations along the floor. They stopped their staring and looked at me.

"Please don't fight. It scares Addle, and she might hear you."

"Where is she?" asked Mama.

"In the bedroom, playing house with her friend."

"This is not a fight. We're discussing things."

Papa patted my head. "Nobody's fighting," he signed. He took the afternoon paper and left the room.

Mama picked up another dish and dried it over and over as though trying to rub out some stubborn dirty spot. "He was a good fighter," she said quietly. "He won fifty fights. I never saw him fight. It was before I knew him, but I heard about him. Everybody heard about him. Everybody talked about him at the Deaf Club."

"Is that where you met him, at the Deaf Club?"

"Yes."

"And then you got married?"

"Well, first we went out, silly," she laughed. "He courted me. Do you know what that is?"

"I think so."

"Everybody told me to watch out for him. He was too handsome, too wild," she told me, putting another dish in the sink. "I was twenty-seven when we got married. Zadie was worried I'd be an old maid. I had another boyfriend, but he wasn't Jewish. Zadie didn't approve of him."

"He likes Papa, doesn't he?"

"Yes, he does."

"And then you got married."

"Yes, in 1928. You were born in '29."

"I know."

"And Addle came in '31."

"Tell me about the wedding."

"It was nice. We got married in Zadie's house."

"Did the rabbi speak deaf?"

"No."

"So you read his lips?"

"Yes."

"And Papa?"

"Well, he knew when to break the glass. It's the tradition for the groom to break a glass under his foot to remember the destruction of the temple in Jerusalem."

"You're happy you married him, aren't you?"

"Of course. What a silly question! Of course."

"Then why did you make fun of him? Why did you call him a bum?"

"I don't understand what you're saying. Speak slower."

She knew what I said. It was a trick she used when she needed more time to answer. "I *said* why did you call him a bum?"

"It was those other things."

"What other things?"

She flicked a dishtowel over a cup. "Never mind. Go play with Addle." She turned her back to me.

I didn't want to play with Adelaide. I knew Shirley and Hannah and Timmy would be sitting on the marble steps downstairs. I had to tell them about Papa. My father—the prizefighter! He wore satin purple trunks and knocked out fifty people. Just like Joe Louis, the champ. I wasn't sure about the purple trunks, but, by the time I got downstairs, I *was* sure. They wouldn't know what color anyway.

They were sitting in a row on one step, knees locked to their chests, heads hanging over their knees. I sat on the step above them and casually related the story. Hannah's jaw fell. Shirley lurched backward in surprise as if I'd just disclosed that Papa was a movie star. But wise Timmy asked, "How did he know when the round was over?"

"The referee poked him on the shoulder," I answered. I didn't really know, but it sounded good. Later I learned it was true.

"Your father's still a Republican," Timmy criticized, looking unimpressed.

It was the worst thing he could have said to me since the whole building voted Democratic on election day. All I could muster in defense was a lame "so what?"

"He doesn't like FDR," Timmy retorted, hurling the final insult.

"Yes, he does, but his brother promised him a job in the party if he voted Republican."

"My father says. . . ."

"I don't care what your father says. I bet he was never a prizefighter."

Shirley, Hannah, and I strolled off to buy an ice cream. We left Timmy there to contemplate.

I wondered about "those other things" Mama had alluded to, but, by the time we came out of Charlie's store with our double-dip chocolate cones, I had forgotten about them.

CHAPTER

8

TIMMY WOULDN'T leave it alone. He was gone by the time we came back from Charlie's, but the next morning when I walked to school with Shirley, Hannah, and Adelaide, he showed up behind us. There wasn't enough room for all four of us to walk together, so Adelaide sprinted ahead. Timmy hung back for a while, then moved close to us and shouted, "My father says your father was a gangster and a boot-legger."

"What are you talking about?" I demanded, walking straight ahead, my knees shaking. The words sounded ominous, at least the gangster part. But bootleggers had no meaning for me. I broke down the word into two parts, still shaking. I figured it must have something to do with shoes and leggings. Did Papa used to make boots? And leggings? I wondered.

"That's what my father said, and everybody knows it. But you're too stupid to know it," Timmy struck again. His face met mine for an instant. All I could see were the freckles on his cheeks. I was shocked and speechless, and so were Shirley and Hannah. We kept on walking, pretending we didn't hear him.

"He's just jealous," Shirley said finally.

"Yeah, I know."

When nobody answered him, he retreated into the street and ran the rest of the way. I didn't talk to him the whole morning and stayed away from him at recess. I couldn't concentrate on the spelling test. Mrs. Tremont glared at me when I missed a lot of the words. After school, I asked Shirley to walk Adelaide home. I turned in the other direction and made my way to Zadie's house. The front door was unlocked, so I let myself in. Zadie was gone. Shul, probably. Maybe even my house, standing nose to nose with Mama. I found Aunt Selma sitting in the kitchen.

"Surprise, surprise!" she exclaimed when she saw me. "What brings you here this lovely afternoon?" She stuck a cigarette in her mouth and blew smoke rings.

"Thought I'd practice 'Chopsticks' on the piano."

"Sure," she said, "but let's have cocoa first."

She heated it in the pot and brought it to the table. While I drank, she blew more smoke rings, then took her finger and poked through them. "So, what's the real reason?"

"I'm confused."

"About what?"

"How come we were rich one time and now we're not?"

"Who told you that?"

"Papa."

"What did he say?" More smoke rings. Then she drank some cocoa.

"Papa said that he had a lot of money, and then it all disappeared. And he said he had a nurse for me and that's how I learned to hear the right sounds."

"That's true. And when the nurse left, Mama brought you here so you could hear us talk."

"Where did he get all the money?"

"Had a job like everybody else."

"What kind of job? I know he was a prizefighter, but Mama says she didn't know him when he was a fighter."

"That's true."

She was waiting for me to say something, but I couldn't bring myself to say gangster. Instead, I looked at her stomach to see if I could see where the baby was. Mama had told me that Aunt Selma was pregnant but not to mention it until she told me herself.

"What are you looking at?" she asked me.

"Nuthin'."

"So, Mama told you," she laughed. "Well, it's true. You can't tell right now, but it'll show soon. And when the baby kicks, I'll let you feel it."

"Maybe you shouldn't smoke, Aunt Selma."

"From the mouths of babes," she sighed, putting her cigarette out. She sounded so clever, and she liked what I said. It made my heart beat faster. "You know all about babies? It's time you know. You're almost twelve."

"Mama told me, but she didn't make any sense. She told me that even the ladies in Africa get periods, and that's all she said. Except she said, 'be careful.' I think she was too embarrassed to tell me everything."

"Why didn't you ask me? I would have told you. Do you understand it now?"

"Sure. Shirley told me all about it. Shirley's mother explained it to her, and Shirley told Hannah and me, right in our living room while Mama and Papa were playing cards. They didn't know what we were saying. Papa would have died if he knew we were talking about those things right in front of him. Shirley got hers already. I guess I'll get mine soon."

She looked at me all soft and sweet like something wonderful was about to happen. I didn't think so. From the way Shirley described it, it seemed like a big nuisance. "Mama has a sign for it."

"What?"

"It's a knock on the cheek. That's how deaf people say it."

"I remember that," she laughed. "That's what she called it when we were growing up. She was always sneaking signs to us. Zadie didn't like it. Didn't want her to talk like a deaf person. Are you sure you understand it now?"

"Yes, but what I don't understand. . . ." The words wouldn't come out. Of all my aunties, I could trust Selma. She was the daring cigarette smoker, the one who bowled and said clever things and gave me the once-over whenever I visited. Nice dress, bad color. What's new? What's old? That's the way she talked. Flip and sassy. Aunt Marian was svelte and cool and private. I would think twice about baring my soul to her. Aunt Nettie was a wonderful ding-a-ling (the aunts called her that) who would listen, twist her eyes around, gaze off, and leave me wanting. It was Aunt Selma who would give me the lowdown.

"Timmy says Papa was a gangster and a bootlegger," I blurted out, my heart beating fast.

"And who is Timmy, and how does he know anything?" she asked.

"Just a person."

"Not a very informed one, I'd say."

"So it isn't true?"

"Your father was a courier. That's a lot different from being a gangster or a bootlegger."

"Please, Aunt Selma, could you talk plain? I don't understand what a courier is."

"A messenger. He was a messenger. There were people who entrusted him . . . gave him certain things to deliver because they were sure he could do the job."

"I'm still confused."

"Let me explain, honey," she said, pulling another chair to her so she could put her feet up. "Some of those men who gave Papa things to deliver, well, they weren't exactly the nicest people, but Papa didn't always know that. He couldn't hear what they were saying to each other, and he couldn't blab anything to anybody . . . I mean talk. And when he found out, well, he gave it up."

I didn't believe a word she said about Papa not knowing. "What's Puddie's?"

She sighed as though I had tried her patience. She rubbed her stomach and considered her words carefully. "Puddie's is a restaurant on Roosevelt Road. Papa worked as a bouncer there."

She could see I didn't know what a bouncer was either, so she explained that some restaurants didn't want certain people in, and it was Papa's job to keep them out.

"Like cops?"

"Oh my!" She pulled another cigarette from the pack, lit it, and stubbed it out without smoking it. Then she got up and strode to the window. I was really trying her patience. She turned away from the window and sat down again. "How do you know all this?"

"Some man told me."

"That's terrible," she groaned. "All right, all right. I don't know if it's my place to tell you, but I'm going to give it to you straight."

"I really appreciate it," I said, trying to act grownup.

"Your father didn't have it so easy. After he stopped boxing, he worked for those bums. I know, I know. But it's hard for a deaf man to find work. When Mama met him, he was working at Puddie's. There was gambling in the back room, and your father is a strong man, isn't he?"

"Yes, very strong."

"So they hired him to keep certain people out and watch for the cops. I know, I know. It sounds terrible, but he was just doing his job. He made good money. Lots of it. That's why you had it so good when you were a baby, but, by the time Adelaide was born, Papa got arrested. He tried to keep the cops from coming in. All of a sudden, he's some hero. Everybody's talking about what Dummy Jordan did as if he saved important people. Uncle Eddie told your Papa it was too dangerous to keep working there and convinced him to stop. After all, he was a father now. He had you two to worry about. And Mama never liked it anyway. Even with all the money, it scared her."

"I really appreciate this, Aunt Selma."

"Your father is a decent and honorable man. Zadie loves him like he was his own son. Better than anyone in his own family

68

ever treated him. He's got an honest job now, so don't go worrying about what people say. It's old hat. And you know what?"

"What?"

"Some people still treat him like he's a celebrity."

"I know. When I take walks with him, everybody's happy to see him—mostly men."

"Living vicariously!" she laughed.

"What?"

"Never mind, honey. 'Chopsticks'?"

"No, I think I better go home. Mama will be worried."

"Good girl. I like that color on you. Yellow is very becoming. It's good for your complexion."

I think she wanted to kiss me, but Aunt Selma never kissed. Nobody in our family did, so she put her hand on mine and walked me to the back door. "I'll call you as soon as the baby kicks."

"I don't have a phone," I reminded her.

"That's right. Well, maybe one day you will. In the meantime, I'll send a message by courier pigeon."

"Can I ask you something else, Aunt Sel?"

"Sure, sweetie, what?"

"Did Papa ever make boots?"

"No," she said, her eyes curious.

"Or leggings?"

Her eyes narrowed, her plump cheeks almost covering them up. "No, no. Now you tell this Timmy to mind his own business. Everything he said was a lie!"

O N T H E way home, I imagined people looking at me, admiring the yellow dress that was perfect for my complexion, ignoring the little voices in my head that whispered that everything Timmy said was true.

CHAPTER

9

M AMA WAS taking a nap when I let myself in.
Adelaide wasn't home, but her dolls were all
lined up on the living room sofa; she'd even taken some of mine
and mixed them in with hers. I didn't care. Dolls didn't excite
me anymore. Mrs. Goldberg must have heard me come in
because she knocked on the door and told me that Mama had
a headache—that's why she was resting—and Adelaide was
upstairs with her listening to "One Man's Family," so I shouldn't
worry. I thanked her and closed the door. It was so quiet in the
house, I could hear Mama's alarm clock ticking under her pillow.
I figured she'd be conked out for at least an hour, so, taking off
my shoes, I pulled a chair over to the closet and climbed up on
it. My arms almost reached the shelf, but I had to stand on tip-
toe to get to Papa's secret box. My heart was pounding like I was
the second-story jewel thief in the new Cary Grant movie showing at the Harmony.

I put the box down on the kitchen table quietly, thinking it
might waken Mama. Then I laughed because that was silly. I
poked through the box. Pictures, mostly. Some I'd seen before.
One I hadn't. A picture of Papa in a flat cap with a brim, sitting
on his haunches in an alley with other flat-capped men. They
were squatting in a circle and staring at something in the center.
One of the men had his hands on something, ready to throw.
Marbles, probably. No more newspaper clippings. Nothing that
said Papa was arrested. Not even a gun. In the corner of the box,
a Hebrew prayer book like the one Zadie had. I opened the cover

and found an inscription: "To Joseph on his sixteenth birthday from your father, Adolph." Underneath the book was a plastic bride and groom. The bride still had her veil glued on, but the groom's black hat had fallen off, and one of his legs was cracked. And a beaded purse my mother must have worn at her wedding.

Then I saw a piece of paper with Papa's handwriting on it. I took it out and laid it flat on the table. There was somebody else's handwriting on it, too, but it was unfamiliar. In the middle of the paper, the stranger had written in capital letters "THE SAGA OF DUMMY JORDAN, THE INCREDIBLE CAREER OF THE GREATEST FIGHTING MACHINE THE RING HAS EVER KNOWN." Below this he had also written to Papa, "Charlie Chaplin could play the part of the manager to make the greatest picture of his life."

Papa wrote back, "Chaplin and his friend Sterling Ford and Chas. Murray, they think I'm dead."

The stranger responded, "You still move like a cat."

Papa: "I fought Chuck Wiggens and Billy Ryan, Leon Roroland, four rounds at Doyle's Gym in Vernon, Cal. Steve Dalton, three times, Johnny Sheppard, where is he?"

No answer from the stranger.

Papa: "Jock Malone. Fatty Arbuckle, Mary Pickford. They used to come see me fight."

The stranger wrote Mary Pickford's address. "Write her a letter. She'd love to hear from you. Write about those times, the glamour of the old days in Hollywood."

Papa scribbled: "My brother sold my contract to somebody else. It wasn't fair. Why would he do that?"

Stranger: "Your brother Dave told me he thought the other guy could do a better job for you."

Papa: "But he was my brother. It was not right. I took care of him when I was making good money fighting. All the brothers came to be with me. I sent money home to my mother. What did the brothers ever do for me?"

A couple of blank spaces, then Papa wrote again: "No matter, I could never be a great champion. Kids don't look up to deaf fighters, only to somebody who can talk."

The stranger didn't answer directly. He just wrote, "Great movie. Chaplin will get sympathy because of his love for the mute."

I put the paper back just like Papa had folded it and stuck the box back on the shelf. I didn't understand most of the writing, didn't know all the people Papa wrote about except Charlie Chaplin and Mary Pickford. But I knew that if they came to see him fight, he must have been somebody special. My heart was pounding even harder, thinking somebody wanted to make a movie about Papa. MY FATHER. All of a sudden, it didn't matter what Timmy said. Let him think what he wants. Let them all think what they want. Let them call him shtimmer. My father was famous once. And I was proud of him for writing all the words down instead of talking short cut.

EVERY FRIDAY after dinner, when all the neighbors went to shul, we had a routine. That's what Mama called it. To me it was just sitting around the kitchen table and talking about anything. Sometimes Papa talked about his younger days, and I hoped that on one of those Fridays, Papa would tell me everything. It had been months since Aunt Selma and I had had our little talk. I never mentioned it to Mama or Papa, thinking that one day, they'd tell me themselves. If they didn't, that was all right, too, because I'd decided that what Papa did for a living when I was a baby was something he had to do. He was right: It was hard for a deaf man to find work. Besides, who else could have done the job as well? Slinking around in dark alleys, not hearing anything or talking to anyone, just handing a package to a stranger and getting paid for it. Who else but Papa was strong enough to cuff somebody who was out of line, shake him about the shoulders to warn him?

Some of Papa's deaf friends were still out of work, even if, according to Uncle Eddie, the Depression was lifting. I wondered if Uncle Eddie knew what he was talking about. When I stood in the grocery store waiting for Mr. Laykin to finish filling Mama's order, I'd hear the neighbors talking about how everything was still bad. The large black notebook where Mr. Laykin kept a record of monies owed him seemed to lie more often on top of the counter than on the shelf below.

Sometimes *we* had an account. Lately, however, Mr. Laykin kept his notebook below when we came in to shop. Papa was lucky. The Roosevelt Chair Company kept him busy six days a week. When he did stay home on a Saturday and rain precluded a trip to the ball park, Zadie would find him playing solitaire at the dining room table. With panic in his eyes, Zadie would ask if Papa was still working. Papa would tell me to tell him he had no complaints. Five days of work was still paying the bills. Zadie said "goot," the panic left his eyes, and he'd be off to shul again. His job may not have been as lucrative and glamorous and thrillingly against the law as his hoodlum days, but it was a job.

ONE FRIDAY evening the following winter, we'd had our dinner, gone to ooh and ah over Aunt Selma's new baby, and come home again. The snow was piled high on the back porch, and we clustered around the kitchen table to talk. My feet tucked warmly under me, I sat waiting for him to reveal something exciting about his past. My belly was aching from my third knock on the cheek, and I felt shivery and sick. It was cold in the kitchen. The janitor generally stopped feeding the furnace at seven o'clock, which caused much grumbling among the neighbors, but it was not an issue for my mother. She trusted in extra sweaters and blankets. She covered my back with a heavy sweater and made some tea. The Sabbath candles were still burning, and the heat and aroma of her Friday night meal still hung in the air.

Mama sat next to me and pulled Adelaide to her other side. Papa had an old flannel shirt draped over his shoulders.

Neighbors' footsteps were crunching down the back stairs; I looked out the window to see how fast the snow was falling.

"Shul waste of time," Papa said, addressing those who were off to pray, only nobody saw him. "There is no God," he added, looking past me.

It seemed a curious thing for him to say, considering the prayer book that lay in his secret box. But then, I'd never seen it or any prayer book actually in his hands.

"Rode the boxcars," he continued as we gazed wide-eyed at him.

"You were only a child," Mama said.

"Old enough to take care of myself."

"It's not right you left home so young," she answered.

"How old were you, Papa?"

He'd told us this story many times, but I could listen to it forever, wishing I myself could leave home and pursue a hobo's existence.

"Hardly older than you," Mama reminded me. "Out in the freezing cold. Can you imagine that?"

"Weren't you scared?" I must have asked him that a dozen times.

"Scared? Why should I be scared? I had plenty to eat. I did some labor. I made some money." His hands moved in graceful storytelling motions. "Shared with the other men on the train."

"You mean the bums," Mama countered.

Papa snickered in response to her attack, then ignored her completely. "Sometimes I went into a saloon, bought some beer, ate the free food. If it wasn't free, I took it anyway," he chuckled.

A quick poke from Mama apparently changed his tune. He leaned over the table and pointed a finger at me. "Don't do what I do. Boys are different."

"I know," I signed, my belly feeling no better with Mama's tea

74

inside me. But the truth was, I didn't understand why it was all right for him and not for girls.

Adelaide had none of my interest in his adventures. She fell fast asleep, her head resting on Mama's lap. Mama gently picked her up and carried her off to bed. When she returned, she poured milk in a pot and heated it for me. The coffee perked, and Mama poured two cups and sat down again. She turned toward Papa and signed, "Knock on the cheek."

Papa hummed in acknowledgment; his eyes became moist, and a faint smile creased his cheeks. He reached across the table and put his hands on mine. "Cold," he signed. "Put under sweater."

Embarrassed that Mama had told him, I signed, "No, not cold" and kept my hands on the hot mug.

"Tell her about the rattlesnake," Mama suggested.

"Snake story is terrible. I don't want to hear it," I protested.

But Papa had already turned into Lon Chaney, the actor he admired because Chaney's parents were deaf. He got out of his chair and played the scene. He stalked through the kitchen, punched the air, and stopped dead in his tracks, signing with his motions. "I was alone in the desert. Just finished a fight in Yuma. You remember where Yuma is?"

"No, Papa, I don't remember. So that's why you were in Yuma. Fighting, right?"

"Of course. I never told you before?"

"No, I thought you were in Yuma, bumming." I looked at Mama and saw her laugh.

"Now you know," he said. "Then I saw the rattler. You listening?"

"Yes, Papa," I yawned. Mama sat enthralled.

"I picked it up with my bare hands and smashed it against a rock." The table shook under his fist.

Mama curled her lips in a satisfying smile. "Wasn't that brave of Papa?" she asked, sending him secret messages with her eyes.

I could hardly keep mine open. The tea and milk had finally soothed my stomach, and I was ready for sleep.

"Then I went to El Paso," he continued. "You know where El Paso is?"

"No, Papa." I never knew where any place was. If it wasn't El Paso, it was Denver, and I didn't know where that was, either.

"I fought in all those places. In all the mining towns."

"Oh!"

"Well, sometimes."

"Oh."

"Do you remember the story of Pancho Villa? Do you remember I saw him. Remember?"

"Yes, I remember." My eyes were growing heavier.

"Okay. Too much stories."

He pulled two coats from the closet and led me to bed. He covered me with one and put the other on Adelaide. The neighbors' voices resounded in the quiet street, signifying that shul was over.

"Tell me again why you left home so young." I knew the answer. He wanted to see the world. But I hoped this time he'd tell me more. He leaned over and explained in very short words. He put his five fingers to his chin and made a shake downward, then pulled his fingers down across his lips. "My mother, sweet lady," he said. He put his five fingers to his forehead, then shook his fingers downward and pointed one finger to his brain. "My father not understand me."

I watched his eyes melt into sadness. I hadn't the heart to ask him any more. He left the room without waiting for a response. The last thing I heard as I drifted off to sleep was the sound of cups being washed, the scrape of a chair, and their soft secret sounds behind their closed door.

Stories of gangsters would have to wait, but I realized Papa would never tell me, no matter how old I'd grown. But after months of keeping Papa's past to myself, I knew I had to tell Adelaide.

76

ONE AFTERNOON, I sat her down on the sofa among her dolls and disclosed Papa's past to her. I compared him to Joe Louis, Jimmy Cagney, and George Raft. I told her about Papa's private box and my discussions with Aunt Selma. I assured her that Papa's choice of work was a reasonable choice under the circumstances. She listened with a ten-year-old's attention, half of her looking no older than her dolls, the other half grownup, her saucer eyes taking in every word. I waited for her to cry or scream with excitement, but she sat quietly among her dolls. "Papa's handsomer," she said, finally.

"That's right, he is."

"Papa's stronger," she said, changing Shirley Temple's dress.

"That's right, he is."

"Did he have a gun?" she asked.

"I don't know."

"Well, he shoulda had a gun," she said. She cupped Shirley Temple in the crook of her arm and walked to our bedroom.

"What color were his trunks?" she asked, returning to the sofa, minus Shirley Temple.

"Purple," I said. She smiled.

Curiously, we kept this conversation to ourselves, never speaking of it to Mama or each other again. It would be years before we divulged our secret to our friends. It would wait until Al Capone and gangsters became as legendary as the cowboys of the West. But we never stopped talking about his purple trunks.

CHAPTER

10

WHILE MY mother sat in her burgundy chair and read her books, I read my comics, which she hated, calling them trashy reading. In 1941, when I was twelve, she became determined to turn Adelaide and me into ladies, to expose us to the finer things in print, so she persuaded my father to buy a set of the classics and a set of encyclopedias. The books cost a pretty penny, but Mama had found a company who would sell them on installment—so much a week for so many months. My father choked on his tobacco when he heard the price. He fiddled with his fingers until he could summon up the courage to form words with them. "Can we afford it?" he finally asked.

"We have no choice," she said. "The girls are getting older. They need them to do their homework properly."

My father sat down at the dining room table and crunched papers. Next to the other household categories, he wrote down "books." He neglected to add Aunt Flora, who had strapped our family's finances because she had lost her job and was flat broke. When Mama had suggested to Papa that Flora move in with us until she could find work, Papa had turned purple, his resentment overcoming his common sense. But Mama had sweet-talked him with a nice cup of hot tea and a slice of her cheesecake, and he had relented. No matter how much Flora's spoiled ways irritated him, he knew he couldn't turn his back on his deaf sister. So she had moved in with her hat boxes and fancy clothes, piled them into every closet in the house, and claimed the hideabed in the dining room as her sleeping quarters.

"Okay, Ruthie," he said after calculating the cost of the books. "Buy them, but I know enough to tell the girls everything there is to know. I've been everywhere in this country."

"You've been nowhere," she said, "and what you know is not what they should know."

The books were delivered the following week. The classics were bound in green covers with gold trim; the encyclopedias were a lovely maroon color. They came with their own bookcase, which Papa placed in the living room next to the sofa. But I couldn't comprehend the stories. *The Last of the Mohicans* was beyond me. So was *The Scarlet Letter*. So I went back to reading "Batman" behind my mother's back.

GOD MUST have seen me reading my "Batman" comic because Papa lost *his* job. He came home one day with a shiner as big as a giant ink blot over his right eye. I was sitting in the dining room with the encyclopedia in front of me, facing the front door when he walked in. As soon as he saw me, he quickly covered his eye and went looking for Mama. I followed as far as the kitchen door, keeping out of their sight while he told Mama what had happened.

"They don't need me anymore," he complained.

"What happened to your eye?" she asked, ignoring his comment.

"I've been looking for work all day," he told her.

"But what happened to your eye?" she persisted.

"I didn't like the way the man looked at me when I asked him for a job. He laughed at me like I was some fool."

"You're not a fool, Joe. What kind of job?"

"A janitor in a factory on Halsted Street."

"A janitor's job!?"

"Yes, Ruthie, a janitor's job. I need a job." He turned his back on her as if he needed time to swallow hard and face her again. I heard the tobacco swishing like a tidal wave. I heard him gulp hard as he turned around to face her again. "Why would the boss let me go?"

"I don't know. It's not anything you did, is it?"

"What would I do?"

"Nothing, Joe. Nothing. Don't worry. You'll find another job."

But she didn't seem completely convinced because she clutched the tip of her apron, wiped her brow, and pulled it over her eyes. Then she got up and put on a pot of coffee.

I pretended I didn't know. Papa left as early as he usually did every day. And sometimes he didn't come home until Adelaide and I were in bed. One night Adelaide and I were jolted awake by a terrible commotion like a train being hauled up the front stairs. By the time Mama saw the light and opened the door, Adelaide and I had run to the living room to hide so we could see what had happened. Aunt Flora jumped up from the hide-abed, wrapped her blanket around her, and pointed her finger to us to stay quiet. We nodded our heads and stood frozen in the dark.

Papa's body was being gently laid on the floor, but, because he was so large, it made a loud thump. Four deaf men whom I'd never seen before started talking to Mama. I couldn't make out the words because everyone was jabbering with their fingers at the same time while Mama screamed and shouted coyote sounds at the men. Then she slammed the door on them and stood over Papa, crying, "You bum. Why must you do this to me?" She turned on her heels and stormed into her bedroom, leaving him prostrate, snoring peacefully.

At least I knew he wasn't dead and told Adelaide, who was shivering with fright, that as long as he was breathing, there was nothing wrong with him. "Let's go back to bed," I advised.

"What do you think happened?"

"I don't know and stop thinking about divorces. I told you Jewish people don't get divorces."

80

"You think you know everything."

"I do, so shut up about it."

Aunt Flora put her arms around us and walked us back to our bedroom. "Don't worry," she spelled. Her blonde hair fell over my face, and I could smell the fancy shampoo she used and the sachet that clung to her nightgown. So, I thought, she can still afford her fancy things. No wonder Papa turns purple every time she signs her troubles. She pointed two fingers—one for Adelaide and one for me—and spelled, "Go back to sleep. Everything will be fine in the morning."

"What do you think happened, Aunt Flora?" I asked.

"Nothing new," she said, which made no sense to me. She was smiling, but her fingers were tense. Because she could sometimes speak like Mama and be understood, I heard her say as she walked back through the darkened living room, "It's not fair for the girls to see. I'm going to talk to him in the morning."

I HAD lied to Adelaide. I didn't know anything. When morning came, Aunt Flora was gone. The hideabed was neatly rearranged, her smells still clinging to the fabric. I knew only that Mama was angry. She didn't even bother changing into her housedress. Her kimono was untied and dragged along the floor. Her hair was still hanging down her back. She hadn't bothered to comb it.

Papa was sitting at the kitchen table, looking sheepishly at Mama, but she wouldn't look at him. She threw the danish on the table and slapped his coffee cup down hard. She wasn't talking to us, either. She just wandered around the house, pretending to dust, and then she sat in the living room chair to read, something she never did in the morning. Adelaide and I ate our danish while Papa poked his nose in the newspaper. There was an unusual smell about him, somewhat familiar, like the Manischewitz on Zadie's table.

Adelaide asked me again, "What do you think happened?"

"I'm not sure."

"He doesn't look so good."

"He didn't shave, so he looks like he just got out of bed."

"Maybe he did just get out of bed. Do you think we should say something to him?"

"He looks pretty busy."

He was reading the sports page, the paper spread out and taking up most of the kitchen table. We stopped talking and finished eating. Papa folded the paper and put his hands up. His eyes were a little drippy, but he blinked them back. "Do you want to take a walk with me?"

"Sure," we both signed.

Papa got up, went into the bedroom, and came out with the installment book on the new refrigerator Mama had just bought. He took both our hands, and we walked down Washtenaw Avenue to North Avenue to Fish's department store to make another payment. Papa didn't stop to talk to anybody. Neither did Adelaide or I. We just walked straight ahead, our eyes on the street before us. I wondered how long it would be before Papa ran out of money and Fish's would come and take the refrigerator away. When we walked into the store, Papa dropped our hands, pulled the book out, put it on the counter, and paid the man, never saying, "Look, I think this is the last payment I can make. Are you going to pick up the refrigerator and take it back until I can pay you more?" I wondered if I should say something myself, make it easier for Papa, come right out and say, "Look, mister, my father's flat broke, and my mother needs her refrigerator. We've already given the ice box to the Jewish charities," but I couldn't muster the courage.

When we got home, Uncle Eddie was sitting on the living room sofa. Mama was next to him. She had changed into street clothes, her hair tied neatly back in a bun. She had lipstick on, and her hands were folded nicely in her lap. When she saw us, she walked into the kitchen. Papa looked a little surprised to see

Eddie sitting there. Uncle Eddie said, "Girls, go into the kitchen, help your mother."

"She's not doing anything," I said. "Just making coffee."

"Go anyway."

He shook Papa's hand, and they both sat down on the sofa and started writing. I heard Uncle Eddie say, "Joe, you're not the only one they laid off from Roosevelt Chair. It's not your fault." When I turned my head to watch him, I saw that he had been scribbling furiously as he spoke. I went into the kitchen and poked Mama. "Why is he here?"

"To visit Papa," she said, pouring coffee into two mugs.

"Is everything all right?"

"Everything is fine." Then she turned away from me and carried the mugs into the living room.

Mama must have made a quick trip to the Rubensteins and told them things were bad. By the time Uncle Eddie left, Papa was smiling. Uncle Eddie had given him a job in his metal reclaiming yard. Papa explained his duties to us while we ate lunch. "I have to separate the metals for your uncle. It's not a hard job. Maybe I'll do more when I understand the job better."

"You'll do fine," Mama said.

CHAPTER

11

ACCORDING TO Mama, Uncle Eddie was paying Papa a decent wage, but Papa still scrunched papers at night. If he was worried about his finances, he didn't tell Zadie when he came to visit. He just nodded his head—fine—and Zadie left satisfied. And when I took an occasional stroll with Papa, he would point to the unemployed men milling about and tell me how lucky he was.

But my own worries filled the summer of my twelfth year. I seemed unable to do anything right for my mother. If I sat on the marble steps with Timmy, she turned crabby. She'd pretend to get the mail more often than the mail was supposed to come. Stockings rolled down to her ankles, she'd come downstairs in her housedress, amble past us, and fiddle with the mailbox as if expecting something important. One day the July heat prompted me to pull my dress above my knees so the marble could cool my behind. Spotting this, she hummed and pinched her lips, gave Timmy a withering look, then opened her mouth wide so I'd get her words. "I think it's time you came upstairs."

"It's too hot upstairs," I said.

"Then sit on the back porch. I'll make lemonade." A fat handkerchief was wrapped around her neck to soak up the sweat. She fanned herself with another and bored holes through me with her eyes.

"Okay, okay, I'll come upstairs."

"With Hannah and Shirley," she said.

"Do you see Shirley and Hannah here? Are you blind or something?"

"Don't get smart. Where are they?"

"At the library."

"Then you should be at the library."

"I've already read three books."

"Read more."

Then she went back upstairs. I didn't move. Most of the time when she got antsy like that she was worried about something. The only way I'd know was to eavesdrop on my parents' nighttime kitchen talks. But there were no nighttime finger fights. Obviously, this was Mama's own agitation, the kind that put her in a mood where she just stared off into space or escaped into her books. She read under the living room window where it was the hottest but where the light was good. When Papa teased her about wearing her eyes out, she waved an angry handkerchief at him. Then she wrapped it around her neck and read some more.

One night after reading about the wonders of the Panama Canal, she coyly suggested to Papa as they played gin rummy that perhaps they could go there someday.

Papa replied with his hands, "Dreamer."

Then she started in about my going to college, reminding Papa that his brother Jake had promised to pay my tuition if we didn't have the money when the time came. He gave her a look that said, "I told you he would, and he will, so stop nagging me about it."

"Pretty soon you'll have to remind him."

He looked at me and turned to Mama, laughing. "She's still a child!"

"That's what you think," she said. She passed her hands over her breasts. I knew she was telling him about the bumps on my chest, and I blushed with indignation.

It was the first I'd heard about Mama's desire to send me to college. I hardly remembered Uncle Jake. All I knew was that he was a big shot in the Republican party, and one day he'd get Papa a cushy job. I hardly knew any of Papa's family because they seldom came to visit. Once in a while, Uncle Jake and another of Papa's brothers would come to the house. They were spitting images of Papa, down to the bald spots on their heads. Mama would serve them cold cuts and potato salad and make small talk. Then they would invite Papa to a day at the track. Mama would put on a polite smile as they left the house, then turn purple with rage as soon as they left the vestibule. On those nights, when Papa returned, there would be a lot of chair pushing in the kitchen.

So if she wasn't crazy about Uncle Jake, why was she nagging Papa to ask him for money? I still hadn't mastered the classics and believed I never would. College was too much to consider. I was thinking more typical thoughts for a twelve-year-old. Like how I'd forgiven Timmy for saying those things about Papa and how much I enjoyed sitting with him. How could I hold a grudge anyway? After all, everything he had said was true. I was also thinking how much fun it was to go walking with Aunt Selma and the baby and listen to her talk to her friends. "Is this Charlotte?" her friend Stella asked one afternoon. "My, how you've grown." I knew that Aunt Selma had said nice things to Stella about me when I wasn't around.

I was thinking how different we Herzbergs were and how—unlike Shirley and Hannah—we had no radio or phonograph or telephone. I should have these things, I convinced myself, but how could I ask Papa for them when they would benefit only two of us in the house?

I was thinking about how I hated walking in Humboldt Park with Mama, Papa, and Adelaide and hearing people say shtim-mer. I thought so hard about that one that, one Sunday, I turned around and told a stranger—a man with bulging eyes—that he shouldn't be so impolite as to talk behind people's backs. The stranger turned purple and twitched his eyes. (He wasn't a total stranger; I'd seen him on Hannah's back porch once, but I didn't know his name.) Papa put his hands up to me and asked angrily, "What did you say to him?"

When I told him, he looked surprised and inquired, "Is that what they call me?" Then he laughed and said, "Well, it's better than calling me 'Dummy.' " I thought he always knew.

I was thinking about all their friends who came to play cards in our dining room, making noises and grunting while their knuckles thumped rhythmically, "Knock, I pass; knock, it's your turn; knock, oh boy, what a lousy hand." One night when their racket kept me awake, I poked my head out the bedroom window to listen to the neighbors who were sitting on the broken bench in front of our building, gossiping about other neighbors. I heard Mrs. Geiger mention Mrs. Solomon's operation. "Two incisions, they made," Mrs. Geiger said, "One for the gall bladder and one for the. . . ." Her voice trailed off, leaving me to speculate where they cut Mrs. Solomon a second time. Because nobody in the building except Mrs. Goldberg ever bothered to tell Mama anything, I wondered if I should. They just passed her on the street and said, "Hello, how are you?" and "Isn't it a terribly hot day?"

I was thinking how Mr. Pierce at the delicatessen on Division Street made a fool of himself every time he tried to talk to Papa, waving his hands, shaking his head, and rolling his eyes. It always surprised me that Papa nevertheless knew just what Mr. Pierce was saying. They had managed to have themselves a conversation when I had absolutely no idea what they were talking about.

Mama never encouraged such displays. She kept her signs to herself and enunciated her words carefully, shouting only when it was a life-or-death matter such as pouring concrete on a beautiful lawn. Or when she gave the salesman at Goldblatt's a good talking-to because the slipcovers she ordered were the wrong color. That was a long time ago when Adelaide and I were little and clinging to her hands, scared because Mama had gone wild. She was so angry, she shouted at him. The salesman looked at me and asked, "What's wrong with her?"

"Nuthin'," I said. "She's just deaf."

"That's right," Adelaide repeated. "Deaf."

Mama finally calmed down and instructed me, "Tell the man I ordered burgundy. These are blue." So I told him. He looked fishy-eyed at her as if he suspected she was pretending she couldn't hear. We got the right slipcovers, but I hated her for making a scene.

I was thinking, as the card playing continued, that I didn't know who I belonged to—the people downstairs or the ones sitting in the dining room, talking with their hands. Somebody downstairs was complaining about the landlord, "Mr. Trask wouldn't spend a dime on this building if we didn't nag him about it."

"You're right," another voice replied. "I have half a mind to move out of this dump."

Half a mind. How do you say that in deaf? Slice a finger across another finger, put it to your head? What kind of meaning would that have in deaf? Or high as a kite or loose as a goose or wait 'til the cows come home? It wouldn't have made sense to Mama or Papa. Deaf talk was too straight. No fancy stuff.

I was thinking how lonely it was only to hear words and not to see them. I crept into the darkened living room, plopped on the floor, wrapped my arms around my pillow, and watched through the haze of cigar smoke that hung over the players. Hands flew in all directions. I caught a couple of words about the janitor. He was lazy. Or was that crazy? Was that an L or a C? Nobody sliced a finger across another or put a finger to their head. Then the talk turned serious. "Wasn't that a terrible thing that happened to Charlie Zimmerman?"

"He was a fool. It was his fault," Louie Friedman declared. "You have to watch out for fire engines if you can't hear them."

Oh, my God. Mr. Zimmerman is dead. Why didn't Mama tell me? Papa peered through the hole in the smoke and spotted me. "Why aren't you asleep?"

I wanted to say I was lonely, but I signed, "Too hot."

Mama went to the kitchen to get me water. The others smiled and waved. I waved back. They were all there: Tyrone, who blew smoke rings my way (Adelaide was right to get starry-eyed over him). And Mama's best friend Sarah, who spoke like Mama, and her husband, Little Joe, curly headed and rosy cheeked. He and Papa spent hours in front of Charlie's discussing politics. He smiled and blew me a kiss. I blew him one back. And Rosie, whose mother fretted about what would happen to her, pencil thin, shy, and unlikely ever to get married, according to Sarah and Mama. I studied Rosie and decided they were right. It was doubtful that Rosie would catch a man, and I felt desperately sorry for her. She smiled her shy smile at me. "Pretty pajamas," she signed.

My mother once said it was hard to find a nice Jewish deaf man, but what was wrong with a nice Jewish hearing man? Why couldn't Rosie sit next to the neighbors on the bench with a hearing man and gossip? But nobody did. Nobody even talked about it.

I sipped my water slowly, not wanting to finish. Polite impatience spread across the players' faces. I was holding up the game. Papa took the glass from me and waved me along. When I didn't move, he took me by the hand and led me back to my bedroom.

"You don't have to do that," I said, but I held his hand anyway. "Did Mr. Zimmerman get killed by a fire truck?"

"No, no. Not dead. Only broken bones. We'll go to the hospital to see him tomorrow."

"Thank God," I signed.

"Yes, thank God."

I closed the window to shut out the noise below, scrunched up against my sister's back, and fell asleep.

IN THE fourth bed in the men's ward at Garfield Park Hospital lay Mr. Zimmerman. One arm and a leg on the same side were all bandaged up. A couple of purple bruises covered the right side of his forehead. His black curly hair was trimmed back where the doctor had bandaged it. After bending over to pat Mr. Zimmerman's good shoulder, Mama kissed Mrs. Zimmerman, who was all dressed up as though she were going to a dance. She was wearing a brown hat and gloves to match. I wanted to laugh, but she looked so miserable, I put on a sad face. When Adelaide tried to jump on the bed, Mr. Zimmerman winced. Papa grabbed her and made her sit in a chair.

Papa put his hands palms up, "What the hell happened?"

Mr. Zimmerman had only one hand free, so all he could do was fingerspell instead of making signs with both hands. Papa, Mama, and Mrs. Zimmerman kept nodding their heads in understanding and shaking them sideways in sympathy. Mrs. Zimmerman started to cry, so Papa took her hand, patted it, and uttered soothing hums.

"Hello, hello."

Nobody turned around except Adelaide and me. A man in a fire department uniform was standing at the foot of the bed. "Mr. Zimmerman?"

"He's Mr. Zimmerman," I said, pointing to the bed.

"Yes, I know." He turned to the patient. "Mr. Zimmerman, I'm here to take a report."

"He's deaf," I said.

"Yes, I know!"

"So you don't have to shout because it won't make him hear better."

"Can he write?"

"Sure," I answered, wondering why he would ask such a stupid question. "But I don't know if he's a lefty, so his writing may not be so good."

"Well, we'll try."

Mr. Fireman wrote a bunch of words on a slip of paper and placed it in Mr. Zimmerman's left hand. But the poor man struggled to balance himself in bed in order to write and finally gave up. It wasn't enough information for the fireman, so he started shouting, "Did you hear the fire truck?"

"How could he hear it if he's deaf?"

"Just asking to be sure the siren was on."

"So what if it was? He still couldn't hear it."

"Listen, little girl. Is there an adult here who could speak for him?"

"My mother, I suppose, but she doesn't say her words too well, so you'll have to listen carefully."

"Which one is your mother?"

"She is," I pointed.

He turned to Mama and said, "Could you ask Mr. Zimmerman if he saw the truck lights?"

Mama asked and said, "He's not sure."

"What did she say?" Mr. Fireman asked.

"She said, he said he's not sure if he saw any lights."

The inquisitor appeared unsure what to do next, so Papa took the paper from him, read the questions, and spelled them to Mr. Zimmerman, who spelled back to Papa for what seemed a very long time. Meanwhile, Mr. Fireman was giving me strange looks as if to ask how I happened into this crowd. I volunteered an opinion, "I really think fire trucks should go slower because deaf people can't hear sirens, and they're busy looking at stop lights, not flashing lights three blocks away."

"That's very true about deaf people," he said, waiting for the latest bunch of words from Papa, "but we can't slow down a truck that's going to a fire."

"Pity," I said, acting grown up. I heard Aunt Selma say that once.

"How old are you, little girl?"

"Twelve."

"Twelve, huh? You talk like a smart . . . you talk pretty grown up for a twelve-year-old."

"Thank you."

The interrogator took the paper from Mr. Zimmerman, read it carefully, and shouted, "We'll be in touch, Mr. Zimmerman."

"He'll be back," I relayed.

Mr. Zimmerman shook his head good-bye.

"With an interpreter," the fireman added.

"He's bringing somebody who can talk and sign," I said. Mr. Zimmerman nodded OK.

It was time for us to go. Mr. Zimmerman was getting sleepy from the shot the nurse gave him, so we all left the hospital to catch the streetcar home.

"Did you smartmouth him?" Mama questioned me, her words carefully enunciated, as we sat on the three-for-a-nickel seats.

"I certainly did not!"

"I wonder," she mused, pinching her lips. "You could have talked for Mr. Zimmerman."

"I guess he thought I wasn't old enough."

CHAPTER

12

CHARLIE MANDEL sent one of the boys who hung around the candy store to our apartment with a message. Mama read it and handed me the note. "Marian is coming at three o'clock," it said. Mama seemed excited, but it wasn't unusual for Aunt Marian to show up. Half our dolls were gifts from her and Mama's other sisters. If it wasn't a doll, it would be a new dress or a pair of shoes.

Adelaide wheeled her dolls around in the doll buggy in high anticipation. I was hoping for a new dress since I was more inclined now to pretty bows and fancy sweaters. I watched my sister cram everything to one side to make room for another doll and laughed.

"What do you think we'll get this time?" she asked.

"I don't know, but we have to remember to say thank you."

"Sure," she said, inching the dolls closer to each other. If they could have breathed, they would have suffocated.

AUNT MARIAN stood in the doorway smiling like Rosalind Russell, dressed in a pleated skirt and an angora sweater draped over her silk blouse. She held a Philco radio in her hands—its speakers covered in brown cloth and its two shiny knobs sticking out from the wooden case. "Look what I've brought you. It's a radio. Where shall we put it?"

My heart pounded at the sight. Adelaide giggled, "Is it really ours?"

"Of course, unless Mama says no. Is it all right, Ruthie? I

thought they should have it. Don't you think?" she winked at Mama.

"I think it's a wonderful gift," Mama said. Then she eyed the living room and took a small lamp off the table that stood in the corner next to her chair. "What do you think, Marian? If we put it here, will the sound come out right?"

"You can put it anywhere. You can put it in your bedroom in the back of the house, and the girls will still hear it."

"What would I do with a radio in my bedroom?" she laughed. But it was a nervous laugh, as if she'd been wishing for this for a long time or, I thought, she'd had some secret meeting with Aunt Marian. Planned this without telling Adelaide and me. I certainly never believed that a gift like this would come from any of the aunts. Taking a second look at the radio, I recognized it as Aunt Marian's own. Another hand-me-down, I thought. Well, that was okay. It was a fine looking radio, and it had to work or Aunt Marian wouldn't have given it to us. Mama kept beaming at the radio, still tittering. I wondered if she knew how the radio worked. She had never encountered anything like this when she was a little girl. I wasn't sure myself how it worked. I'd listened to one in Hannah's living room, but I'd never fiddled with it. This radio didn't even look like Hannah's. Hers was a giant box that stood on the floor and had so many knobs even Hannah got confused. Aunt Marian dropped to her knees. "This is the volume knob."

Suddenly sound filled the living room. Adelaide ran back to the kitchen. "Aunt Marian's right," she shouted. "I can hear it all the way back here."

"Of course, I'm right," Aunt Marian said.

Mama was confused at first at the way Adelaide ran past her but soon figured it out. She laughed again. I'd never seen her look so happy. Tears were forming in my eyes, but I decided it was silly to cry over a radio. Aunt Marian would never have cried over such a simple thing, so I said, "Thank you, Aunt Marian. It's the best present I ever got."

I kicked Adelaide in the behind. "Yes, thank you," she parroted. "I love this present."

"Well now, you know how to work it. Just move this knob to the station you want. That's all you have to do." She turned to Mama and spoke nose to nose. "Ruthie, can I have a cup of tea?"

Mama led her into the kitchen. Adelaide fiddled with the radio. "Where's *The Green Hornet*?"

"I don't know if it's on right now."

"Well, how are we gonna know?"

"I'll have to ask Hannah."

"That'll take too long."

"Then move the dial. We'll find something."

Adelaide turned the knob, and Rudy Vallee's voice came through loud and clear. Too loud. I wasn't used to noise in the house. I could walk around the house for days and hear nothing but Adelaide's voice talking to her dolls. I could talk to myself if I wanted to, and Mama and Papa wouldn't know. "Adelaide, turn it down; it's too loud."

"How?"

"Here, stupid."

I turned the knob. Rudy Vallee's voice became soft. Adelaide and I sat on the floor and listened to Mr. Vallee. We were waiting for *The Green Hornet*.

WHEN PAPA walked in the door, we were still waiting. I wished we had a telephone so I could call Hannah and ask her for instructions. Instead, I asked Adelaide to yell out the back porch to Timmy and ask him, but she wouldn't leave the living room. She was afraid she'd miss the Hornet. So we were still sitting cross-legged when we should have been helping Mama set the table. When Papa saw us, he put up his hands, palms up.

"Aunt Marian brought us a radio."

"What for?"

"Everybody has one."

"Why?"

"Oh, Papa."

"Don't need."

"We need! Aunt Marian thinks so."

"Mind her own business." Then he walked into the kitchen.

So Mama hadn't cooked this up. It was as much a surprise to her as it was to us. Or maybe it *was* her idea, but she didn't tell Papa. Mama yelled "Sha and Addle, come to dinner." *The Green Hornet* still hadn't come, but we obeyed. It was very quiet at the table. More than usual. In between mouthfuls, nobody signed anything. Papa was definitely not happy. He cut up his serving of roast and stuck it in his mouth, never looking up. I tried to get his attention just to talk about anything, but he stayed glued to the roast, mashed potatoes, and, afterward, the Jell-O salad that Mama had made earlier that morning.

After dinner, he went into the dining room and played solitaire, pretending he wasn't interested, but I caught him watching us while we sat waiting for something interesting to come on. Mama sat down at the dining room table, and they played gin rummy. Papa took out his cigar, lit it, and filled the dining room with smoke so thick he could have hidden behind it.

Mama must have said something to him while she dried the dishes because he seemed miffed. He slapped the cards down hard, one, two, one, two, as though jabbing a hard right to someone's jaw. The table shook. She left him and came to sit in her chair next to us. He went back to playing solitaire. Hours passed like that—Adelaide and I squatting on the floor, Mama pretending to read her book and sneaking looks at Papa and watching us with curiosity until we finally found *The Green Hornet.*

"Green Hornet? What kind of insect is that?" she asked.

"It's really a man."

"I never heard of such a thing."

"It's pretend, Mama."

96

After a while, she looked at her watch. "Time to go to bed."

"We're in the middle."

"Of what? The living room? So what?"

"In the middle of *The Green Hornet*."

She didn't understand radio time—when a program ended or began. "It's time," she stated.

"A few more minutes."

She sneaked a look at Papa. "Well, a few more minutes."

Papa shook a finger at us. Ugly smoke clouds loomed above his head. I turned off the radio, and we went to bed. A couple of chairs got pushed around the kitchen. I pulled the blanket over my ears and tried to sleep.

THIS WAS the first time I can remember being angry with Papa, but something else was troubling me. He looked hurt most of the time; his eyes clouded over and tears began to well up when he thought I wasn't looking. He brushed them away before they had a chance to fall down his cheek. I thought it was silly for him to behave like that. Finally I understood that this new activity wasn't like going off and playing with my dolls. This wasn't sitting on the porch to play Monopoly with my friends. He could see all of that. He could watch me stuff my winnings in my socks or change my doll's dress. The radio was something he couldn't see. When Adelaide and I swooned over Rudy Vallee or bit our fingernails anxiously while listening to *The Shadow*, Papa had no notion of what was coming out of the box. I wished he would leave the house to see his friends, talk to them, like he belonged somewhere. I would even walk to the corner with him, if it didn't interfere with my programs, but I was determined not to give up my radio.

MAMA SAID he would adjust. That word came out so garbled I didn't understand it, so she spelled it for me. We were sitting in the kitchen having lunch one Saturday. Papa was at a ball game. We were finishing last night's chicken soup and left-over chicken. Adelaide and I ate it like Papa did—the leftover pieces of chicken in the soup along with a piece of challah bread and catsup over it. Emboldened by the presence of a radio, Adelaide and I put thoughts into Mama's head. We talked about telephones.

Mama asked, "Expensive, isn't it?"

"I don't know."

"If you get a job baby-sitting, could you pay for it?"

"You mean baby-sit Aunt Selma's baby?"

"Maybe."

"Aunt Selma hasn't asked me, Mama. I don't think I'm old enough."

"We'll see," she said. "Do you need a phone?"

"Addle and I could make calls for you. You know, to the doctor or Zadie."

"But do you need a phone?"

"Sure."

"What for? To talk to your friends?" She drummed her fingers on the table. "Well, we'll see."

"Forget about it, Mama. It's too much trouble."

"I said, we'll see. Read a book. Do your homework. Enough radio for today."

PAPA STOPPED looking angry after a couple of months, but he didn't talk about the radio, and he never cared about what we were listening to. Then suddenly one day, every-thing changed. Maybe Mama said something to him—the final blow, a strong push of a chair, or a quiet reasoning with him.

One night he asked us what we were listening to. Adelaide, surprised, got all excited and explained that Dick Tracy was after someone. She moved her arms around, shooting imaginary peo-ple, and Papa laughed and shot her back. The next day he asked again, and we explained *The Shadow*. He rolled his eyes upward and pretended fright. Then he sat down at the dining room table, put a plug in his mouth, and played a nice game of gin rummy with Mama.

But the biggest surprise was the day he came home and stopped me in the middle of my Monopoly game. He waved hello at Shirley, Timmy, and Hannah. Turning to me, he said, "Come inside. I have to talk to you. Important," he signed.

Taking my "money" with me, I stepped into the kitchen. "What, Papa?"

"The Joe Louis-Billy Conn fight will be on the radio. Will you listen for me?"

"Sure, Papa. When?"

"Soon. Don't go away. I'll be back." He rushed past Mama to the front door. Mama looked at him as if he'd gone crazy, and her eyes narrowed when she understood what he was up to. She shouted with her hands, "No, Joe. I don't want the girls to listen." But it was too late. Papa was already out the door. I went back to the porch and told my playmates we'd have to end the game. I had something important to do.

Papa returned, bringing his friends with him: Little Joe, Mr. Zimmerman (all healed from the fire truck accident, his hair still missing from the spot on his head), some men I'd never seen before, and Tyrone, who looked at me and smiled. I thought I would faint.

"Get Addle," Papa signed.

"Why? I can do it."

"Please, get Addle."

"All right. All right."

I had to leave the house to find her. She was two doors away, playing with a friend who lived on the third floor in the next hallway. She wasn't happy about listening to Joe Louis and Billy Conn. But I didn't want to make Papa hurt or angry, so I grabbed her by the hand and pulled her back to our apartment. Papa had placed the dining room chairs in a circle in the living room. The men were already in their seats when we walked in. They were looking at the radio as if something was already happening. I found the station. "It hasn't begun yet," I told Papa.

"Not yet?" he asked, disappointed.

"No, not yet."

"Then why did I have to run up the stairs like a crazy man?" demanded Mr. Zimmerman. "My legs still hurt!"

"I'm sorry, Charlie," Papa said. "I'll tell Ruthie to make you some tea." He left his chair reluctantly, afraid of missing the beginning, but, as soon as he stood up, he ran into the kitchen. I could hear Mama screeching and humming at him. She was probably calling him a fool for dragging Mr. Zimmerman away from his comfortable rocker just for a stupid boxing match. I could only guess because my ears were glued to the set, worried that Papa might miss the beginning. Adelaide and I took our places on the floor in the center of the circle. Eight heads bent down to watch us. The announcer's voice finally cracked through the speaker. Adelaide and I split up the group, she facing one side and I, the other. We signed and fingerspelled so fast our fingers fumbled.

But Papa had grander ideas. "You will be Billy Conn," he told Adelaide. "And you. . . ."

I was the Brown Bomber. I threw a jab at Conn. Conn grazed my cheek with a blow. The men hummed and fussed in their chairs. Lightning jabs came through the box and through our bodies. Bam. Bam. Bam. With a strong upper cut to Conn, I flattened Adelaide. She fell backward, her dress wrinkled, her hair ribbons twisted and turned. She moaned. The men groaned. She picked herself up. Came up punching. I hit her again. I won the fight.

Eight pairs of hands patted our heads. Eight pairs of hands spelled "thank you." Adelaide straightened her dress, tied the ribbon back in her hair, and stamped her foot to get their attention. "Next time I get to be Louis," she insisted. They roared with laughter. "Sure, sweetheart, next time." They walked out the door, shaking Papa's hand.

THE FOUR of us sat in the kitchen, drinking cocoa, winding down from the excitement. Mama had a smirk on her face. I couldn't tell if she was annoyed or trying to keep from laughing. "Shame on you, Joe, for teaching them to fight," she said finally, rolling her eyes. Papa chuckled. Mama covered her mouth to stifle the laugh. "This is so silly," she said. She slid her fingers through Adelaide's hair, turning the ribbons right. And then she laughed a real horse of a laugh. Because Mama sounded so funny, Adelaide and I laughed, and Papa made his funny chuckles, and we were hitting the table, our sides hurting from all our laughing.

"Enough," she said. "It's time we went to bed."

She took the cups to the sink. Papa sat for a while, shaking his head up and down and sideways. I knew he was reliving the fight. I was sure there would be no chair shoving tonight. I changed into my pajamas. Adelaide was already in bed, still charged up from the evening. She kept pawing an old stuffed dog. I was about to turn off the light when Papa showed up at the bedroom door.

"What's wrong, Papa?"

"Nothing is wrong. I want to ask you. How much does it cost to have a telephone?"

"I'm not sure, Papa, but I'll find out."

"Find out."

He turned his back and walked into the living room, but he reappeared just as I was pulling the blanket up. He turned on the light.

"What, Papa?"

"Mama thinks you should have a piano."

"Really?"

"Would you like?"

"I would love! Adelaide, he's talking about pianos."

Adelaide sat up straight in bed and tossed the stuffed dog into the doll crib. "True, Papa?"

"Will try. Good night."

"Good night, Papa."

ADELAIDE AND I never missed a fight. I can't remember how many times we did this for Papa. I figured we'd be doing this forever, never imagining television would take our place.

After years of stroking Aunt Selma's piano as if it were ours, Mama persuaded Papa to look for an old upright. He found one for thirty-five dollars and hired a truck and driver to bring it home. It was scarred and dirty, but Mama polished it to a high sheen, laid a flowered shawl over the top, and put family pictures on it. It looked grand in the corner of the living room. Adelaide and I took the streetcar to Uncle Morrie and Aunt Ethel's house to take lessons from cousin Paulie's piano teacher.

Mama came to my first piano recital, dressed in her best suit and her rose-covered hat, and beamed while I played "Claire de Lune" so poorly that I wanted to die on the spot. I took my bow to lukewarm applause, my body trembling with shame. But Mama smiled as if just seeing me at the piano was enough for her. Adelaide wasn't any better, but I lied and told her that her performance was wonderful. And Aunt Ethel lied to Mama, "Ruthie, the girls did very well."

And Mama said to Papa later that evening, "Joe, the girls were fantastic." Papa smiled. The telephone would have to wait until Adelaide and I could earn money baby-sitting.

CHAPTER

13

O N DECEMBER 7 that year, the radio blared
dreadful news, and I ran to my father to tell him.
The *Tribune* was spread before him on the kitchen table, his eyes
busy with reading. "Papa, Papa," I poked him, insisting he turn
to face me.

"What?" he demanded impatiently, throwing his hands in the air.

"The Japanese bombed Pearl Harbor. I just heard it on the
radio. Where's Pearl Harbor?"

He moaned loudly, which frightened me, and his eyes were
bright with surprise. He didn't answer. He looked back at the
paper, then realized that the radio had told it that very instant
and the paper was as useless as yesterday's news. He folded it up
and hurried into the living room to tell Mama. She'd been sitting
in her chair reading, fidgeting with the lamp, turning it first one
way and then the other to get the best light. The sun hadn't
come out yet. It was cold and ugly outside. He pulled the book
out of her hands and informed her.

"Pearl Harbor?" Mama asked.

"Yes, Hawaii," Papa told her.

"I know. I know."

So that's where it was. The announcer's voice sounded hyster-
ical. His words came in a clip clip, repeating the news again and
again. "The radio's still talking about it, Papa."

"What else does it say?"

"Bombs from planes. An airfield. I didn't get the name. What
does it mean?"

"It means war," he said. "Turn it off. I don't want you listening anymore."

"Listen to music," Mama suggested.

I switched the dial. Everything was the same. "There is no music. There's nothing but the news."

"Then turn it off."

I turned the radio off while Papa slipped a coat over his shoulders and left the house. I watched him through the window as he walked toward the candy store. Some of his deaf friends were coming out of their buildings and walking in the same direction. They would meet at Mandel's to discuss the situation. This time he didn't want me along.

I followed Mama into the kitchen. "Is there going to be a war, Mama?"

"I'm afraid so," she cried.

"But we don't have to worry, do we?"

"How do I know?" she said angrily. "This is terrible."

In a frenzy of activity, she began pulling cans from the pantry, putting them back, sponging down the sink, and wiping it. She turned to look at me and forced a smile, "This is nothing for you to worry about. I'm sure it will be over soon. Why don't you read your comics? Maybe later we'll go to Pierce's for corned beef sandwiches." As if this last spurt of calming energy had drained her, she sank into the kitchen chair and neatly folded her hands. I knew by the way she sat, eyes focusing internally, that she wanted to think, so I walked back to the living room and opened the window to look for Papa on the street. A blast of cold air blew the lace curtains up and over me. Papa was nowhere to be seen, but there was plenty of activity on the street. Neighbors were pouring out of their buildings, huddling in groups and talking. Men mostly. The women, like Mama, were probably sitting in their kitchen chairs with their hands folded.

Mama had been muttering "terrible" for months, every time she read the newspaper. She said it when I told her Timmy's grandmother had died. It was the second time in my life that death had become something to talk about, but this time it was far away, and I handled it with courage and, I thought, understanding.

One afternoon Timmy had come to sit on our steps with a bewildered, sad look on his face. "My grandmother's dead," he explained. "She lived in Germany. I never knew her, but now she's dead, and everybody at home is crying about it."

"I'm sorry to hear it, Timmy. Germany is very far away. I don't suppose you'll be going to the funeral," I said, trying to make him feel better. Using my own experience as a connection, I told him I wasn't allowed to go to my grandmother's funeral. "Too young," I explained.

"Are you nuts? Nobody can go to Germany. Don't you know what's happening over there? Don't you read the papers?"

"You don't have to get all mean about it," I answered

"Well, sometimes you're stupid." He got up and opened the vestibule door and walked out.

No, I didn't know. Well, maybe I did. While I sucked the butter off my popcorn at the Harmony Theater, chorus girls danced up steps that went nowhere, and smooth-talking matinee idols held slinkily dressed blonde bombshells, and Flash Gordon took off in his space machine. Then the Pathe News came on with scenes of death and destruction in places I'd never heard of. Or if I knew about them from Papa's sometime geography lessons, I didn't care. It all seemed too far away.

I felt close to Timmy. When I sat in the darkened theater watching passionate embraces, I thought of him. I suspected he thought of me, too, in that way, and now I had angered him. I felt awful about my stupidity.

Mama had hummed sadly at Timmy's news. "You tell Timmy to tell his family that I'm very sorry. I'd go there myself, but it's hard for them to understand me. But you know how to do it. You understand."

"No, I don't understand. Why don't you write it on a piece of paper?"

"Just tell them I'm sorry."

Annoyed with the burden she had put on me, I walked over to Timmy's house and knocked on the door. At least I would have a chance to make it better with Timmy, tell him I'm sorry. But the family was another matter. Remembering my mother's screams and Aunt Selma's fainting dead away when Bubbi died, I knocked on Timmy's door, prepared for the worst. Timmy answered.

"My mother would like your mother to know she's sorry to hear the news about your grandmother."

"Thank you," he said. "I'll tell her."

I was relieved he didn't invite me in because I could hear wailing in the back rooms. "I guess you're busy," I said.

"I'm not allowed to go out today."

"Okay, then."

He closed the door. I walked away, thinking his grandmother's death must have something to do with the scenes I saw at the movies, but I didn't ask Timmy. By the time I was back upstairs again, Mama had her nose in a book and looked up only to thank me.

When Papa returned from Charlie's that Sunday morning, he carried a special edition of the *Tribune*, its headline underscored by a strong black line. His head disappeared from my view as he stretched out the new edition on the table to read. He didn't need me anymore. The radio sat quiet because Mama insisted I keep it off. She sat next to Papa and their fingers flew. There was nothing for me to do except play hearts with Adelaide at the dining room table. I figured that eventually they'd let us back into their conversation, but, by bedtime, they were still engrossed with each other, so we turned off the lights and went to bed.

FOR DAYS the paper boys roamed the streets with special editions, screaming their headlines. Papa, sensing their calls, looked out the window every morning. Discovering one on the street, he rushed down to buy his new paper. One evening he let his food get cold while trying to convince Mama of his plans. "I'm still strong," he said. "I could work in the kitchen."

"Don't be a fool," she answered. "You're forty-eight years old, too old to go to war. If they didn't take you last time when you were the right age, what makes you think they'll take you now?"

"I could peel potatoes," he insisted.

Mama almost laughed but thought better of it and covered her mouth quickly. She stroked his hand. Then, with a sweet look on her face, she said, "Joe, you have a family now. I know it's not fair. You should have a right to fight for your country, even if you are deaf. But, Joe, we need you here."

"Is it fair?" he asked me. "If I can't fight, if I can't hear the orders, why can't I peel potatoes?"

"I don't know why, Papa. It doesn't seem fair."

He stabbed the cold meat with his fork and put it to his mouth, but he had no appetite and asked Mama for his coffee. We didn't talk about it again.

Every day as I walked to school, I looked up at the sky, wondering when the bombs would fall, wondering if Papa was right to be angry because they wouldn't take a deaf man. After much thought, I decided that it was unjust. He was still strong. So what if he couldn't hear somebody yell, "Shoot!"

When nothing fell from the sky, when no bombs made craters in the middle of Washtenaw Avenue, I relaxed. Nothing was going to hurt me, and, since the government didn't want my father, nothing would hurt his flesh, only his pride.

THE NEIGHBORHOOD soon filled with men in uniform. As we walked the street, Papa stopped to pat a soldier on the arm, turned to me, and gave me a message for him.

"He wishes you good luck," I said.

"Thank him for me, honey."

Papa tipped his hat. He stopped every man in uniform, young men, hardly older than me, dressed like toy soldiers in spanking new khaki, patted them, and gave them his message of good luck. Sometimes he scribbled a note. I suppose in his thoughts he was fighting the war every time he touched a uniform. He pulled himself up straight when we walked, as if to prove to himself he could do it, if anyone asked.

Mama had said once, when she heard the news of a friend's death, that it broke her heart. I'd never heard the expression before. I figured it was deaf talk and pictured a heart on a Valentine card split in two. It seemed comical to me, the way some deaf talk was, but the look on Mama's face was anything but happy. I didn't want Papa fighting a war, but every time I saw him touch a soldier's hand, it broke my heart. When cousin Jerry came to say good-bye, eighteen years old and still in civilian clothes, ready to report to camp, my mother's heart broke again.

Papa's brother Lou came to our door to take his leave. He looked splendid in his army uniform and moved his fingers in a simple good-bye. He was thirty-nine. They held on to each other for a while, their faces awkward with the intimacy; then Uncle Lou left.

As THE war continued, I allowed Timmy to hold my hand. My heart was strong and whole. But the mood in the kitchen was somber, and in the neighborhood, cold and gray. Papa and Mama pored over their newspapers. In the quiet of our dining room, while the radio spewed out encouragement, Papa drew Indian faces—powerful, quiet and brave. Service flags appeared in the front windows of our neighbors' homes, their blue stars proclaiming that a family member had gone to war.

PAPA POKED Adelaide on the shoulder one morning. "Your doll buggy is good metal. We should give it to the scrap drive."

She whimpered, but Papa prevailed. "There's plenty of room in your doll crib," he said.

"He's right, Adelaide," I agreed. "There's plenty of room. I'll take my dolls out and put them in the closet."

My willingness to support the war effort was a sham: I simply didn't care about my dolls anymore. I stuffed them in the closet— legs twisted and hair matted—and never took them out again.

We walked the buggy to the corner of Evergreen and Washtenaw where a pile of steel, aluminum, and rubber tires was stacked. Adelaide's brown eyes filled with tears in a last attempt to hold on to her past, but Papa put his finger to his lips. "Shush, don't be sad," and then he moved his hands upward and promised, "The buggy will become something new, something to help us win the war."

Mama was so pleased with his beautiful words that she squeezed his hand.

"Pretty soon," I assured her, "you won't care where your dolls sleep."

SOME OF the stars in the service flags turned to gold, a sign that a member of the family behind the flag had been a battle casualty. Papa shook his head whenever he saw the symbol of death, then returned one day with a flag bearing two blue stars in the middle. I don't know what possessed him to do it. I didn't think we had a right to hang a flag because nobody in our immediate family had gone off to war, but Papa insisted and hung it proudly in our living room window.

One day, Mr. Jacobson, our neighbor across the street, yelled up to me from the street below. "You have no business hanging that flag. Tell your father to take it down."

"I will not, Mr. Jacobson. We can hang anything we want in our window."

Anger flooded his face at my impertinence. "You're sassing me? A smart kid like you. Where are your manners? Listen, honey," he softened, "I know your father doesn't understand. Just tell him."

"What right do you have to say he doesn't understand? And what business is it of yours anyway?"

The blood was rushing to my head from hanging out the window too long.

"Oy, a smart mouth. I'm gonna tell," he chided.

"You're not telling anybody," I answered dizzily.

Mr. Jacobson's body disappeared. Only his head bobbed in front of me, his eyes aimed at mine. Pulling my head back into the room, I ran to the kitchen, filled a bucket of water, hurried back to the open window, and poured the water straight down toward him. Mr. Jacobson did a quick hop, narrowly missing the torrent. His eyes bulged with disbelief as he retreated, shaking his head. Adelaide jumped up from the sofa where she'd been reading a comic and ran to my side. "What did you do that for?"

"I dunno," I said, my hands trembling. "I just don't know."

"What did Mama say when she saw you filling the bucket?"

"Nuthin'. She was reading the paper. She never saw me."

"Lucky. But he's gonna tell Mama and Papa."

"I don't think so, and don't you tell either."

She went back to the sofa, shaking her head. "Well, get rid of the bucket, or Mama will know you've been up to something."

I sneaked past Mama, whose face was hidden by the newspaper, and put the bucket back in the broom closet. I was nervous the whole afternoon, thinking Mr. Jacobson—bent on revenge—would run to tell somebody. I didn't care if he told Papa. Unsure if we were breaking the law, however, I brooded over the possibility that he would inform the authorities about our flag. But even if he did, nobody was going to tell my father he was wrong and get away with it.

MR. JACOBSON apparently never told anyone because nobody came knocking on our door to haul Papa and me off to jail. The only neighbor who knew about the incident between Mr. Jacobson and me was Mrs. Goldberg, who had seen the whole thing. She had told Mr. Jacobson, right on the spot, that he should leave us alone, the poor dears, and mind his own business.

I began to read the newspapers, thinking Timmy was right; I was stupid, but the real reason for involving myself in the news was to keep the kitchen talk going. Papa, it seemed, was not interested in anything else, and he kept Mama occupied with his thoughts. But, no matter how hard I tried to sound knowledge-able, Papa took little notice of my interest. I wondered if he would have acted differently if I had been a boy.

There were shortages everywhere—of food, gas, silk stockings, and men to fill jobs left empty by other men who had gone to war. Papa took us to school one day to apply for food ration books. After supper that night, I took a walk with Timmy to Humboldt Park.

"How is your mother feeling?" I asked.

"As well as can be expected," he said.

"I can well imagine," I answered, remembering Aunt Selma saying that once to a friend. I suspected that Timmy's words were also a repetition of some grownup's utterance. They sounded too perfect. We held hands and talked for hours under a perfect sky, afire with twinkling stars. The blue stars in our flag stayed blue.

ADELAIDE TOOK over my baby-sitting duties while Hannah and I applied for work at Woolworth's on North Avenue. We were barely fourteen, but the manager welcomed us, our brand-new Social Security cards making us feel very grown up. "Can you cook?" he asked us.

"I can scramble an egg," I told him. He wasn't impressed.

"I've cooked hamburgers," Hannah said.

"Well, now we're talking," he smiled. "Don't get me wrong.

I can use the both of you, but I need someone who knows her way around the kitchen."

That was decidedly Hannah, so she put on her hairnet and served hamburgers at the luncheon counter. I sold bridge mix and jelly slices at the candy counter. I measured the amount on the scale and calculated the price, which required concentration, but I figured it was better than being a cook. I was in the retail business. I came home and informed Papa that I might consider doing this as a career when I grew up. After all, it was better than baby-sitting, I told him.

"Sure," he waved his hand, "if that's what you want to do the rest of your life."

The rest of my life seemed distant. My father had determined then that my initiation into big-time work was just a passing thing. When the war was over, I would concentrate on school and where I'd go from there. He was still counting on Uncle Jake to bail me out of retail work. He went back to his reading, confident that better things were in store for me.

Flushed with pocket money even after I'd given a portion of my salary to Papa for "rent," I searched Marshall Field's and Carson Pierie's for the latest clothes. It was a waste of time, for the fashion of the day was to wear a man's shirt over rolled-up slacks. I borrowed Timmy's. My dirty saddle shoes completed the look.

Papa's fortunes took a turn for the better. Tired of waiting for Uncle Jake to get him that cushy city job, he pressed another brother into finding something more substantial than his job at Uncle Eddie's yard. His brother Sam found him a position at Drewry's Brewery, where he worked on the bottling line. He was a union member now and paid his union dues like a true soldier, forgetting the days back in the twenties when people paid him to break up strikes.

I sold candy every day after school and on Saturdays. I'd never had so much money. Papa insisted that I buy bonds to help the war effort. Besides, he winked at me, "It's a good start for a nice wedding."

"I thought you were pushing for college, Papa."

"So, after college."

"Why should I bother going to college if what you want for me is a wedding?"

He put his hands palms up. "Just in case."

HANNAH, SHIRLEY, and I were too young to help out at the USO clubs. We were in between, too old to stick to the past, too young to be adults, too naive to understand the true horrors of war, so we spread our blankets in Humboldt Park and looked at the sky. We talked of boys and the new Spanish teacher and how handsome he was and the latest styles in clothes and left the worrying to the grownups.

I knew that when the war ended, I'd be out of a job. The war was going well. Politicians focused on the problems of postwar recovery. For weeks, I'd been hoarding my money, afraid to diminish the healthy lump of capital. That's what Papa called it. "You have to have a little capital," he'd say. I wondered how much capital he had. My paying rent must have swelled his worth.

THE WAR ended with a blast of bells and sirens throughout the city. Papa's friends patted each other on the back and whooped along with the neighbors who stood in front of Charlie's. There was a holiday spirit everywhere. Shirley and Hannah were there. And Timmy. He stood close to me so that our hands could touch without anyone seeing us. Papa insisted we all take the streetcar downtown to State Street to celebrate.

"I'd rather stay home and listen to my music," I told him. (A phonograph now sat in our house.)

"But this is a big celebration. The war is over. We should be happy about it."

"I am happy, Papa, but I'd rather stay home. Well, all right, if Timmy can come along."

He looked at me strangely and chuckled. "OK," he waved his hand. "He can come." Mama gave me a knowing smile.

State Street was crowded with people, all shouting with joy, kissing perfect strangers on the mouth. Confetti fell from above, coating us with bits of color. I sneaked a kiss to Timmy. It didn't seem to matter to Papa anymore that he couldn't have joined in the fight. His emotions were given over to the war effort in the best way he could, and he shook hands with strangers and smiled, happy it was over and that Uncle Lou and my cousin Jerry were safe. We were all in a festive mood. My mother looked up at the falling confetti, shielding her eyes from the glare of the sun that had finally poked through the clouds. She lurched, losing her balance for a moment, and grabbed Papa's arm. My father was ready. He held her tight. I knew by the look on his face that something was wrong. Seeing me, he smiled and signed, "She's just a little dizzy."

I don't know if he knew then what was happening to Mama. I know that I didn't know, but soon it would become apparent to all of us that Mama was going blind.

PART

2

CHAPTER

14

I T S E E M E D logical that those a generation older than me would begin to show signs of aging. Mama was sprouting a few gray hairs, and Papa had developed arthritis in his knees. He rubbed them on cold winter nights with a mixture of alcohol and witch hazel that he had made special at the corner drugstore—a reminder of the magic potion massaged into his sore muscles during his boxing days. It was the only remedy he used, and he used it on us every time we developed a cold, rubbing our backs when we were little, filling the bedroom with fumes that made us drowsy. When our modesty and his understanding of our maturity prevented him from doing the massage personally, he asked Mama to take the job over, insisting it was better than Vicks VapoRub.

Zadie had progressed to infirmities faster than anyone. He was bent over when he walked, the red in his mustache had disappeared, and he wore a strong pair of glasses. He looked perpetually tired and unhappy, missing Bubbi, I supposed, and adrift from Aunt Selma's and Uncle Eddie's modern ways. My talk of high school, hayrides, and movies only confused him more. When he came to the house to poke Mama on the shoulder for his usual "Nu, how are you?" he seemed depressed, even when she said, "Fine."

Aunt Selma had given up smoking because a decent smoke was hard to find during the war. She still made snap decisions about my clothing. "Nice. No good. Great color. And how's your love life?" she'd ask. My love life at seventeen no longer included Timmy. Instead, there were good-looking older students who turned my head, one of whom found his way to my marble steps. We talked until three in the morning until Papa glowered above me from the second floor landing, his eyes filled with anger. A shake of his finger sent my friend running into the night. Humiliated, I cried on my sister's shoulder, cursing Papa for his shameful behavior.

"He's deaf," she said. "What other way can he explain his feelings? It doesn't take a genius to know that he was upset. He's been pointing fingers at us since we were babies."

"That's no excuse."

"And what's your excuse for staying out until three in the morning?" she challenged.

"So you're on his side."

"I'm not on anybody's side. Go to sleep and leave me alone."

Preoccupied with my own teenage rebellion, I ignored the signs around me. There were no more chair shoving episodes in the kitchen. If Mama tried his patience with nervous shrieking and hand waving, my father ignored it, an unusual way for him to behave. Giving up without a fight and ignoring her nagging fingers should have told me something. But I took it to mean that he was settled into a job that paid well, eliminating the need for frantic arguments about late nights out with strange deaf men or where to spend his money. I missed Papa's worried look every time he took Mama's hand and patted it.

I listened halfheartedly as the women in the bridge club sat tightly in a corner of our living room while Mama prepared coffee and donuts after their game, talking secret talk, mouths open and forming words only for each other to see. Monotonous droning about "It won't help" and "Joe told me the doctor said. . . ."

Who's sick? Who's in trouble now, I wondered, but I walked past them without questioning, down the steps and out into the street, trying to find my own way.

ONE AFTERNOON when I was almost eighteen, my father's callous behavior gone from consciousness because I had found myself a beau (as Aunt Selma called him), I saw Mama sitting in her chair, reading a book with a magnifying glass. I poked her. She lifted her eyes to me. "What's wrong?" I asked her.

"Just old age," she laughed.

"You're not old. Timmy's mother is old. She's fat and gray all over and can hardly walk. You're forty-six. That's not old."

"Well, you make me feel old, staying out late at night, going out with someone I don't know."

"I'll ask him to come tonight to meet you," I promised.

"We're having a poker game tonight."

"Well, I guess he'll meet everyone." Won't that be fun? I thought.

"Does he know about us?"

"Do you mean, does he know you're deaf? Of course, he does."

I had told him on our very first date. It was something I had done when I met new people from the time I was fifteen. "Hello, how are you? My name is Charlotte. My parents are deaf." Maybe not right away. Two or three sentences down the line. "Come over and listen to Frank Sinatra in my living room. We can dance and make as much noise as we want to. My parents are deaf."

Mama's eyes were back on her book.

"I really think you should see an eye doctor," I insisted, pulling the book away from her face.

"I'm going tomorrow," she said in a voice flatter than usual.

"Tomorrow? But I'm going to school. Why didn't you tell me sooner? Who made the appointment for you?"

"Selma," she said. Flat. Very flat. Almost a whisper. I could hardly hear it.

"Selma?"

"Yes," she nodded.

"Why? I could have done it. That's why we have the telephone now. Is Aunt Selma going with you? You know you get all excited when you talk to doctors."

"Yes, she's going with me."

"I could have done it if you let me pick a date."

"It's not your business!" she shouted in a surprising burst of emotion. "You've got your own worries. Papa says he found you sitting in the living room again late at night. All alone. Why? What about this new boy you have? Why isn't he with you? Where did you meet him?"

"He's a friend of Timmy's, Mama. I have no worries. I like to sit in the dark and think. He has homework. He can't be with me all the time."

"Is that the truth?"

"First, you're angry with me because I come home late. Then you're angry with me because I'm sitting alone in the dark. Then you tell me Aunt Selma is taking you to the doctor—after we went to all the trouble to get a telephone in the house. Don't you want me to do this for you anymore? Maybe we should get rid of the phone!"

"The phone was never for us. It was for you and Addle. To talk until two in the morning. To keep things from me like new boyfriends. If I want, I can ask Charlie Mandel to send a message, just like in the old days. I don't need your phone, so don't make empty threats. As long as you pay the phone bill, you can keep it."

She got up, closed her book, tossed the magnifying glass on the end table, and walked to the kitchen muttering. I followed her, demanding an answer, but it was useless. If she felt my steps behind her, she purposely avoided turning to face me. A twinge of fear gripped my stomach. This was strange. This wasn't ordinary. I usually made the appointments for her, and, when she couldn't understand the complicated talk—too stubborn to use pen and pencil—Adelaide or I interpreted for her. I pushed the tight feelings away. Okay, if that's what she wants, fine with me. I picked up the telephone, called my beau, and insisted he come to the house to pick me up. I was nervous about dumping Al into an unfamiliar world of deaf ears while they sized him up, but it was now or never. I was serious about him. It was time they got to know each other.

I HAD just finished putting nail polish on my baby finger, the poker players watching with interest, when the doorbell rang. Everyone stopped playing and stared at the bell light. I opened the door and let Al in. Papa turned the bell light off. The poker group now focused their attention on Al, who was dressed in a khaki shirt, brown pants, and a plaid jacket. A bow tie filled the space between his shirt collar. They kept on gaping. Papa shook his hand. I giggled while Al solemnly shook back. He was trying not to stare at the others. He had prepared for this meeting, understanding my parents from the picture I'd painted, but the others sitting quietly had surprised him. He tugged at his bow tie with nervous fingers.

Tyrone saluted hello. Rosie got all shy and couldn't look at him. Mama walked back into the dining room through the kitchen door, barely missing the sides of the door. She took her seat at the table, then waved her fingers into the air in a command. The players averted their eyes to the table. "Happy to meet you," she said, her words perfect. Al nodded his head. He didn't say anything, although he knew my mother would understand his words. He just nodded his head again and looked anxiously around the room.

"She bumps into things sometimes because deaf people have a hard time keeping themselves straight when they walk. Something to do with signals to the brain, or is it the other way around? I'm not sure which way it's supposed to be. I get confused."

"Of course," he said.

"Where is it we're going, Al?"

"To the State and Lake. I hear the vaudeville act is pretty good."

"He's taking me to the State and Lake," I told the group.

The group smiled. "It's supposed to be a great show," Tyrone said.

"Tyrone says he heard it was great."

"His name is Tyrone—like the movie star?"

"Not really," I laughed. "It's a private joke."

Papa smiled politely waiting for his turn to say something. He made a stab at writing his question on a piece of paper but crunched it in a ball and instead asked me, "Does he work?"

"No, he goes to school. To college. To be an engineer."

All the men nodded with approval. "That's a very important job," Papa explained to Tyrone, who nodded back yes. Then everyone got quiet. I could tell that not one of them knew what an engineer was. Neither did I, and I hoped that Papa wouldn't ask me.

"I'll get my coat, Al, and we'll go."

"Sure."

I hurried to the hall closet, pulled the coat off the hanger, uneasy about leaving Al alone, and rushed back. Papa had paper in front of him, and he and Al were "talking." Papa looked up and spelled, "I know his father. Long time. Nice man."

"How do you know his father?" I asked, surprised.

"Well," he said, embarrassed, but Al was pushing me out the door before Papa could answer. I waved a hurried good-bye and went down the stairs with him. "I suppose he's bought newspapers at your father's newsstand."

"Yeah. And placed a couple of bets on the horse races."

"Your father's a bookie?"

"I wouldn't call it that," he laughed.

"I would," I laughed.

122

WHEN I came home from school the following day, Mama was sitting on the sofa next to Aunt Selma, a pair of glasses perched on her nose, one lens frosted opaque. They both watched me as I put my books down on the dining room table.

"Hi, honey," Aunt Selma said, smiling. "I was just about to leave, but I'm glad you're here. She needs to wear these all the time. Doctor's orders. Make sure she does. She's not happy about it."

"Sure," I answered, watching Mama. There wasn't a hint of worry, just annoyance with the glasses. She fiddled with them, trying to adjust them to her face. Aunt Selma pulled herself up from the sofa, smoothed the hennaed hair that covered her own beginnings of gray, tucked her purse under her arm, and said, "You'll get used to it, Ruthie. It just takes a little time."

Mama tilted her head to the left to get Aunt Selma's face in her view. She nodded. "If I can walk all right, I'll be over to see Pa tomorrow."

"Give yourself a few days to get comfortable with walking outside." She headed toward the front door. "Char, there's nothing to worry about."

"That's good to hear. And if she can't get used to it, I'll walk her to Zadie's."

"She'll get used to it. Don't worry." She closed the door behind her.

Mama pulled the newspaper in front of her, blocking her face from my view. "Al seems like a nice boy," she said, her voice muffled behind the pages. Her hand came down and the newspaper with it. "I'll get used to this in time."

"Sure you will." I spread my homework on the dining room table thinking this wasn't the first time she'd seen the eye doctor. Glasses didn't just appear on the first visit. This has been going on for a while. When Adelaide came home, I was still sitting at the dining room table doing my homework. Mama's eyes were closed, her head resting on the back of the chair. She looked at

Mama and twitched her nose like a frightened rabbit. "What's happened to her eye?"

"Nothing's happened. She went to the eye doctor. I told you that."

"You never told me."

"I certainly did. You didn't listen." The dates of the Civil War popped out bold and black from the pages of the encyclopedia. I shut the book and asked calmly, "What are you getting all riled up about? It's nothing."

"Why is one lens frosted?"

"Something to do with making the other eye stronger."

"You never tell me anything!"

"That's not true. I told you. Well, maybe I didn't, but you're never home, so how I can tell you anything? I said it's nothing to worry about."

Mother's uncovered eye opened. "Why are you fighting?"

"We're not fighting."

"Good, because I won't have it," she demanded, pulling the glasses off.

"Sha says you have to wear the glasses all the time. Don't take them off," Adelaide said.

"Of course, I won't," she said, putting them back on again.

"Good," Adelaide said and left me there, feeling guilty.

BUT MAMA pulled them off regularly in the first few weeks. Adelaide worried and screamed at Mama, "You have to wear them or your eyes won't get better."

She screamed while I talked on the phone to Al. She screamed while I put curlers in my hair. She screamed while I pulled up my nylons, hooked them up to my garters, and put on my pancake makeup. She had turned into the worst of neighbors, shrill and demanding, her eyes darting in fear.

"Leave her alone. She only takes them off when she's cooking. I can understand that. They get all steamed up."

"You don't care."

I threw my curlers at her and walked out of the apartment.

BEFORE THE year was up, Aunt Marian took her to a specialist. "Nothing to worry about," she said, depositing Mama at our front door. "Have to run. If you need me, give me a call."

Empty offer, I thought. Aunt Marian would tell me nothing. They would talk about it to each other—Aunt Selma, Aunt Marian, Aunt Nettie, Uncle Morrie, maybe Zadie—but they wouldn't tell me, I knew. They would keep the doctor's words to themselves, fix it themselves. As if they could throw more Shirley Temple dolls and pretty clothes our way to soften the blow. I was past their mothering and wanted to know, but I couldn't pick up the phone and ask. So I stuck my head in my books and fell more deeply in love with Al—and pretended to Adelaide that I wasn't worried.

The glasses stayed on Mama's nose. Still opaque. She adjusted to her one-eyed vision, cooking, cleaning, and ironing. Once in a while she brought the iron too close to her fingers, burning them.

"Let me do this," Adelaide begged one morning before we left for school.

"No. Leave me alone. You do what you have to do. I'll do what I have to do." She stuck her finger in her mouth to cool it off. "I'm fine."

Mama and Papa didn't talk about it. We sat at the kitchen table ignoring it, talking about our days as if nothing was happening. He spit his tobacco out in the toilet and sprayed the wall. She hung her laundry on the line. They visited friends, played cards, acted normally. But, by the time I was nineteen, Mama no longer shopped on her own. She walked through the house, her arms outstretched to keep from bumping into walls. Papa took her to the fish market and Mr. Laykin's grocery store. They stopped going to the movies because the bright lights of the screen hurt her eyes. One night I watched Mama play cards with her friends, the cards almost to her nose. Her friends paused to talk, their lips close to Mama's face. Mama finally asked that we sign to her because it was too hard to see our lips. Sometimes when it was even too difficult to see our fingers going at full speed, she asked us to go slower or sign in her hands. I finger-spelled in her good hand and formed her hand around mine while I made signs. For a while it stayed that way. My mother had changed, but not so much that she still wasn't Mama. We just changed the way we talked to her.

CHAPTER

15

"**A**RE YOU serious about this boy?" asked Mama.

I laid the bag of groceries down on the table and handed her the cans. "I'd like to marry him. As soon as he graduates from college."

"Which ones are the green beans?"

I put the green beans in her hands. She brought the can up to her face to read the label, then disappeared with it into the pantry. Returning to the kitchen table, she looked at me hard. "Your hair is too long. You should cut it."

"Good idea, Mama. I was thinking the same thing."

I was thinking, thank God she could see my hair. It was hard to tell what she could and couldn't see. She was still cooking, cleaning, and vacuuming, shouting to us with pinched, determined lips that she could see well enough to do it herself when we offered to help.

"Have you forgotten about college?" she questioned me, pulling up a kitchen chair.

"Have you heard one word from Uncle Jake?!"

She nodded no.

"Then what are you talking about? Papa is so gullible. He believed that nonsense about sending me to college, just like the nonsense about getting him a city job."

"What kind of fancy word is that?"

"Which?"

"Gulla."

I spelled it in her hands. "He's a fool sometimes—the way he trusts certain people and doesn't trust others."

"Don't talk about your father like that."

"Sorry. Please, Mama, I know there's no money for college. Besides, I like my job. I like being a secretary. The boss thinks I'm great." It was tedious, spelling in her hands. I had to go slower while she wrapped her good hand around mine to feel my fingers.

"When will he finish college?"

"Next June."

"Then I think it's time we had his family over. Why don't you invite them for this Saturday?"

"So soon?"

"I think so. He seems like a nice boy."

"He's a man, Mama. Almost twenty-one."

"And I think he'll make a good living. Rosie says engineers make good money."

"So the poker group approves?"

"Yes," she laughed.

I made a pot of coffee for us and poured her a cup.

"I can do that," she said, taking her cup.

"I know you can. Just trying to help."

"You don't have to worry."

"I'm not."

"Addle will be here."

"I know. I'm tired, Mama. I'm going to bed. Will you be all right until Papa comes home from bowling?"

"Of course," she said. "I'm going to take a bath now and go to bed myself."

"Aunt Selma called earlier. She wanted to know how you were feeling. She wanted to know if you were too tired out from the trip to the doctor this afternoon."

"Call her back in the morning and tell her I'm fine."

"What did the doctor say?"

"Nothing's changed. He's given me a new prescription for glasses."

"That's good."

"Yes, that's good. Tomorrow we'll make plans for the wedding. Go to bed."

"Good night."

"Good night."

She went into the bathroom. Water gushed from the faucet. She left the bathroom and went into the bedroom to get her robe; she didn't see me standing in the kitchen. Her face was placid, unlined with worry. She had taken her hair down and let it flow around her shoulders. She looked young. Her body had grown plump, but her figure was still good, her legs firm. The muted rose color of the chenille bathrobe reflected a soft glow on her face—the way she looked over the Sabbath candles, except she didn't light them anymore. Adelaide and I took turns every Friday night. I left the kitchen light on, walked to my room, and fell into bed, dead tired. Adelaide's legs were spread across my side. I shoved them away from me and fell asleep.

I HAD forgotten my nighttime dreaming; my bed floating through the ceiling and into the darkened sky, looking for a place to land. I hadn't done it since I was very little. But that night I dreamed—only this time I didn't want to leave. I was in the park, where the bright green willow trees hung close to the banks and puffy clouds made pretty animals in the sky. Papa sat close to me on a bench under one of the willows.

"Papa, I'm scared to leave her alone."

"Adelaide's here," he assured me.

"You spelled it wrong, Papa. It's Addle."

"No," said Papa. "It's Adelaide."

"You're speaking, Papa. I didn't know you could do that."

"I can do it in your dreams."

"But one day Addle—I mean Adelaide—will go to work and

get married. It's lonely in the house for her. She can't go outside by herself."

"Rosie will come. Sarah will come. And Zadie and Selma and Marian and Morrie."

"But Selma and Marian and Zadie and Morrie can't sign to her. She gets tired reading lips."

"That's true," he said, holding me. "Well, they'll have to learn to sign in her hand, won't they?"

"They won't learn. They never learned before."

"They will."

"No, they won't. Zadie forbade the aunts to sign. And Zadie's too old to learn. Sometimes you're so stupid, Papa. You think everyone is around to help you, but nobody will help."

I pulled away and raised my hand to strike him. He looked at me, his blue eyes dripping. I pulled my hand back and cried. Papa, angry with me for challenging him, turned me over and slapped me hard on the back. Then he turned away, ashamed to see me cry.

"You're dreaming," Adelaide said. "You're shouting. What's the matter?"

I bolted straight up and grabbed the blanket to wipe my tears, but there weren't any. Then I heard crying sounds coming from the back bedroom. I put my feet on the floor and into my slippers. Adelaide sat up and wrapped her arms around me. "Don't go. She thinks we're asleep. Don't embarrass her."

I WAS asked to come along to a specialist that Uncle Morrie had found. Mama couldn't see Uncle Morrie's lips well enough to make out his words, and, since none of the Rubensteins could fingerspell, he needed me. Adelaide insisted on accompanying us.

Dr. Campbell, the best in town, according to Uncle Morrie, was number five on the list of specialists Mama had gone to (or was it six? Nobody had told me how many others she'd seen).

After the examination, Mama, Adelaide, and I sat in the outer office. Dr. Campbell was deep in serious conversation with my uncle. Through the crack in the door, I could see their faces lined with worry. I listened intently. "I think the girls should know," Dr. Campbell said. Uncle Morrie opened the door wide and motioned to us to come into the room. "Tell Ruthie to wait on the couch."

The words came to me in fragments, shattering me like shards of glass. Dr. Campbell's face was a blur. I couldn't focus on it or the chair with all its gadgets or Uncle Morrie's body turned away from me, his shoulders sagging with despair.

"Retinitis pigmentosa," the doctor said. "At least, that's what we suspect at the moment."

The name sounded impossible to imagine.

"Dark pigments forming on the retina," he continued.

"Can they come off?" Adelaide asked.

Uncle Morrie turned to us, his face twitching with emotion. Dr. Campbell looked at us with discomfort. "I'm sorry, but there's nothing we can do."

"The glasses aren't working, are they?" I asked, trying not to cry.

"I'm afraid not."

"Will it get worse?"

"We can't tell. It might. Or it might stay just the way it is. We have no idea."

Adelaide took my arm, and together we went over to Mama to tell her. I spelled the diagnosis in her hand, and Adelaide explained the doctor's thoughts. Mama shook her head, nodding in understanding and shrugging her shoulders, then got up from her seat and offered her hands. "Come. Let's go home."

We held on to her hands as we walked from the streetcar down Washtenaw Avenue.

"She can barely read her books," Adelaide commented, her

eyes straight ahead of her so Mama wouldn't feel the turn of her body toward me.

"I know."

"It's not fair."

"I know."

"Why didn't they tell us before? Why did they wait?"

"They didn't want to worry us, I guess."

"It was selfish of them."

"*We* were selfish. We hardly paid attention."

"So why didn't you and I talk about it? Why did we pretend that nothing was happening?"

"We were all pretending. I don't know how long this has been going on. Maybe they didn't tell us because they didn't know themselves. Maybe they thought it would get better. Be careful how you move. She'll know we're talking."

The corner was filled with neighbors crossing the street as we passed Charlie's store. Adelaide started to cry.

"Please, Adelaide, not on the street. I don't want them to see the Shtimmers crying."

CHAPTER

16

I NEVER saw my father cry. The blue eyes that misted at the slightest emotion—the smile of a baby or the death of someone's pet—stayed dry. In June, 1949, just before my twentieth birthday, he stood proudly in the reception line at my wedding, my mother's arm wrapped around his, pumping hands and patting guests on the back. His rented white tuxedo did marvelous things to his blue eyes, but it didn't mask his slight paunch. Still, he looked virile and handsome. My mother's glasses were now clear, the thought of another specialist who prescribed yet another treatment, hoping something would come of it. Her hips had widened, and her hair was partially gray, but she looked lovely in a floor-length pale blue dress with a lace peplum. The bright slash of red lipstick that she had given up wearing because she couldn't see her lips in a mirror was back on her mouth, carefully molded by Adelaide. A touch of rouge and penciled brows brightened her happy look.

Aunts and uncles from both sides of the family were there to watch me walk down the aisle. We had decided on the shul where Aunt Selma taught Sunday school, a domed building that would one day become a Greek Orthodox Church. It was the largest building in the neighborhood and the most beautiful. Aunt Selma approved of the rabbi, and both families agreed that it was a proper site for a happy event. We hadn't visited Bubbi's shul since her death. The Maplewood Avenue shul where Zadie still prayed was a hole in the wall, in Aunt Selma's terms.

It was hot that day. The temperature still hovered at 90° when the sun went down. Tall ceilings made the shul even hotter. My borrowed gown of heavy satin was wrong for a June wedding, but it was the most glamorous thing I'd ever been dressed in, so I was happy to wear it. Adelaide, my maid of honor, wore the sea green dress I had worn to my high school prom, and Hannah and Shirley wore their prom gowns as bridesmaids' dresses. The ceremony went on too long. The heat stored up inside my dress like a furnace. As the rabbi motioned to Al to break the glass under his foot, I swayed, and the room swayed with me. Adelaide propped me up. Then it was over, and we all went downstairs for the dinner reception.

Zadie took his place of honor at the head table, which was draped in white cloth down to the floor. Pink flowers were arranged in the middle of the table. Chicken soup, matzo balls, and brisket of beef were served in dishes too hot to handle. The waiters put them down quickly and blew their fingers with their lips.

I had dreamed of a garden wedding with dainty finger sandwiches, champagne, and a flowing chiffon gown that billowed in the afternoon breeze. But there was no garden, and we couldn't afford champagne. My savings were just enough to cover a shul—a traditional—wedding. In the frantic weeks leading up to the wedding, Aunt Selma hovered over me, advising me, assuring me that champagne wasn't necessary.

"Schnapps is good enough," Aunt Marian added, and that night she placed one bottle on each of the tables. "Enough to make a toast. That's all you need. Are you happy with the sweet table?" she asked me, spreading her hands wide in presentation. The aunts had baked for days to fill up a dessert table of cookies and tiny cakes; my mother-in-law had made her famous strudel. "It's just beautiful," I sighed. I didn't care anymore about my dream wedding. It was tradition to have chicken soup and all the other courses, and it was tradition to serve a hot meal, no matter what the weather, and to put one bottle of schnapps on the table—just one. I couldn't break tradition.

Uncle Morrie

Zadie and Bubbi

Aunt Marian and Uncle Leon

Aunt Selma and Uncle Eddie

Aunt Nettie, Albert and Uncle Simon

Mama, Ad, and me (left)

My graduation picture (1948)

Aunt Flora

Papa with his brother Lou

Al and me on our wedding day (1949)

Ad and Arthur's wedding (1950)

Mama's 50th birthday (Sarah is holding Mama's hand and Rosie is standing behind her, 1951)

Ellen, Andy, Larry, and me with Mama and Papa at Disneyland (1963)

Mama and Papa's 50th wedding anniversary (1978)

Mama and Papa with Mama's family at a wedding (1978)

Mama and Papa conversing in front of Pilgrim Tower

Al dancing with Mama (1978)

Mama and Papa visiting the Queen Mary

My bridesmaids had deserted me. They swung open the doors of the banquet room and left to fan themselves outside. I couldn't blame them. At first one friend and then another deserted the festivities in search of a cooling breeze. Then a strange figure appeared in the doorway, reversing the exodus, someone who apparently could stand the heat. His face was indistinguishable in the shadows of the outside light. Then he moved closer to the brightness of the banquet room, and I recognized him. It was the janitor.

"Papa, what's he doing here?" I protested.

"I don't know."

"We didn't invite him!"

"It's all right," he patted my shoulder. "I'll talk to him."

He left me with Mama, walked to the door, and scribbled a note. He handed it to the janitor. The janitor wrote back. Papa smiled. I was surprised at Papa's familiarity. I didn't even know the man's name. Maybe Papa did. I had never said more than hello to the man. Papa escorted him to one of the tables and made a space for him next to Rosie, Sarah, and Little Joe. After spelling something to them, then pouring a glass of schnapps and offering it to the man, he returned and spelled words into Mama's hand. She nodded in understanding.

"Papa, he looks like a slob," I complained. "He doesn't even have a jacket on. Or a tie! Why did you let him come in?!"

"Zimmerman couldn't make the wedding, so I offered him his place. He's known you since you were a child. He wanted to wish you well. Wave to him. Make him feel at home."

"I don't even know his name."

"It's Bernie. Wave hello."

Mrs. Goldberg, sitting at the next table, put her handkerchief to her face in surprise. I smiled at her to let her know it was okay, then waved hello to Bernie, thinking it was such a normal name for a man I'd been afraid of all my life. Papa took a few drinks of the schnapps himself, careful about overdoing it, and passed the bottle to Zadie and Al's father. He took Mama by the arm to make the rounds of the tables, playing the perfect host. Relatives and friends scribbled notes to Papa and smiled. Papa relayed the messages to Mama in her hand. Mama smiled at Marian's shadow and Selma's shadow and the rabbi's shadow and asked Papa to identify the people whose hands she shook and to whom she said, "I'm glad you could come."

THAT'S WHAT her sight had come to: shadows. In familiar surroundings, like our apartment, she could still walk without bumping into things or tripping. Knowing who lived there, she could tell if a particular shadow was Papa, Adelaide, or me by its size. She could walk straight to it and talk. She could also walk to the stove, cook, pull out the ironing board, put finger to tongue to test the readiness of the iron, and do a perfectly decent job of ironing Papa's shirts. She could scrub the floor on her knees, wash the insides of the windows with her vinegar-and-water mixture, fold the linens left at our front door by the neighborhood laundry, and sit with us and talk. If we weren't in the house, she could sit on the back porch and smell the fresh air, hang out the hand wash, and go downstairs to get the mail. What she couldn't do anymore was read.

If she missed that diversion, she didn't complain. She walked around with a smile on her face, thrilled that she had another man in the family. She fussed over him, cooked him meals, puffing up with pride as she laid dishes before him. She hummed pleasantly when Al painted the apartment, applying a triple coat of white paint to the bathroom wall. Papa's tobacco drippings finally disappeared. She glided her hands over the smooth enamel in approval of this handiwork. Clearly, I had made an excellent choice in husbands.

Maybe we were pretending again. It is hard from the perspective of many years gone by to understand why there was so much happiness in the house when we should have been distressed by

Mama's losses. There was no more gloom. There were no more tears, at least that Adelaide, Al, or I could see. If it happened in the privacy of her bedroom, only Papa knew, and he seemed happy while he entertained Al and learned from him things that concerned men. One day he said to me, "Your husband doesn't know a thing about baseball."

We had formed a new way of life. My mother had one lifeless hand, deaf ears, and obscured vision. To my in-laws she had never appeared sighted; they accepted her readily. If they clucked their tongues and murmured "what a shame," I never knew it. It seemed easier for me to walk the street with her now, her dark glasses shielding her eyes from the sun as if we'd done this all our lives. There was no need for us to pretend deafness and play silly games in front of strangers. No listening hard for "Shtimmers" to reach our ears. It was my mother, who held our hands straight—her two fingers stuck in my palm—who made it easier. When Papa walked with us, men still glad-handed him and shared their memories. Mama smirked when I told her what they were saying and maintained, "He's still a bum." We all shook our sides, laughing.

I WAS still living at home because Al and I couldn't find an apartment. The war had stopped all new building, while soldiers returning from the war, married now and with children, scooped up all the vacancies. We searched every Sunday for a modest apartment, wondering why we were turned down. We were a respectable young couple, I thought. Any landlord would be proud to have us.

It was Aunt Ethel who explained the facts of life. "I have a lead on an apartment," she said over the phone one day. "He wants $250.00 under the table—a bonus," she said with a catch in her voice. "Apartments are hard to find nowadays. Landlords have their choice of tenants, and they also choose to make a little extra."

"It doesn't seem fair."

"Welcome to postwar reality," she laughed.

Al and I hadn't an extra penny to our name, so I shared my double bed with Al, and Adelaide was banished to the hideabed in the dining room. This arrangement lasted for a year until we had saved up enough money to put under someone's table. We located a two-room apartment on the West Side overlooking the El tracks and moved in with some of Aunt Marian's hand-me-down furniture and a brand-new tomato red sofa bed. My sister was glad to be rid of us.

PAPA, MAMA, and Adelaide rode the streetcar to our apartment for their first meal in my new home. While the roast stayed warm in the oven, I took Mama's hand and described every detail in the apartment. She rubbed her fingers on the sofa and tables and measured with her feet the distance from the kitchen to living room. She even remarked on the fresh smell of our bathroom. Then she took the chair Papa offered her, and we sat down to eat.

"I should buy one of those," Papa said, pointing to the television set on the small table next to the sofa.

"Good idea, Papa. Sha's not around any more to help me with the fights," Adelaide laughed. "I can't do both parts."

"What do you mean, both parts?" Al asked.

"Family joke," Adelaide answered, winking at me.

"I'll tell you one day," I whispered. "But let's not talk to Papa. His food will get cold."

We ate in silence until I served the dessert. Mama tapped her fork on the table. "Sha, the dessert is delicious." I shook her hand in a thank-you sign. Then she put her hands in Papa's and waited for him to talk.

"I'm thinking we should buy a television set," he spelled. "I could watch the fights and the baseball games."

"And you can tell me all about them," she responded.

My heart stopped. She would never see the screen. Was it a good idea to bring something in the house that she couldn't share? Another deprivation?

"Now you won't be running off to ball games," she added.

Good. She won't be alone on Saturdays while he's off to Wrigley Field. He can bring his friends to the house, and Sarah and Rosie can sit with her and talk.

"How are Sarah and Rosie?" I asked Mama.

"They're fine. They say hello."

"They stink," Papa said, putting his fingers to his nose. "They ignore her when we play cards."

"How can they talk to her and play cards at the same time, Papa?"

"One of them can stay out of a game once in a while."

"I'm sure they try their best. Mama says they visit her often."

"They do," said Adelaide, finishing her strawberry shortcake. "Papa's got it in his head that they're treating her differently."

"Are they?"

"I don't think so. But then I'm at work, so I'm not sure, and I'm not home that much in the evenings."

The answer was not to play cards, I figured. Have them over for cake and coffee so they could take turns talking to her while the men watched television. But would Sarah and Rosie want to sit and watch television, too? "I hope you didn't tell Mama how you feel about Sarah and Rosie."

"Why not?"

"Stop spelling in her hands, Papa. I don't think you should feel that way. They're good people. And how about Selma and Marian. Have they've been to see her?"

"Only when I'm home. They can't talk to her anymore. She can't make out their lips."

And Zadie? What did Zadie do? But I didn't ask Papa. I knew without asking that he climbed the stairs, put his key in the door, stood right in front of her, poked her shoulder, and asked his predictable question. Because she knew what the question would be, she would merely answer, "Fine, fine."

My head was bursting. Al got up and got me an aspirin. "How did you know I had a headache?"

"Because I'm getting one, too," he patted my hand.

"What's the name of this television set?" Papa asked Al.

"An Admiral," Al spelled. He was clumsy with his fingers, but Papa waited patiently. "The appliance store on North Avenue has a good stock of them. And it's a good price."

"Then I'll go there. Ruthie," he spelled, "we're buying an Admiral television set. We'll see the games together."

"HE JUST hit another homer."

"That's wonderful," she said, only she didn't say it. She took Papa's hand and slapped it up and down on the arm of the chair to show her enthusiasm. She sat close to him with her hand outstretched so he could spell it all to her. If she had never been a baseball fan before, she was now. She rooted for the Cubs. The television sat on the small table where the radio had been. Adelaide had taken the radio and put it in her bedroom, and, since Papa watched television with the sound off, it didn't interfere with Adelaide's entertainment.

I had come by myself after work one evening to get a first-hand look at how they were managing. Adelaide couldn't get over it. "In many ways, it's better for them," she told me as we sat at the kitchen table drinking coffee. They've forgotten about going to the movies since Mama can't make the figures out too well, and the lights are too bright for her. And you know," she said laughing, "Papa hates Technicolor movies, anyway. He can't get used to it."

"How is she managing in the kitchen?"

"See for yourself."

My mother had abandoned Papa. The fights were on and she

hated boxing. She would not be a party to grown men slugging each other. She went to the pantry, took out some canned goods, and brought them over to us. "Which ones are the peas?" Adelaide put her hand on the proper can.

Mama walked over to the sink, took the can opener, pried open the lid, put the peas in the pot, turned on the gas, moved her hands carefully over the larger pot on the second burner, pulled the lid off, bent over to smell, took the spoon, and stirred.

"You staying for dinner?" asked Adelaide.

"I can't. Al's waiting for me."

"She's managing fine. If I'm not here, she asks Papa to read the cans for her. She's even tried new recipes. Papa spots them in the paper and reads them to her. It's become a partnership in the kitchen."

"What does she do when he's watching other things on TV?"

"She sticks to him like glue. Except when the fights are on. It's her only entertainment now, but she's enjoying it."

"No more cards."

"Not any more."

I thought of all the times we had played together, the four of us at the dining room table, Papa teaching us one game, then another, helping Adelaide to find a nine in Go Fish, and I wept.

"Please don't," Adelaide begged, her voice breaking. As she took hold of herself, I stopped my crying.

"Once in a while she can make out the shadows on TV, the fast movements. Of course, Papa has to explain what those movements are. They still come over."

"Sarah and Rosie?"

"All of them."

"That's good."

My mother walked over to me, discerning the difference, and asked, "Are you staying for dinner?"

"Al's home waiting for me."

"Call him on the phone and tell him to come."

"It's too much trouble for you."

"No trouble. Tell him to come!"

She stood right in front of my nose, the spoon in her hand, her apron neatly tied around her, her hair tucked smoothly into her bun, her pinched lips pulling the hollows of her cheeks even further in.

"Okay, I'll call him."

In the living room, Papa was engrossed in the fights. I picked up the phone and called Al. Papa poked me on the arm.

"Wait, Papa, I'm talking."

"She has no friends anymore. They never come to see her," he spelled.

"Wait until I'm off the phone, Papa."

"Well, maybe they come, but they talk to each other, not to Ruthie." He went on spilling out his thoughts. I knew he wasn't talking to me now. He moved his hands in front of the TV, talking to himself. "Sarah says she would kill herself if she was going blind. What kind of thing is that to say to me?"

I put the phone down. "She didn't say that to Mama, did she?"

He pinched his nose. "They stink, damn them. What am I supposed to do when I'm at work, worry about her? What kind of friends are they?"

"Papa, please."

"Adelaide shops. That's good," he spelled, fingers down to his side. Then he stopped. He rubbed his hands and fingers together, smoothing and flexing them in the air.

"What's the matter with your hands?"

"Spelling everything in her hands is hard work. She likes TV." He laughed, and the tobacco dripped down his chin. He pulled his tongue over it and scooped it back in his mouth. "Who are you calling?"

"Al."

"Coming for dinner?"

"Yes, if I can get the time to ask him."

"Sorry," he laughed. "I hope I have some witch hazel left in the medicine cabinet. That'll fix it. I'll rub it on my fingers, make them good as new, then I'll help Mama in the kitchen. Ask him if he wants to play pinochle. Ask him if his father wants to come. I'll get one more person. We'll play after dinner. You can talk to Mama."

"Sure, Papa."

CHAPTER

17

M Y FATHER did not watch Steve Allen. There was too much talking, he explained, and the few magic or dancing acts on the show weren't enough to keep them up late at night. Talking on TV—like talking in the movies—was a waste of their time.

But there was plenty of action on TV. All he had to do was turn the channel to find something: an old western, cartoons (which were difficult to explain to Mama), baseball games, and the news. He also read the *Tribune* to her. His fingers flew constantly. When he was at work, she did the cleaning and cooking.

A few more specialists were consulted throughout the year. Expensive doctors in fancy offices at downtown addresses. Her condition remained unchanged. Adelaide didn't worry. Zadie didn't worry. The aunts didn't worry. But Mrs. Goldberg worried. She called one afternoon while I pounded on the typewriter, my attention on the invoices before me, oblivious to Mama's world. "I don't wish to bother you," she said, "but I don't hear her in the house. It's quiet."

"You're not bothering me, Mrs. Goldberg. It's all right. I'm glad you called. She's probably napping. Believe me, she didn't walk out of the house to go shopping."

"Would you mind, Charlotte, if I took her to the store?"

Where are Rosie and Sarah? I wondered. "That would be nice, but Mama would hate to bother you."

"It's no bother. I'll tell your father to make a list. If he tells her I'm coming, she'll open the door for me. I have to knock hard sometimes before she comes. She could use the walk."

"That's sweet of you, Mrs. Goldberg, but Adelaide can do it when she comes home from work."

"I want to do it. I don't like her staying in the house all day." She hung up. Papa would probably call her a busybody, I decided, mistrusting those who weren't like him, but I made myself a note to convince him that it was a good idea.

DINNER WAS all prepared when I got home. Al had broiled steaks and baked potatoes. But I had no appetite.

"You have to keep up your strength," he said, looking ridiculous in my frilly apron. The colors clashed with his navy suit and plaid bow tie.

"You sound like my father. Meat and potatoes. The only healthy food. I can't eat it. Truly. My stomach won't take it."

"The baby needs it."

"The baby isn't due for a long time."

"Then try this," he offered, pushing a bowl of steamed vegetables in front of me.

I retched at the sight of it. The El clattered by outside, shaking the apartment and making my stomach queasier. I ran to the bathroom to heave the bitter stuff.

"When can we leave this dump?" I asked, falling into the open sofa bed.

"Have to save up enough money first. Here, take the wet towel and put it on your forehead. It'll cool you off."

"I'm not hot. I'm sick to my stomach."

"When are you going to tell our parents?" he asked, propping a pillow behind my head.

"When I'm sure this one is real. When I'm not surprised by another knock on the cheek."

Puzzled, he looked at me. "Another family joke," I explained. "One day I'll tell you, but right now I'm feeling miserable."

145

"You and your family jokes. When are you gonna let me in?"

I smiled, "I didn't think you minded. You're a good finger-speller. Slow, but you'll get all the business that goes with it. Lots of knocks and raps and looks and, oh, too much to explain now."

I pulled the pillow from under my head and covered my face with it. My eyes were open, and I envisioned a snow-covered mountain—white and serene and ice cold—wetting the insides of my mouth like an ice cube. I pulled the pillow away from me. "Go ahead and have your dinner. I'm not hungry."

He sighed and went back to the cubicle we called our kitchen. When he stood in the middle, everything disappeared: the stove, the fridge, the small counter, everything. Just his back, his black hair, and his rolled-up shirtsleeves filled my view. I hadn't purposely meant to leave him out. Deaf ways came naturally to me. It took time for outsiders to understand.

"They'll be thrilled when they hear about it," he said. "Well, try to rest."

I must have fallen asleep because Steve Allen was saying goodnight when Al turned off the light and crawled under the blankets with me. The smell of steak permeated the room. I wanted to run to the window and breathe fresh air but was too tired to lift my head. I fell asleep again.

When the phone rang, I thought it was the alarm clock and reached for the button to stop it, but it was only four in the morning. Terrified of hearing bad news at the other end, I poked Al. "Get up. The phone's ringing. Something awful's happened. Zadie! It's probably Zadie. He's dead."

I couldn't rouse him. "Al, please get up. The phone's ringing."

He opened one eye. "Then answer it." He closed his eye again, and I got out of the sofa bed and stumbled to the phone. The El rumbled through just as Adelaide's voice came through the line.

"It's Zadie, isn't it?"

"No. It's Papa," she shouted. "Can't you hear me? The hospital called. The police found him in the gutter in front of a diner. He was beaten up. I didn't know he hadn't come home from his bowling game," she cried. "I came home from a date and thought they were both asleep. Then the phone rang. He's at County Hospital. I don't want to leave Mama alone. She's moaning and humming. I can't leave her alone!"

"How bad is he?"

"Oh, I can't remember exactly. Yes, I remember. Not bad, they said. What does that mean?" she cried.

"I'll call the hospital. You stay with Mama. Stop worrying. Hang up the phone, Adelaide."

I turned to see Al sitting up in bed. "What's wrong?" he asked.

"Papa. County Hospital. Beaten up." I gave the operator the name of the hospital.

"Why?"

"How the hell do I know?"

"Bastards. Let's go." He jumped out of bed and put his clothes on, stumbling over his shoes in the dark.

"Put the light on, for heaven's sake."

He switched on the lamp and looked for his car keys.

"Hello," I shouted. "I'm inquiring about Mr. Joseph Herzberg. What's his condition? You need to tell him that I'm. . . ."

"You mean the deaf and dumb man?"

"Yes," I whimpered.

"Nothing serious. Swollen nose, broken fist. A couple of bruises. He'll be fine. He's not talking. Won't tell us anything. Won't talk to the police."

"I'm coming to get him. You write him a message that we'll be there as fast as we can."

"You can't take him home until morning, so you might as well get a good night's sleep."

"We're coming. Give him the message." I hung up the phone and it rang again.

"It's me," Adelaide said. "Mrs. Goldberg's going to stay with Mama. I'm going."

"We'll pick you up."

THE ELEVATOR made a terrible racket until it reached the ground floor. It was quiet in the building. I'd never been up so early. Nothing seemed real. It was like one of my dreams, floating off to nowhere, being carried to a line of parked cars, looking for our brown one, Al's keys dangling from his hand, getting in the front seat, wondering how long it would take to reach Adelaide. Should I say something to Mama, or let Adelaide get in and speed away, leaving her alone with Mrs. Goldberg, not understanding anything, just having her wait? "Should we take my mother with us, Al?"

"It's better that she stay with Mrs. Goldberg," he said.

The streets were empty. Tall apartment buildings, dark in the white sky, still sheltered the workers, the nine-o'clock people who were asleep in their beds. I was a nine-o'clock person, one who showered, dressed, and took the streetcar at 8:30. There were no streetcars, not even a taxi. There was nothing but white skies, stray dogs, and trees—a melancholy, empty city.

Adelaide was waiting in front of the house, a sweater loosely draped over an old blouse, no stockings on her feet, just open-toed sandals. I, too, was haphazardly dressed. My sundress was tight around my waist. I pulled the two curlers out of my hair. Adelaide climbed into the back seat.

"Is she okay?"

"She's sitting in her chair with her hands in her lap. She's not making a sound. Mrs. Goldberg made her some tea."

"Okay, then. Let's go."

"This couldn't have happened at a worse time," she said, reaching over the front seat to talk to us. "Arthur's asked me to

148

marry him, and I told him I would. We'll be looking for our own apartment soon. If this had happened after I moved out, how would Mama know that Papa was beaten up? It's too terrible to think of, Char."

"Does Papa know you're leaving?"

A car appeared in the intersection. The driver looked surprised. Who else would be out in the early morning? his face said. He hit the horn as Al put on the brakes. "Damn him."

"Does Papa know?" I shouted.

"I told him two days ago."

Al's hands trembled on the steering wheel. "That settles it. They're moving in with us."

"You're crazy!"

"No. I'm the only sane one around here. Look at your sister. She's bawling in the back seat. What do you think is going to happen when you're both gone? You'll go crazy with worry, that's what. I'm worried about your father. I don't think he can take the pressure."

"Shut up and watch where you're driving. Where are we going to live? In a no-bedroom apartment with a sofa bed and no porch where my mother can sit outside for a while? I'm not moving back to Washtenaw."

"And I'm not staying," Adelaide said.

"And what about me? And the baby?"

"Selfish," he said, speeding up.

"How dare you call us selfish?"

"What baby?" Adelaide asked.

"I'm pregnant."

"Oh, that's wonderful," she sniffed. She blew her nose into her handkerchief. "You should tell them. It'll make them feel good. It's about time we felt good about something."

We slammed all three car doors and walked to the hospital entrance. The sign in front listed the visiting times; it didn't include five o'clock in the morning, but we barreled into the hall and up the steps to the third floor ward. Papa was sitting in bed, dressed in his hospital gown, his nostrils caked with dried blood. The bottoms of his feet were filthy. He must have been pacing the floor all night. The ward was disgustingly dirty. The room reeked of urine. Patients, bleeding and coughing, were lined up in the corridor.

"Why didn't you come?" he signed.

"We just found out. Didn't you get our message?"

"No," he waved angrily. "No message. I've been here all night waiting for you!"

My sister rushed out of the room. Her screams rumbled through the corridors. "Why didn't you tell him? Why didn't you write it on a piece of paper? Why didn't you call us sooner?"

No one answered her questions. The nurses were putting patients in their beds and checking their wounds, ignoring her. "County's nothing but a rat hole," she said, coming back into the ward with papers in her hand. "I'm signing you out of here, Papa. Let's go!"

"It's about time," Papa said. And then he shut up. Blood was pouring from his nose. Al packed it with bandages he found on the stand, and we walked him out.

MY MOTHER knew. She had known him longer than any of us. She understood. Her body was stiff with anger as we helped him through the front door, but when she saw Papa's shadow, she rushed to him and put her arms around him. When he gently shoved her away, she knew. She stood in the doorway of their bedroom while we washed the blood from his nose, cleaned his feet, and helped him on with his pajamas.

The doctor who lived down the street came in answer to Adelaide's knock on the door. Papa lay strangely still as the doctor poked and prodded every inch of his body. "We'll get that fist in a cast tomorrow. Tell him to keep it elevated. As for the rest of him, well, he's badly bruised, but a few days in bed and he'll be fine." He waved a finger at Papa. "You stay put, you hear?" Papa barely nodded his head.

Mama left the doorway, walked into the kitchen, and sat down, hands in her lap, staring into nothingness, her expression chiseled into marble. There was no sign of compassion on her face, only anger darting from her eyes. She knew what my father was made of. Strength and enormous love and emotional eyes, anger at those who hurt him and things he couldn't control. She didn't have to hear the details from the police officer who knocked on the door moments later and went to Papa's room for a report. She didn't have to see my father put his finger to his nose when I ushered the officer in.

"Stinking cops. Keep out of my business," he spelled hurriedly. He closed his eyes, shutting off further talk. I listened to the officer's words, my heart full of shame.

"Seems he was looking for trouble. Threw a mustard bottle at the cook in the diner. I could book him for drunk and disorderly."

"I didn't know he was drunk. You mean he started the fight?"

"Yes, ma'am, but what those punks did to him! Doesn't your father want to sign a complaint?"

"Why, Papa?" I demanded, poking him on the shoulder. "Why?"

"Made fun of me," he signed. "Won't talk to cops," he stormed with his hands. "Get him out of my room."

I led the officer to the front door. "I'm sure he'll pay for any damages."

"No damage done. Just a fight that got out of hand, but I need to make a report. Maybe when he's cooled down a bit." He looked through the kitchen door at Mama and turned to me. "I've heard about your dad. I don't mean to make light of this, ma'am, but your father sure gave those punks a helluva fight. I hear he managed a couple of good punches. Pretty tough for an old guy." He raised his hand in a small salute and left.

Mama knew. She sat quietly, hands tapping the chrome edge of her brand new kitchen table. Tapping, tapping, her eyes filled with shadows.

"It'll be all right," we told her. Adelaide took her hand and spelled the words over and over. "It'll be all right."

"No, it won't be all right," she said. "Nothing will be good now." Her fingers tapped the chrome with an infernal deliberate beat. Al hunched his shoulders and stuck his hands inside the pockets of his golf pants. "I'm going home to change. Then I'm going to work. You stay with your mother. I'm going to talk to my folks after work."

"Don't tell them. It's not necessary."

"I'm going to ask for a loan. Maybe we can buy a small house, big enough for all of us."

"We'll talk about it later."

"Okay, but think about it."

He closed the front door quietly, still forgetting that nobody would be disturbed. I went to the bedroom to check on Papa. He was fast asleep, his swollen fist on top of a pillow, his nose packed with fresh gauze. He looked like a referee had given him the count of ten and was too tired to get up again. I mentally replayed the officer's words of praise and tried to laugh at the absurdity. Another legend in the making, I thought. Another story the men in the neighborhood will tell when they see Dummy Jordan strutting down the street. Papa opened his eyes. He looked ashamed to see me standing in the doorway.

"You forgot your purple trunks, Papa."

"Why do you think I wore purple?"

"I always imagined it."

"Never wore purple. Only black. One time, red. Purple for sissies." He tried to smile, but his lips moved painfully. "Mama okay?"

"She's okay," I lied.

"You stay with her?"

"Sure, Papa. Addle and I are here. Go to sleep."

He closed his eyes. I walked into the kitchen where Adelaide sat next to Mama, spelling assurances in her hand. I gave up all pretense of holding myself together and, as long as Mama couldn't see me, allowed myself to cry.

CHAPTER

18

THIS TIME Mama couldn't run to the Rubensteins. She couldn't leave the safety of her apartment and walk down Washtenaw Avenue to get help. Even if she could, I didn't know what she would have asked for. Papa hadn't lost his job; he had lost his courage, weary from the burden, afraid of the future, angry at those who hadn't supported Mama. I believed it was all in his mind. Her friends hadn't abandoned her, but I wondered with deep hurt why the Rubensteins hadn't made that one concession: learning to fingerspell and sign in her hands.

While Al and Adelaide went off to work, I sat with Mama in the living room, feeling sick to my stomach, the nausea rolling in waves over me. Mama was still holding her hands in her lap, unwilling to talk, so I curled up with my knees to my chest and tried to weather the battle in my stomach. What did I expect the Rubensteins to do? They had had their share of shtimmer calling all their lives, and they had protected her from the time they were children. Zadie had seen to it. Aunt Nettie had gone to school with her, holding her hand while crossing the street to protect her from unheard cars and taunting children. Aunt Selma and Aunt Marian had made sure we wanted nothing. And it came to me, as I wiped my forehead of the sweat that poured down to my ears, that it was our turn now. Al was right. But could we convince my father? Would I strip him of his manhood with offers of caring? It was too much to sort out, feeling my own misery now.

It was a big one this time—a tidal wave of bile working its way

up from my stomach to my throat. I sat up and ran to the bathroom to heave the bitter stuff.

Mama, feeling my footsteps through her feet, ran after my
shadow. She caught up with me as I reached the toilet. "What's
wrong?"

"Nothing, Mama. I'm pregnant."

"A baby? Oh, that's wonderful," she said, clapping her hands.
"My first grandchild. Come. I'll take you back to the kitchen."

"No, want sit on the sofa."

"All right. You sit on sofa. I bring you tea."

"No, don't want tea."

"All right. I bring you tapioca pudding. Settle your stomach."

We were talking deaf talk. I was the child again, feeling miserable. She was in a hurry to comfort me. All the little words got
lost. I laid my head against the sofa arm and let her feed me. The
tapioca pudding went down, the tiny bits of fruit cocktail shimmering in a sea of white.

"I know this good. I eat myself when I pregnant. Feel better?"

"Yes."

"Good. You sleep. I sit chair, wait for Papa get up. You sleep.
Wait." She walked to the closet and brought out the afghan that
Mrs. Luft had given her for their twentieth anniversary. Rows of
colors, burgundy, rust, green, beautifully crocheted. I wondered
if she remembered the colors. She draped it over me and went
back to sit in her chair. "Wonderful," she said to the Persian rug,
"Sha have baby. Addle get married." Then she folded her hands
in her lap and smiled. The window behind her was open, and the
buzzing from the neighbors who were sitting on the front bench
filtered through the living room. I tried hard to listen to their
noises, and then I didn't care anymore. I fell asleep.

MY MOTHER made dinner, turning on gas jets,
pulling dishes from the pantry, counting out the silverware, and
setting it on the table. She tore the head of lettuce apart and put

wedges in each dish. The cabbage soup smelled wonderful, but I knew I couldn't eat it. Adelaide walked into the kitchen and sat down. "My new ring," she said, waving her finger. "Got it last night. I was going to show it to you earlier, but well. . . ."

"It's beautiful."

"It is, isn't it?" she said, polishing it with her napkin.

We could hear Al and Arthur, Adelaide's fiancé, laughing in Papa's bedroom. My God, they were laughing! About what? Man talk, I heard. "Did you hit him from the front or the back?" Arthur asked. Arthur must have swung his arms mimicking a prizefight. More laughter. And then it got quiet, except for shuffling feet and drawers opening and closing. They helped him out of the bedroom and brought him to the table. He was wearing a clean robe and slippers, still looking tired, but the nosebleed had stopped, and he was clean shaven. Papa straightened his back in the chair and put his swollen fist on the table. A tiny black-and-blue mark covered the corner of his lip.

"Well, have you decided?" Al asked, reaching for a roll.

"Adelaide and I talked about it. She offered to stay with them, but I don't think it's fair. They're just starting out. Besides, I'll be home with the baby. It makes more sense."

"Then it's settled," Al said. "Now we have to convince your father."

"And my mother. I don't think she'll take this well."

Adelaide held Arthur's hand. "Maybe we should discuss this with the Rubensteins."

"There's nothing they can do. We have to make the decisions from now on. We'll tell them when we're ready," I said.

"Then let's eat," she decided. "No more talking while we're eating. I don't want him to think we're talking about them." She walked over to the stove where Mama was ladling soup into the bowls, feeling the rims for their fullness. She took them from her, one by one, and brought them to the table. We ate in silence.

After dinner, Papa put a plug in his mouth and chewed carefully. His right swollen cheek was only half full of the stuff. It was too bitter to chew, and he spit it out in his napkin. He didn't look at Mama or Adelaide or me. He turned to Al and Arthur and smiled, rubbing his tongue over his wounded lip, as if only they could understand. Man stuff. A good sock and everything is solved. I could see it in Al. I could see it in Arthur. I could not see it in Mama. Half of her smiled, the part that swooned with joy over the new baby; the other part stayed locked in anger, frozen, like her two fingers.

Angry myself but terrified of his reaction, I translated Al's thoughts to Papa with trembling fingers. Al was clumsy, too slow to do it by himself. Papa looked stunned for a moment as he watched my fingers. He let his tongue roll inside his cheek as if he still had the tobacco in his mouth. "We don't want charity!"

"He says he doesn't want charity," I told Al and Arthur.

"No charity. We expect you to pay your way," I translated.

"Not a good idea," Papa said.

"He says it's not a good idea."

"Maybe it's not a good idea. We're mixing in their lives," Adelaide said.

My soon-to-be brother-in-law put in his two cents. He and Al weighed the pros and cons. There had never been so much hearing talk in the kitchen. Papa waited out the conversation, his eyes tense. Mama sat, oblivious to our words. Eventually it was time to stop the words that Papa didn't understand. Positive that we'd made the right decision, I turned to Papa to ease his frustration. "I could use help with the baby," I said. "Mama will be happy about that."

"Baby? You pregnant?" he asked, making a big circle over his stomach.

"Didn't Mama tell you?"

"No," he said, raising his hands in elation. "Wonderful," he signed, then took my mother's hand. "Why didn't you tell me?"

"Not my place to tell you," she smiled. They held on to each other's hands, smiling with happiness. The look of their eyes seemed private, so we turned our faces away.

"Did you talk to Ruthie about this?" he asked.

"No. You first. I want you to think about it."

"I pay my own way? I pay rent and food and help with other expenses."

Yes, Papa, I thought. You can scrunch papers in the middle of the night with us. We all nodded our heads: yes.

"I'll think about it. If it's a good idea, I'll tell Mama when we're alone."

"What's everybody talking about?" asked Mama.

"About the baby," I lied.

She walked to the pantry and brought back a bottle of schnapps and put it in Papa's hand. "To celebrate," she told us.

We raised our glasses in a toast. "To Adelaide and Arthur. Congratulations."

"To the new baby," Adelaide toasted.

"To Papa. Here's hoping he can use his persuasive charms on her."

We laughed. Papa looked puzzled. My mother cleared the table.

ADELAIDE TOLD me Mama and Papa talked about our proposition together in the privacy of their bedroom. No talking with us, no tears, no more anger from Papa. Just a calming quiet in the house as Papa shook Al's hand in agreement. The first thing my mother said, when Sarah, Little Joe, and Rosie came to visit, was that she was expecting her first grandchild. The second thing she said was that Adelaide would be getting married. Then she sat back and beamed.

"Mazeltov," Sarah said to me. Her z came out like a d. "Your Papa says you're moving in together. I think it's a good idea."

"And what does my mother think?"

She shrugged her shoulders. "Has to be done. I'll miss (the

esses were gone) her. But if it's not too far away, of course, we'll come to visit."

"Any time. You're always welcome."

Sarah's eyes filled with tears. "And what about your aunties? What do they think?"

"I haven't told them yet."

"You should."

"Yes, I should. Maybe today."

Little Joe came out of the living room and walked over to Sarah. He put his fingers to his head to say good-bye and bent over to kiss Mama on the cheek. Then they left. I picked up the phone and called Aunt Marian. Her smooth silky voice asked, "Hello?"

I told her everything as if I had written the words on paper, dry and remote. I could hear her sigh with relief. Then I dialed Aunt Selma's number. Zadie answered the phone, but I told him only that I was pregnant. He shouted, "Goot, goot," and yelled, "Selma, quick, on the phone. It's Charlotte. Goot news."

She listened carefully as I told her everything, and when I was done, there was silence. Finally, she said in a strong voice, "Well, kiddo, I think it's a good idea. I know a mover who would charge very little. His name is. . . ."

"It's okay, Aunt Sel. We've figured it all out." And she, too, sighed a big sigh of relief.

IN THE following months, Al and I negotiated a loan with his parents. We searched for suitable housing. Papa's wounds healed, but his emotions seemed fragile. He wavered between happiness over Adelaide's coming marriage and shame over the way he had disappointed Mama. Mama, distracted by feverish wedding plans, showed no obvious anger. Occasionally, she exhibited a nervousness, but I attributed this to the excitement over the wedding and her concern for my pregnancy.

We found a house only weeks after Adelaide and Arthur's

wedding. I was eight months pregnant. Mama's demeanor changed then. Closed, keeping out of our conversations when we came to visit, she showed interest only in my welfare.

I opened her hands wide one day to brighten her mood, to talk of pleasant things. "We're going to name him Andrew after Papa's mother, Anna," I spelled.

"That's very thoughtful," she said.

"If it's a girl, we'll call her Anne."

"That's nice, too." She was sitting in her burgundy chair, stroking the fabric, thinking, I suppose, of the changing events ahead of her. She'd lived in this apartment since I was five years old. It would be a wrenching transition. I took her hand again. "We'll be signing the final papers next month, Mama. I can take you to the house then to show you around."

"That's good," she replied.

MAMA AND I took the streetcar back and forth to the new house, figuring what furniture we would keep and what we would discard. She held on to me as we walked through the rooms, feeling the walls and the placement of the doors. When she was comfortable with the layout, she pulled away from the walls and walked alone through the house.

"I think we should put the sofa bed here," she said, touching the long wall of their new room. "And the television here, so Papa can see it while we sit on the sofa. Is that all right, Sha?"

I shook her hand yes.

"Then, while he's at work, I could stay in my room and sit on the sofa. I won't bother you unless you need me."

"No, Mama." I led her to the big kitchen. "You stay here with me, not by yourself."

"We'll see," she said tentatively.

"It's a good idea for us to live together," I assured her.

"Maybe. Maybe not," she said, her face stony.

I changed the subject. "Addle thinks you should learn braille."

She pushed my hands away. "I'm not completely blind."

"But you can't read anymore."

"I'm much too old. I'm in my fifties. I have one bad hand. It's no use."

"Maybe you'll try."

"Never. I can do my work. I suppose I can help you in the kitchen. I'll be busy."

"We'll be happy together. I know it."

"We'll see," she said again, standing in the middle of the kitchen and waiting for me to take her home.

AT THE apartment, the secondhand dealer and his workmen carried the old sofa down the stairs. They took the dining room table and the six chairs next, then the lamps that Aunt Marian had given us years ago. When they had finished, nothing was left. The wood floors, scratched from years of dragging our toys across them, the walls where Mama's pictures left their marks, the clothesline on the back porch where the wash had hung, all looked strangely empty. Papa walked down the stairs for the last time, his cigar box of personal papers under his arm. Mama tucked Mrs. Luft's afghan under her arm and took my hand. I closed the door behind us and gave Mrs. Goldberg the keys. "Will you give these to Mr. Trask?"

"Of course," she wept. "I didn't do enough, did I? I should have paid more attention."

"Mrs. Goldberg, you were the best friend Mama had in this building. Of course you did enough. It's just time we moved on." She leaned over to kiss my mother's cheek.

"Good-bye, Mushes Gobug," my mother said. "Joe will bring me back to visit. I promise."

"With the baby? Ask her, with the baby?"

I spelled into Mama's hands.

"Of course, with the baby."

But we never came back.

19

WHEN I was about eleven, I heard one of the neighbors say to Mrs. Goldberg, "You can't have two women in the same household. They're sure to kill each other."

I pulled three four o'clocks out of the flower bed that day, sat on the front stoop, and listened with great interest as Mrs. Goldberg debated her position with the neighbors. The three of them were sitting on a bench, crossing and uncrossing their legs, then spreading them apart to let the breeze flow up their dresses.

"Especially if one of them is the mother-in-law. Oy, what a mistake that is," the middle neighbor declared. Then they unwrapped their white handkerchiefs from their necks and wiped their brows. Nobody paid attention to me because I was just a kid, sitting on my front stoop, picking four o'clocks, and crushing the petals between my fingers. They uttered a couple of swear words in Yiddish and went back to wiping their brows.

The reason for this discussion was Mrs. Mandleman's heartless behavior with old Mrs. Mandleman, a tiny lady with a face like the wrinkled leather of a worn-out shoe. She was even older than Zadie, I had determined. She wore old-fashioned dresses down to her ankles, a shawl over her shoulders, and what appeared to be a wig—one of many, apparently, because their shades of brown seemed to change every couple of days. I would see her shuffling along with her cane to Laykin's grocery and come back with only a small bag because she couldn't carry anything larger. One strong breeze off Lake Michigan could have blown her over.

What had happened the previous day, according to Mrs. Goldberg, was that young Mrs. Mandleman threw old Mrs. Mandleman out, left her on the street, crying and wailing in Yiddish. When nobody came to rescue her, Mrs. Goldberg called the police, who had a heart-to-heart talk with the younger Mrs. M. Somewhat later, the older Mrs. M. shuffled back upstairs, and peace settled in again at 1309.

Mrs. Goldberg's intervention came as no surprise; she was always rescuing somebody. But what astonished me was the fact that one of the neighbors attacked Mrs. Goldberg for butting in. How could anybody fault Mrs. Goldberg? I tossed the crushed four o'clock petals behind the bushes and went upstairs to tell my mother.

"I'm not surprised," she commented, swirling chocolate frosting in a bowl. "Mrs. Goldberg is a saint. The others wouldn't help a dying man into his bed. And Mrs. Mandleman, well, Mrs. Mandleman is a horse's arse."

"A horse's what?"

"Arse. Arse. A-S-S," she spelled. She looked at me, giggled, filled a spoon with the frosting, and gave it to me. "Don't tell Papa I swore."

"Which Mrs. Mandleman is a horse's arse?"

"Well, now that I think about it," she mused, swirling the frosting again, "they're both horses' arses."

When the movers placed the last piece of furniture in our new living room, Mama and I sat down on the sofa. We were determined not to be horses' arses. We didn't have a big discussion about it. We just held hands, her two icy ones firmly grasped by mine.

THE "NEW" house was not new. Built in the early thirties, it boasted high ceilings and old-fashioned wainscoting, unlike the modern trilevels sprouting in the suburbs. There were three small bedrooms, a kitchen large enough to accommodate the five of us, and an antiquated bathroom with black and white hexagonal tiles halfway up the walls. Mama inspected the kitchen cupboards one by one, poking her fingers in them—dishes here, cans there, pots and pans under the sink. These were her markers.

Instead of a back porch, she now had access to a large back-yard with grapevines dangling over an arbor. She could negotiate the back steps without trouble, guide herself to the lawn chair under the arbor, and poke her face up to the sun that filtered through.

When we stood at the counter at the new drugstore to pick up Papa's potion of alcohol and witch hazel, the sights and smells were familiar: the soda fountain along the middle of the wall, the sweet sickening odor of dishwater lingering on the cloths used to wipe up ice cream spills, the strong aroma of cough medicine, and powdery tablets in apothecary jars on a shelf in the back room. Even the pharmacist looked the same. Bald, with coke-bottle eyeglasses and a short white coat. Only his name was Mr. Swenson, not Mr. Kaplan.

Mama sniffed and felt at home. But the A&P that replaced Laykin's friendly grocery store shocked her. "Do you mean," she asked incredulously, "you have to pick your own groceries?"

"That's right, Mama. I put everything in my own cart and bring it to the counter, and the lady totals it up on a cash register."

"Very modern," she said, holding on to the cart. "What will they think of next?"

River Park—a fraction of the size of Humboldt Park—was where Mama and I walked the baby. I missed the willow trees, and perhaps Mama missed them, too, although she hadn't walked in Humboldt Park in years. Holding on to the side of Andrew's buggy while we shopped or resting on a bench by the small river that ran through our new park, she seemed surprisingly happy. After all, a park was a park. The trees may have been different and the scenery less stimulating, but the benches were the same, and the smell of flowers reached her nose as readily as before.

We had weathered our test of togetherness. Mama's icy tentacles clung to me on the outside and felt their way with freedom through the house. She did Papa's and her own wash separately, putting the wet clothes through the wringer like a professional laundry woman, ironed his shirts on Tuesdays, keeping some of the same routine she had at the old house. I cooked, she washed the dishes. I mopped, she made the beds.

She played blocks with the baby, laughing every time he knocked them down, and told him nursery rhymes that I had to retell. If I hadn't, Andy—just learning to say "Mama" and "Dada"—would have recited, "Eensy spider climb up the bathroom wall," leaving all the esses and the little words out. He looked confused at the difference in words that bounced around him. When Papa said (poking a finger in his chest), "Ome," and I said, "Grandpa's home," he swiveled his head from him to me, his mouth open, as if to ask, "Now which is it, 'home' or 'ome'?"

But, just as I had learned their differences, so did Andy, and he waved his hands and arms to Papa and led Mama to the places he wanted to go and put toys in her hands so she could play games with him.

At five o'clock Mama removed her tentacles from me, hung up her housedress, and put on her walking dress. She then pulled off her slippers, eased into her Cuban heels, put a comb through her hair—one last smoothing touch to it—applied lipstick by feel, and waited for Papa. Joe would be coming home soon. And after Joe said "ome" to Andy and put his empty lunch box on the kitchen counter, Joe would take her out walking. He would sit with her in their room and spell the news into her hands and then, the door would close, not fully, because if Andy wanted to crawl between them, they welcomed him while they spelled over his head and turned the sound up on the TV so he could hear it. And I was free to sit in the living room with Al.

So the neighbors on the bench were wrong. In fact, Mama was a big help to me. She turned Andy's crabby times into holding times, putting up with his nonsense with monotonous hums and jiggling him in her lap. "Hum, hum, ma, ma, ma, ma, oowee, oowee." Bouncing and hugging him, it didn't matter what she said to him because I was ready to tear my hair out and leave him to cry alone in his prison of a crib.

From dawn to dusk, we women ran the household. But who was this woman who shared it with me? This woman who sat with me at the kitchen table, asking if the baby was crying in his crib or if he'd eaten all of his lunch. This was not the woman I called my mother. I never knew what she really felt. And I missed her. I wanted her back in her burgundy chair, reading books and ignoring me because she had something to do, not because she felt she was in my way. I hated it when she said, "you're the boss" every time I made a decision about meals.

"What do you think about Russia?" I asked her one day while Andy napped, trying hard to pull thoughts from her imprisoned mind. "You could never go back there, you know."

"Why are you asking me such a silly question? Is the baby crying?"

"No, the baby's not crying."

"And why couldn't I go back?" she asked.

"The Cold War. You know about that, don't you?"

"Of course. Papa tells me everything. And why would I want to go back anyway?"

"To see where you came from. To remember your child-hood."

"My childhood seems so far away."

"Did you dance like a flapper?"

"Oh my, you move so fast. From childhood to when I was grownup."

"How was it when you were grownup? Before I was born."

"How should it be? Different from you?" she said, waving her hands in the shadowy space in front of her. "Yes, I danced like a flapper."

"I didn't." Maybe it wasn't fair to remind her of the past, but it got her to smile.

"Very funny," she laughed. "Oh, yes. I danced like a flapper. We dance, you know. Deaf people can feel the drums, the vibration on the floor. Did you know your father was a good dancer?"

"No, I didn't know."

"There's a lot of things you don't know about us."

"Papa moves like a cat, even now, Mama." Indeed, he walked out of our house every morning, free from tension, and bounded down the stairs like he'd knocked out the world for a ten count. He was happy. I heated the coffee, poured two cups, and put her hand on the cup. She brought it to her lips and drank.

"The baby looks just like Papa," I told her.

"Yes, Rosie says so."

"Can you see anything of him?"

"A little. His face is round. Chubby."

"You feel it?"

"Yes, of course. With my hands."

"He's crazy about you and Papa."

She beamed and shook her head in agreement.

I wanted to ask, "Do you miss your reading?" Instead I said, "Hannah is pregnant. She's having a hard time with the pregnancy."

"Oh, too bad," she sympathized, opening her eyes wide as if she could see the trouble. "I had it easy with you. Addle was hard. That's why the doctor said, no more. Papa was disappointed. He wanted six."

"Six!?"

"Yes. Can you imagine? A boy. He hoped for a boy."

"Of course!"

"But I'm glad we didn't have a boy. He'd teach him to fight. Be tough with his hands. Men think they can solve everything with their fists." She put her hands in the middle of the table, searching.

"What, Mama?"

"Where are the graham crackers?"

"I put them away because the baby made a mess of them. I'll get you some." I went to the cupboard, brought the box down, and handed some to her. She took one cracker and ate it daintily with her good hand. "Men are a lot of trouble," she confided.

I laughed, but she couldn't see it, so I took her hand and waved it yes.

"Al doesn't give you trouble, does he?"

"Not at all."

"Doesn't help much in the house, does he?"

"He works hard every day. I manage. You help me. Did Papa help you?"

"Papa made the money. I cooked and cleaned," she said, sweeping graham cracker crumbs into her lap. "That's the way it's supposed to be, but I didn't have Bubbi in my house to make it worse. To make my job harder."

"It's not harder. You're a help."

"I still talk to her in my dreams."

"Bubbi?"

"Yes," she smiled.

I wanted to ask, what did Bubbi say when she found out you were deaf? Instead I said, "I guess you and Bubbi were the closest because you were the oldest."

"I suppose," she replied dreamily. Blind eyes will do that. Stare off unfocused, picturing some imagined scene. "I was a big help to her. After the little boy baby died, the one that came after Marian, she was depressed. I watched over my sisters. I made sure they didn't run into the street. It was hard for her. I was too young to know how it feels, but I saw the way she looked. I think she never got over it."

I looked at my watch. "It's two o'clock. The baby's still sleeping. My program is on."

"Which one?"

"Hawkins Falls. The one where the man was killed in the plane crash."

"Oh yes. That one. Do you want to watch it?"

"Come with me. I'll tell you what happened."

She got up from her chair and accompanied me to the living room, hands out in anticipation of misplaced danger. I turned the TV on. The music and the credits had started. I took her hand and asked, "What do you think about Adelaide's idea that you should learn braille?"

"Silly idea," she said, taking her hand away from me.

The screen showed Hawkins Falls, Hollywood's idea of a perfect small town, with elm-shaded streets and perfect cottages with front porches and rose bushes along the walk. The camera panned into a living room. The actors moved and spoke. I spelled the dialogue into Mama's hands.

"Oh my," she said, filling herself with someone else's life. "Where is Hawkins Falls?"

"It's an imaginary place. Just a story, Mama. A fairy tale like the ones you used to tell me." Only fifteen minutes long, it wasn't a soap opera that drew national attention. It was, in fact, a filler for the local station. Still, its story riveted me. The plane crash, the tumult of the aftermath, the despair on the heroine's face. I turned it off and sighed. Mama got up, smoothed her dress, and walked away from me toward the back door. "I'm going downstairs," she called out into the void. "Let me know when it's time to change my dress. I want to get the sun before Papa comes home."

She closed the door behind her. I could hear her steps, one after the other, until she reached the bottom. I ran to the back door and watched her, half wanting to run down and guide her to the lawn chair, but she had already turned the corner and taken off like a rooted bird, her wings in motion, marking the spaces around her. She sat in the lawn chair and lifted her face to the sun. I went back into the kitchen, washed the coffee cups, and put the graham crackers back in the cupboard exactly where they had been before and closed the cupboard door tight so it wouldn't fly open. Mama had bruised herself one day, thinking the door was closed. She caught it with her forehead, creating a slender gash, but Papa went into a rage when he saw it. Mama had stamped her foot and called him foolish for carrying on about it, but I was soberly reminded of what could have happened if she had moved her head up even an inch.

Chairs stayed where she remembered them. Soap stayed in the soap dish, not in the middle of the tub. Glasses belonged in the cupboards, not waiting to be washed in the sink. Golf clubs in the closet, not resting on the wall in the hallway. Nothing in the middle of the rooms. Everything where she had memorized it.

The phone rang. It was Rosie's mother with a message. Can Rosie come to visit?

"When?" I asked.

"Tomorrow? One o'clock?" her mother said after a small silence. I envisioned her signing it to Rosie, waiting for Rosie to sign back.

"It should be okay," I told her mother, "but I'll ask my mother to be sure. I'll call you back."

More silence. More unseen signing. She came back on the phone. "She'll wait to hear from you." Then she hung up. I imagined Rosie nodding her head at her mother's signing. I imagined her doing whatever single deaf women do who have no family of their own to care for and no jobs to go to every day. Did they fret because their mothers worried about dying and leaving deaf them all alone?

Of course, it was all right to come. Mama wasn't going anywhere. Maybe to the A&P or the barber shop with me. It was time to cut the Shirley Temple locks from Andy's head, Mama holding him in her lap while I soothed his tears. I walked down the steps into the backyard and gave her the message.

"Is it all right with you?" she asked.

"You don't have to ask me," I spelled.

"Don't you need me for anything?"

"Not tomorrow."

"All right. Then tell her to come."

I sat next to her on the small wooden bench that Papa had painted bright yellow last weekend. Our backyard was in motion from weeds to new flowers. Papa had dug little trenches in preparation, and Al had laid out the garden.

"How long have you and Rosie been friends?" I asked, offering her a rose to smell.

"We went to school together. Papa's sister Flora introduced me. That was before Flora went to the state school. We were best friends, Flora and Rosie and I. Poor Rosie. It's too late for her. She'll never get married."

"And Sarah? How long have you known her?"

"Forever," she sighed. "Like my own sister."

"She hasn't been to see you lately, Mama."

"Papa and I see her and Little Joe! We saw them last week at the club."

"But Sarah doesn't come alone. Is it too far for her?"

"Sarah can be moody," she said. "Now, if you want to see a flapper dance, you should have seen her. Her cheeks were painted all the way up to her eyes, and her hair was very short in a bob. And her dress was above her knees. Her mother didn't approve. She came to my house, crying one day that her mother didn't understand her. To tell the truth, I didn't either. I would never have shamed Zadie by looking that way. I kept my dress down to my knees. That's as far as I would go. She's so silly, Sarah is, sometimes. Worried about her wrinkles and her hair. Little Joe spoils her like a princess."

The phone rang again. I touched Mama's hand to tell her to wait and ran up the stairs. It was Adelaide with her daily call of worrying and fretting and pushing me for an answer.

"I tried again today, but she's not interested," I told her, over the sound of her typewriter keys.

"Well, keep trying. I think it'll do her a lot of good."

"Maybe Mama's right, Ad. It might be too hard for her with one bum hand."

"How many hands do you need to read braille?"

"Is that a question or a statement?"

"Char, you only need one. That's a fact. Well, if you can't convince her, get Papa moving on it."

"Are you kidding? He's so protective of her, he won't let her cut her own meat. He takes care of everything when he's home."

"He's wrong."

"Then you tell him. I'm not gonna have his eyes turn to steel."

"You're an idiot," she said, banging the keys.

"I love talking to you, too," I laughed. "I'll see you Sunday. Roast beef and mashed potatoes. An American dream. The family together, just like in the movies."

"Ha, ha," she said and hung up.

I knew it was hard for her. Stuck in her cubicle of an office, typing and taking shorthand, our mother's welfare filling her thoughts. I walked down to tell Mama it was time to change into her walking dress. "Braille is for blind people," she snorted as we returned to the house.

"Your mother is not blind," my father had said the day we moved in. "She sees light and shadows."

Even the Rubensteins had given up. No more specialists to see. No need to butt into our lives any more. They phoned and visited and went back to their own world. It seemed only right. But I never asked Mama if she cared—if she missed reading their lips.

SHE WAITED, hands outstretched at the kitchen table, her apron covering her clean dress. Papa dropped his lunch pail on the kitchen counter, tweaked Andy under the chin, said "ome," and took my mother's hand. She smiled. He sat down next to her and patted her back.

He cut her chicken into little pieces and put her fingers on the fork. They ate in silence while Al and I talked. Same table, two different couples split down the middle by silence. Andy gurgled and dribbled chicken down his bib. Al laughed. Papa looked up to see what was happening and laughed himself. He told Mama what Andy had done, and she smiled. We finished our dinner. Mama helped with the dishes, took off her apron, and let Papa guide her into her mouton coat.

"It's getting cold outside, Papa. Maybe you should stay in tonight."

He grunted an unpleasant sound, ignoring me. She put her arm through his, and they left. I returned to the living room, where Al had spread himself on the floor, legs stretched out, head resting on his arm. Andy was on his back, riding him like a horse.

"It's working out okay, isn't it?" he asked.

"He's very happy."

"And your mother?"

"She loves him."

"But is she happy?"

"I don't know."

CHAPTER

20

I N TWO years' time, the garden fulfilled its promise.
Tulips and crocus pushed through the snow in early
spring. In the summer, green onion and carrot tops waved at the
side of the house. The old shed that hugged the alley had been
painted shiny white and gleamed in the sun. Because it was only
a lean-to, propped up by rotting boards, it seemed wasteful to
put good paint to it, and, indeed, in autumn the shed burned to
the ground. As it did, my father put his hand to his forehead in
dismay, then put his fingers down to his side, muttering that his
son-in-law was a fool, even dangerous, for burning leaves so close
to the shed. "Doesn't know a thing about anything," he spelled
to his pants leg.

I wondered whether to interrupt his internal thoughts and
defend my husband, for Al could do anything he wanted. He
could wield a hammer or screwdriver, change the wiring, turn
the basement into a rec room, and I was proud of him. So
what if he burned leaves too close to the shed? Papa was aware
of my loyalty. It would take only a flash of indignation on my
face to cause him to back off. But I thought the better of it.
As long as he didn't confront Al face-to-face, as long as he
kept it to himself, as long as he complained only to me, I let
it pass.

Papa had invited Sarah and Little Joe to our Garden of Eden,
so they showed up one Sunday to help harvest.

"Take," he said, shoving carrots into their shopping bags.
"Take more. No, Little Joe, don't run off just yet. We'll have a

glass of lemonade under the grape arbor. Be careful not to step on the grapes. Sha forgot to clean it up."

What did he think I did all day? File my nails? But I let this one pass, too. Sarah walked down the grape-stained path and sat next to Mama. I ran in to make lemonade and dashed back outside, pitcher and glasses tilting to one side of the tray. I was in a rush to please my father, happy that he felt secure enough to offer carrots and green beans. Sarah spelled in Mama's hands, and Papa and Little Joe talked of the old days. When they had finished reliving the Depression, they turned to baseball, and when that topic was exhausted, they started discussing the deaf club and its current president and the new temple everyone was hoping for. I'd heard it all before. In fact, because the Depression had assumed legendary proportions with them, I began to mistrust their stories—tales, for instance, about Papa moving us out of our apartment in the middle of the night because he couldn't pay the rent. "When was that?" I had asked years ago, and he had answered, "You were just a baby. That's why you don't remember." Little Joe would nod his head in agreement, and Papa would puff on his cigar, pleased at being backed up.

My father's tales of hoboing through the country and seeing Pancho Villa and Indians (drawing his Indian heads for Andy now) were reduced to folklore, even if Little Joe always backed him up. How would he know? He didn't ride the rails with Papa. And baseball was something I had no time for, but a temple—now that was something! I interrupted their talk, "What new temple?"

"There's a rumor going around that a temple for the deaf might be formed."

"That's wonderful," I exclaimed, watching Sarah spelling into Mama's hands. Because Sarah's fingers were covered by my mother's hand, I had no idea what those two were talking about. When Mama had something to say, it was usually "Really?" or "Isn't that something?" or "No, I haven't seen her. How is she?"

Bored, I walked back upstairs to find Al reading in the living room. Andy moved himself from the sofa and toddled to the coffee table. He had wonderful comedic talent, shredding old newspapers and scooping and dropping the bits neatly in a pile again, mugging constantly, then walked downstairs to perform for the others.

"So, what are the old folks talking about now?" Al asked me.

Was it the old folks' talk or was it deaf talk I was bored with? I wondered. "The old folks are talking about the old days," I told him and picked up a book to read.

SUNDAY VISITORS and lemonade got to be a habit. If it wasn't Sarah and Little Joe, it was another deaf couple, and Papa shoved carrots and green onions their way and offered them my lemonade. The talk was always about the same. If it wasn't a deaf couple, it was Leo and Rebecca—Al's parents—who came, along with Al's Uncle Bennie and Aunt Olga. While Papa chewed his tobacco and Mama put her face to the sun, they, too, sat among the grape splotches and talked of the Depression and who was the president of the B'nai B'rith. Only when the deck of cards came out did the deaf men and Uncle Bennie and Leo and Al blend together in pinochle. I sat next to Mama, Rebecca, Sarah, and Aunt Olga while the speaking women spoke and the deaf ones either talked around Mama or spelled in her hands.

My father was happy. He poured lemonade for our guests and sometimes beer for Leo and Little Joe. He came home late every Thursday night from bowling, always dropping his magenta team jacket on the chair that he claimed as his own coat hook. He stashed his ball and shoes in the hall closet, slightly annoyed at having to share it with Al's golf clubs. The smell of stale cigar smoke and beer permeated the hallway. He was calm and relaxed. He didn't have to shop or help Mama clean the house. He didn't have to go to work with a fluttery stomach, worried

Mama might fall over a stray chair or burn herself. He had me to do the worrying for him.

When I walked past their room on occasion, I'd spot a word about the baby's antics or how well Papa bowled the night before. But when Papa asked, "Ruthie, what did you do today?" she'd turn her hands upward to say "nothing" and lay them back into her lap.

Sometimes, as I watched, I'd spot boredom on my father's face. He'd shake her hand up and down, pretending he was listening, but his eyes were glued to the television set. I wanted to tell him, "Papa, listen to her. What else does she have in her life?" but the child in me was too afraid to scold him. So I would speed past him as a train meeting up with another at a crossing, saying no more than was necessary, tipping my head hello, assuring him that he was wanted and respected.

But Mama had turned passive. She would lower her eyes in embarrassment when he poked her hard on the shoulder for breaking a glass in the sink. As if the glass were a precious diamond. What did I care about broken glasses? I wanted to shake him up and down and tell him to be quiet about it. Instead, I placated him with an assuring pat to the air. "It's nothing, Papa, just a glass."

He'd chew hard on his tobacco as if it would be his last chew before I threw both of them into the street, like old Mrs. Mandelman. I could see he thought it. His steely eyes turned whimpering blue in fear. Yet he could be filled with rage when he thought Mama was abused, when a chair was left in the middle of the dining room and Mama met with pain. His flip-flopping from scared child to my mother's ferocious protector made my stomach tight. She patted the air when she fell over toys that Andy had laid out as strategically as a minefield. She spelled wildly after she had steadied herself, "Don't worry, Joe. It only hurts a minute. Don't worry, Sha. I'll be fine."

I saw too much: his inattentiveness when they were alone, his unspoken rage, his eyes flashing with anger at the broken glasses, and his hands flung wildly to the air at her black and blue marks, no matter how hard Mama and I tried to smooth it over. I kept it to myself. It was none of my business. I hoped that in the privacy of their room, they would straighten it all out. When Mama came to breakfast, smiling, I was sure they had.

CHAPTER 21

"RUTHIE, THIS is going to be a big party. The biggest one of the year," my father said, as I retrieved Andy from their sofa one night. "I haven't seen my New York friends in years. Tell Sha to take you shopping for a new dress."

My mother took his hand and waved it "OK."

"What kind of party?" I asked her.

"The annual convention of the Hebrew Deaf," he interrupted. "It's going to be at the Edgewater Hotel. I want you and Al and Addle and Art to come, too. My treat," he waved.

"Sure, Papa."

I put Andy to bed and walked into the living room. "How would you like to spend a Saturday night in a ballroom filled with deaf people? My father's treat," I proposed to Al.

"Sounds intimidating," he said, putting down his newspaper. "I can't manage one single conversation with your father without getting fingertied. How will I ever manage with a crowd of strangers?"

"It'll do you good. You'll have plenty of people to practice on."

"What's it like?"

"I don't know. I've never been to one, but I'm happy Papa wants to go. Mama could use a fancy night out."

"How is it that you've never gone before?"

"I suppose he couldn't afford it before."

"Your father's a sport, you know."

"My mother said that once when she told me how he courted her. This is how you say it in deaf: I put my thumbs into imaginary suspenders on my chest and puffed my fingers out. "Now that's how you say 'a sport.' Or you could call it a big timer, or a boaster, or someone who's full of it."

"You're full of it," he quipped. " You made that all up."

"No, it's true."

"Well, how is one supposed to know which of those a person is?"

"You have to pay attention to the rest of the conversation. When my mother told me my father poured coffee out of a silver pitcher in their first-class train compartment on their honeymoon, and she stuck her thumbs into her chest, she definitely meant he was a sport."

"Gotcha."

"And when you go around telling everyone how smart Andy is, I'd say you were a boaster."

"Gotcha."

"Did you really get it?"

"I haven't the foggiest idea."

"I thought so. Let's go to bed."

"I'm going to look like a fool," he said, holding my hand.

"No one will notice."

FINGERING THE dresses on the rack at Marshall Field's, Mama seemed unhappy. She felt the collars, zippers, buttons, and sleeves, pinched the material between her fingers, then decided none of them were suitable.

"But this one is perfect," I spelled, putting her hand back on a particular dress. "It's your size. It's blue, your favorite color, isn't it?"

"All blue?" she asked, feeling the cuffs.

"White cuffs and a white belt."

"I'd rather have blue cuffs and a blue belt."

"There aren't any like that."

"Then let's pay for this one and leave," she said. "Here's the money Papa gave me. She reached into her purse and pulled out a roll of bills. Papa was definitely acting like a sport.

"Is it enough?" she asked, seeming uneasy with her bounty.

"More than enough. But you have to try it on first."

"No, I don't care to try it on," she said, closing her hands over the money. "If you say it's fine, it's fine with me."

"But Mama!"

The store clerks were staring at us. My frantic fingerspelling had attracted them. They were bunched behind the cash register, pretending not to notice. One of the clerks leaned over and smiled. "Perhaps she'd feel more comfortable trying it on at home. If it doesn't fit, bring it back."

"Thank you, but we'll try it on here."

She had stuffed the bills back in her purse, shut the clasp, and waited for me to take her arm. I pulled the dress off the rack and led her into the fitting room.

"It fits," she said after a quick slip into the dress. "Let's go," she said, pulling it over her head.

"I don't understand you, Mama. What are you upset about?"

"Nothing."

"Nobody's paying any attention to us, if that's what you think."

"Don't be silly. What do I care what people think?"

"Then what?"

"Take the money. Here," she handed me the purse. "Now let's go home."

She waited like a statue while I paid the clerk, took my arm as we walked out of the store, stood with her face to the sun, her dark glasses shielding her eyes while we waited for the bus. I slipped my fingers into hers as we boarded the bus. She slid into the inner seat next to the window.

"Something's wrong," I said, sliding in after her. "Why don't you tell me?"

"Nothing," she whispered.

ON THE day of the affair, I fluffed her salt and pepper hair into the latest style and misted it with hair spray. "What do you think, Mama?"

"Feels like a beehive," she said, running her fingers over her head. "I hate it. It feels awful."

"It's very becoming. You'd better hurry. We only have an hour. The babysitter's due any minute."

Something was said in their room, I figured. Something that had made her angry and unwilling. Something that was none of my business. She was still in her pink slip, sitting on her sofa when I returned ten minutes later. I poked her gently on the shoulder to remind her of the time.

"I don't want to go."

"Why!?"

"What am I going to do there?"

"Papa says it's a good show and there will be dancing."

"I'm not going to dance. I'm not going to see the show. People will stare at me. I look blind, don't I?"

"You don't look blind. Besides everybody knows you're blind." Everyone, I thought. The grocer, the druggist, the people on the streetcar, the milkman, the mothers with their babies in the park, and she had never once revealed that she was uncomfortable with it.

"His friends from New York don't know I'm blind. I don't want to embarrass Papa."

I pulled her new dress out of the closet. "You won't embarrass anybody. Please, Mama. Put it on."

She didn't move.

"I'll fix your face. Give me your makeup."

"I threw it out," she laughed.

"Damn it, Mama." I reached into my purse and took out my makeup. Her face was stiff and hostile. I worked the powder around her cheeks and nose. She grabbed the lipstick from me and smeared it on her mouth herself. A line of red caked the corner of her lower lip.

Papa came out of the bathroom in his undershirt and shorts. He put on his trousers and laid the dress shirt, tie, and jacket on the bed, behaving as though he didn't know. He poked her hard on the shoulder with his ring finger. "Will you please hurry? I don't want to be late."

"I don't care, Joe," she said.

"But I care," he said, poking her hard again.

"All right," she waved. "All right." She stood up and pulled the dress over her head, then sat back down again and laced up her black walking shoes.

Papa stared, horrified at the clodhoppers. "Why aren't you wearing your good shoes?"

"Who cares what I wear?"

His face turned red. I wanted to pick up the corner lamp and hit him on the head to stop his angry poking. Strike him dead so he wouldn't do it again.

"What's the matter with her?" he asked me.

So he didn't know. Mama had never said a word to him.

"Papa, she's afraid she might embarrass you. People will stare at her. Especially your New York friends. And she won't see the show!"

He sank into his chair and breathed hard. "Stupid. Sometimes I stupid," he said in deaf talk. "I no think of her." He put his hands in hers, prying her fingers open, insistent on conversation. "Ruthie, you look beautiful. Put on your good shoes."

She shoved his hands away.

"Ruthie," he demanded, prying her fingers open again. And then he spelled something I didn't see. Mama looked at him hopefully and put on her good shoes. I ran to my room, and fished out a pair of fancy sunglasses, and brought them in to her, wondering what Papa had said. Whatever it was, it had perked her up. "Try these on, Mama. All the movie stars wear them."

She fingered them and perched them on her nose, then slid them into place. "Do I look like a movie star?"

"Just like Hedy Lamar!"

The dress was very becoming; it flattered her body. Her hips had spread these past years, but she still had her nice bustline and slender legs. Her skin was smooth with only tiny lines around the mouth. She ran her hands gently over her hair again. "Still feels like a beehive."

"Trust me, Mama. It's very becoming."

"Do you have some rouge?" she asked, turning her cheeks into round balls. "Just a little, Sha. Don't make me look like a foolish flapper."

You don't look like a foolish flapper, I thought. But you were foolish for not making Papa understand. Why must you make things so difficult? Why must you behave like a prisoner in this house? I walked away, thinking that if I'd stayed in the bedroom with her one more minute, I would have poked her hard myself.

ADELAIDE AND Arthur were at the front entrance of the hotel when we arrived. My sister looked uncomfortable in her shapeless maternity dress. Her pregnancy had turned her into a large pumpkin. She waddled over to us and took Mama's hand, but Papa gently shoved her away, locked my mother's arm into his, and strolled off with her. He weaved through the crowds, Mama's arm still in his, then sat her down and held her hand. She smiled like a queen, nodding politely as he introduced her to everyone who came by. It was magical. The hands that had scooped pennies from Hannah's ears long ago had worked their miracle once again in my mother's palm. I didn't know if she was truly happy, but she was putting on a pretty good show.

I searched for gawking strangers, but no one seemed to notice Mama. The room was filled with people signing in deaf. Whoops, groans, and moans permeated the air—the sorts of sounds Adelaide and I were used to. Our husbands, however, were astounded at the noise level.

"Who said deaf people were quiet?" Arthur laughed. He walked to the far side of the room at my sister's urging, so she could prove a point.

"Honey," she said, her voice only slightly elevated, "Can you hear me?"

"Yes, it's amazing," his voice came back. "There must be five hundred people in the room, but I can hear you!"

Then we lost sight of him as he struggled back through a crowd of flying fingers and clumps of threes and fours whose hands were shielded from prying eyes. It was hard for deaf people to talk privately.

"Some good looking girls here," he remarked, sitting down next to Adelaide.

"Don't get any fancy ideas about running off with a deaf girl," she warned.

He looked surprised at the thought, even uncomfortable. "Can't hang a man for looking."

Someone else's spoken words filtered over the deaf sounds. It was coming from the bar about fifty feet away. One of the bartenders cupped his chin in his hands, surveying the scene. "Never been in a room with a bunch of deaf and dummies before."

"They sure look like normal people," his partner said.

"Yeah, except when you jab one. They sound like animals." He dropped his hands to the counter and laughed. It was a moment of discomfort for us. Old feelings of being stared at and mocked when they thought we couldn't hear them. Adelaide gave a long sigh and stroked her stomach. Al and Arthur looked at each other with loathing in their eyes.

"It's the kind of thing we're used to," Adelaide said. "Don't let it get to you."

"I detest it," said Arthur. He pulled Al out of the chair, and they walked to the bar.

"Don't make a scene," I muttered to myself. "Please don't make a scene."

We sat frozen, waiting for the roof to fall in, but Arthur calmly sat on a stool. Al did the same, locking his legs around the base. Arthur turned to Al and fingerspelled. My sister started to giggle. He was so bad with his fingerspelling that Al almost laughed, too, but he sobered his face and spelled back. The bartenders leaned against the cash register, hands folded across their chests. Amusement filled their faces.

"What are they trying to do?" Adelaide whispered. "They're so clumsy. I can't imagine why they're even trying to sign."

"They're setting a trap."

"You mean like we did when we were kids?"

"Yeah. Watch for the fireworks. I hope you don't go into a fit of laughter so you start labor right here."

"I promise I won't," she said, clutching her stomach.

Arthur turned to the bartender and ordered, "Three Black Russians, please."

"Yes, sir," the bartender gulped. "Coming right up."

He poured the drinks, hands shaking with embarrassment, and put them on the counter. Al took two, Arthur one. Al leaned over and poked the fat one, whose cheeks were beet red, and said something to him. Please, no fighting, I prayed. Just tell him off and come back.

"I'm proud of you," I said as Al offered me the drink.

"I sure told him off, didn't I?"

"I'm proud of you for not putting your fist in his face."

I glanced at Papa, whose back was to us so I couldn't make out what he was saying. He was intent in conversation with Little Joe and Sarah, but he still held tight to Mama's arm.

A parade of smartly dressed men and women sauntered past us. They smiled, waved, and went off to their own chairs to watch the parade. I couldn't see another blind person. No one walked with a cane or held on to someone's arm. If they hadn't waved their fingers, they would have appeared like any other ordinary group: no wheelchairs, no missing limbs. Normal-looking people. I'd read somewhere that the deaf were called the Silent Minority. What did they call Mama, I wondered? Were she and Helen Keller the only deaf and blind people in the world? Hardly, I thought. But then where were they? Hiding in their homes?

And then I saw what Mama had feared. A woman I'd never met before was talking about Mama. Hands up, fingers out, not caring to keep her words secret. She stared at my mother's back and let her fingers fly to the blonde sitting next to her. "I'd kill myself if I were blind," she fingerspelled. "I'd swallow some pills and let my husband go free."

The blonde moved her eyes up and down my mother's dress and spelled, "It's too bad about Ruth. She was a nice lady. I feel funny talking to her. I don't think she understands everything I say."

"He should have kept her home."

Adelaide sobbed, and her belly heaved up and down. I grabbed her hand. "Stop it. Just stay calm. They're stupid bitches. Forget about it."

"Did you see what she said? Mama *was* a nice lady. What is she now? Dead? What if Papa saw them?"

"He didn't see them, but if he did, he'd have smashed their heads against the bartenders."

Adelaide dried her eyes with her handkerchief. "I only wish he had!"

"You don't mean that! You're just excited now. Your hormones are all fired up."

"I do! I hate this. I hate what's happened to us."

Everyone in this room had gone mad, I decided. Hearing people mocking the deaf, the deaf deriding the blind. All of them puffed up with their own sense of wholeness. Even my sister, who suffered most from intolerance, who had cringed at the sound of "Shtimmers" as a child, had muttered indecencies at the fat bartender. A fat slob, she had called him. And I had called the arrogant women bitches, feeling superior because I had ears. Stupid deaf people. That's all they were.

The orchestra started to play, and people moved onto the floor, keeping time by the drums. It was so loud the chandeliers shook and the walls trembled. Arthur winced at the thunderous beat. He put his hands to his ears, then put them back in his lap again, and smiled. "Come on," he said, taking my sister's hand. He guided her pregnant body into a slow jitterbug. Papa guided my mother onto the floor and did a couple of fancy movements, but my mother's balance left her, and he caught her tight and almost carried her in their dance. One step, two step, then a tight swing with his powerful arms into a whirl. Her dark glasses reflected the chandelier's lights. Her feet moved above the floor. Her blue dress swung in graceful swirls. People watched.

The lights dimmed off and on in a signal, and everyone rushed to their seats. Not wanting Mama to feel left out, I hurried Al toward seats next to them. As soon as the magician entered center stage and bowed deeply, Papa began a running commentary in her hands. "First, he took the rope, Ruthie, then he cut it right in the middle. Then it came out in one piece."

"Oh," Mama said. "That's wonderful. I remember that trick."

"The cage was empty, but all of a sudden, the bird appeared. A dove, Ruthie, a big white one."

"Oh, that's a good trick. How do you think he did that, Joe?"

Memories of skinned knees and broken dolls and my father's hand on mine, telling me not to feel bad, flooded my brain. I remembered why I loved him so much. The lights went on full force, and everyone prepared to leave. Papa wanted to stay a bit longer. There were still more friends to see. We walked over to the bar where Little Joe, Sarah, and Rosie were lined up. The bartenders respectfully filled their glasses, wondering, I supposed, who spoke and who didn't. Mama said some things to Rosie. Sarah made a fuss over Mama's dress.

Papa found one more friend from New York. Barney Foster, I think his name was, someone who saw Papa fight back in the old days, Papa said. He spelled it so quickly I couldn't make it out, but I shook Mr. Foster's hand like a dutiful daughter. Papa spelled the name to Adelaide and Mama, and then he turned to the man and said, "Yes, she's blind, but I take care of her."

As we were ready to leave, my mother's cheeks still pink from excitement, a group of young men in their twenties formed a tight wedge. Brash, brazen in their good looks, they walked in unison and stopped in front of Papa. "You're Dummy Jordan, aren't you?" one of them signed.

"Yes," Papa signed back, looking twenty years younger.

"You see, I told you," one of them spelled. They melted in awe. They shuffled their feet and made shy, reverent talk. Mama put her hands out, and I told her what was being said.

"Still a bum," she laughed. "When will people stop remembering?" But there was no animosity in her voice, just a sweet look on her face. We walked across Sheridan Road to the steak house and ordered supper. It seemed reasonable that the waiter would know my father. He was a few years younger, I supposed, but the same vintage Puddie's card-playing look about him. The waiter socked Papa hard on the back and turned to us. "I knew your father back in the old days. What a guy he was!"

Translation was unnecessary. My father accepted his admiration as he had done with other strangers: a sock on the back, a bear hug, a tip of the hat, and smiling eyes. Papa shook the waiter's hand and imperiously pointed to a steak on the menu. So this was the way it was, I thought. Papa, with his fedora and velvet-lapeled suit and a stogie in his mouth, sitting in speakeasies with Mama, dressed in shimmering silk and feathers in her hair, smoothing her good hand over her fancy beaded bag and smiling at him.

My sister raised her ginger ale in a toast. "Good show, Papa."

"Yes, it was a good show," he answered, clinking his glass against ours. He didn't get her meaning.

CHAPTER

22

MY FATHER had made a brave attempt to make my mother belong. I thought it had gone well, but deep inside, I suspected her loneliness, and the thought of it hung over me like a black cloud. I began to wonder how she perceived things—little things like the latest styles in clothes, the shape and design of new cars, changes in street corners, a new deli, or the disappearance of a gas station. Little things I didn't bother to tell her about (did Papa? I wondered). There were only her memories of how we all looked. As the years passed, the changes would be so dramatic that, if her sight returned, she'd be shocked. And if her ears came back (that same old dream), how would singing sound to her? Or my voice? Depressed, I blundered through the following weeks, thinking I should have stuck by her side, demanding that Papa leave her alone. I wanted to wrap her in my cocoon of safety, protected from unseen changes. I would keep her with me.

Mama didn't appear to be upset, but she had developed a new habit, patting the air as if telling herself it was okay to think whatever she was thinking. Internal thoughts like Papa's, only she didn't spell to herself, she patted the air. Then one week, months after the affair, it all came out, an avalanche of emotions. We were sitting at the kitchen table finishing the last of our coffee. Andy was asleep, and the air outside was blustery cold. There was nothing for us to do but fiddle with our danish and make small talk about tomorrow's menu. Aunt Selma and Aunt Marian were expected for lunch.

"Tuna salad is fine," she said in response to my question.

"Something warm. Piping hot," I suggested. "It's so cold outside. Soup?"

Yes, she nodded. There was a pause in the air, and she said, so matter of factly, "Who did he talk to at the dance?"

"You know. I told you."

She nodded.

"Mrs. Zimmerman is getting old, Mama. She has wrinkles in her face. You don't."

She nodded again. "He'd be better off without me."

"That's silly." I shuddered at the thought. Perhaps she did, too. A look of fear crossed her eyes as if she'd been caught in the woods, a frightened deer blinded by headlights.

"And maybe apple pie," I offered.

"Fine."

"Don't think about such things, Mama. Papa would never leave you. Why should he? You're a beautiful woman."

"Fine."

"No. Listen to me!"

"No. *You* listen to *me*. It's better that you keep out of this. I know you told Papa how I felt. Maybe I was wrong. He wanted to go. To be a sport. Maybe I was wrong. But it's not your business."

"Then don't tell me what you think. Don't talk nonsense about Papa leaving you. He'd never do it."

"Fine."

"Are we finished with this talk? With your silly talk and your gloomy mood?"

"I'm going downstairs."

"It's too cold."

"Then I'm going to the bathroom to swallow some pills. What kind of pills do we have?" she asked.

"Nothing that will kill you," I screamed. I shook her fingers until she pulled them away. She laughed as if what she had said seemed ridiculous now, and she patted the air.

192

"No, it's not enough, Mama, to pat the air. You can't talk like this and expect me to forget it."

She swept the danish into the plate with a swift movement. She took the coffee cups, put them in the sink, and walked to her room. This was just crazy talk, I figured. But I walked to the bathroom and opened the cabinet. Aspirins, cough medicine. Nothing dangerous. Or was it dangerous? I pulled them out and stored them on a shelf in my closet. I slept badly that night, thinking I should have said something to Papa or at least to Al.

EVERYTHING WAS on the table when Selma and Marian arrived. Mama waited on the sofa while Selma draped her coat over the corner chair, then took Selma by the arm as she bent over to kiss her. Marian bent over to kiss her, too, and guided her to the dining room table. We sat down to lunch. Aunt Marian made small talk. Nice pictures. Pretty drapes. I passed it on to Mama. "Baby sweet," I spelled to her and for the first time since yesterday, she offered a smile. I passed more talk to her, angry that I had to do it, irate that they still hadn't learned to sign, to spell in her hands like the rest of us. But I smiled until my cheeks were sore and my elbow stiffened from remaining in one position as I spelled. My stomach turned to knots from gulping my food while I acted as interpreter. When they were finished, the aunts patted their lips with their napkins and sat with their hands folded neatly on the table.

"Listen, Ruthie," Aunt Selma said. "Pa's in a lot of trouble."

"You mean Zadie?" I asked.

"Yes, of course. Listen, Ruthie, Marian and I are sure Pa's getting senile. Remember I wrote you that he forgets to eat and leaves the stove on at night?"

"Yes," Mama recalled. "Joe told me what was in the letter." She said it loudly as if the shouting would make them understand better.

Aunt Selma continued, "Well, he left the house last week and couldn't find his way back. Mrs. Killansky saw him three miles from the house. He was dirty and his pants were. . . ." She stopped to sniffle, and Aunt Marian took over.

"Thank God for Mrs. Killansky. If she hadn't found him, I don't know what would have happened."

"Someone has to stay with him," my mother spoke.

I continued to spell Marian's words into Mama's hand. "But who can stay with him? We still have our children at home. Nettie lives too far away."

My mother cut off her fingers from me. "Are you saying he has to go into a home?"

"What did she say?" Aunt Selma asked.

Surprised that she couldn't make out my mother's words, I began to speak.

"No, it's all right. I'll tell Selma," Marian said. "I understand her words. Ruthie asked if he has to go into a nursing home."

"What else can we do?" Selma sobbed.

"I see," Mama said. "If that's the way it has to be, I have no objection."

Empty dishes and apple pie crumbs. Remnants of a family gone. It was not the family I remembered. After they left, I poked Mama hard on the shoulder. "How could you let them put Zadie in a home? I would never do that to you. Never!"

"Maybe someday you will."

"Never, never," I protested.

THE LETTERS had come regularly. I saw the return addresses, thought nothing of it, and had passed them on to her so Papa could read them. She had never mentioned the contents to me. No one had discussed by telephone Zadie's state of senility. I wondered why nobody had thought to tell *me*. I was a grown-up now, but, I thought, I was still a child in their eyes. Someone who couldn't be trusted with grown-up problems.

Well, let them have their secret world. But at least I would never ship my mother off to a nursing home.

IN THE following months, Mama became fervently interested in Zadie's welfare. She stopped patting the air. I saw her once make the motion for "crazy" as if she was explaining Zadie's dilemma to herself. I knew that she hadn't meant crazy. I figured there was no true sign for senility. It was her shortcut way of saying that Zadie had lost touch with reality.

In the summer, when Zadie had been settled into the home, Mama requested a visit. I called the home to arrange it, and the following Sunday we all headed for Elgin. The ride was long, over bumpy country roads. There was nothing but open space and the smell of corn ready to be harvested. We closed the windows to keep out the dust and sweated on the mohair seats, saying nothing, keeping our fingers to ourselves. Mama made comments as we rode, expecting no answers: "The corn is ready for picking," she sniffed. And then she sniffed the dust as it seeped through the floorboards. She was marking the territory, imagining the terrain through her sharpened sense of smell. I promised myself that I would tell her about everything she couldn't see as soon we got there.

An imposing three-story brick building came into view. I told Mama. A snaking driveway brought us to the front gate. "Big lobby," I told Mama. "Lovely chairs. Green. Sit down."

Presently, an orderly brought Zadie to the main lobby. He was dressed in his three-piece suit as if he were on his way to shul, walking the old neighborhood streets again. I told Mama.

"Too hot," she said. "Tell the people here he shouldn't be wearing all those clothes."

"I'll tell them."

His eyes were glazed with confusion. He stared at Mama but didn't recognize her.

"Are you Ruthie?" he asked. "Is Ruthie all right?" he asked me in that singsong Yiddish way he had. I didn't tell Mama. "Yes, Zadie," I answered. "This is Ruthie and Ruthie is fine. And I'm Charlotte. You remember, Zadie. And this is Joe, and here's my husband, Al."

"This is a terrible place. You see," he pointed, "there are bars on the windows."

There were no bars on the windows. There were only pale gray curtains and white shades that hung halfway down.

"They won't let me leave," he cried. "They make me eat pork."

I didn't tell Mama. "Zadie, they would never do that!"

He stared at me without recognition now. I put Mama's hands on him. She made soothing noises and said, "Don't worry," but I don't think he understood her. Papa patted her hand reassuringly, and Mama repeated her demands. "Tell them he's dressed too warm for this weather."

"I will," Papa assured her. "You're right. It's too hot. But he looks good, Ruthie."

VISITING THE home was not enough for her. Unsure of his well-being and not trusting our words, she decided that visits in our home would jog his memory. Her arms around him and the smell of home-cooked food would make him feel better. I arranged for a Sunday pass. Al drove alone to pick him up. Mama cooked dinner, rejecting my offer of help. She cut the chicken herself and put it in the oven. "Turn it to 350," she ordered. I told her when the hour was up. She took the chicken out and laid it on a fancy platter. Then she cut the potatoes and put them in boiling water. I stayed close by, worried she might spill something hot on herself. All the while she talked to herself, remembering what he liked for dessert and how he liked his coffee—black with two cubes of sugar. No, maybe tea, she vacillated. She felt the air outside the window and decided it was still too warm for soup, so she covered the pot and asked me to remove it from the stove.

ZADIE WORE the same three-piece suit. His cheeks looked dangerously red. I helped him off with his jacket, sat him at the table, and looked at Al.

"Out of it," he motioned, his thumbs down. "Completely gone."

Mama stroked his arm while I served dinner. "How are you?" she asked.

But he was too distracted by the strange surroundings even to know us. He spotted Andy and put him on his lap, smiled and said something in Yiddish, as if he had turned the clock back to his own fatherhood. He bounced Andy up and down, then let him slide down to the floor but caught him in a scissor-like vise between his legs. It was the same old trick he had used on me when I was a child. I would scream, "Let me go," and, when he did, I begged for more. It seemed like only yesterday. How was it, then, that he had turned old almost overnight?

The afternoon was a failure of communication. Zadie was uncomfortable, smiling frantically, but wanting, I believe, to be someplace else. If Mama understood it, she didn't say. She went back to her internal thoughts, patting the air while she sat next to him, close enough so their heads touched, and smiled. As Al helped him into the car, Mama stood at the window with me, waiting for me to turn away so she could ask, "How does he look? Is his mind all gone? What did he say?"

Some things I told her. Some I didn't.

"You know," she said, walking back to the sofa, "if I wasn't blind, I could help him, but I'm useless, aren't I? I can't even help my own father. I can't even be a good daughter to him."

It was the first time I heard her refer to herself as blind.

"You made a wonderful dinner," I reminded her.

"But he didn't eat it, did he?"

"He doesn't have much appetite. But he tasted everything."

"And I can't even be a good wife."

"That's not true. You're not useless. Don't talk like that. If you want to cook dinner from now on, I'll agree. I'm a lousy cook, anyway."

"You don't understand. I live in a house that isn't mine. I don't know where to walk, where to sit. I hurt. I hurt all the time."

I began to cry. Tears I hadn't shed in years spilled down, and I shook so hard that Mama felt it. She said quietly, with her hand on mine, "It's not your fault. I'm sorry. I should keep my words to myself." She got up and put her hands into her apron pockets. "Well, I still have my mind, don't I? Maybe it's better if we don't bring your grandfather here again. We'll visit him in the home."

I got up and poked her on the shoulder. "I thought you didn't like it there."

"It doesn't matter anymore."

WE MADE the trip every month, bouncing up and down the roads through the summer's heat, then the fall when the leaves began to turn gold and red. The only one who enjoyed our visits was Andy, who climbed the trees and rolled in the beautifully manicured lawn. Zadie died two winters later as he sat in the chapel with his prayer shawl wrapped around his shoulders and his prayer book in his hand. He was eighty-three.

Mama, Selma, Marian, Nettie, Morrie, Adelaide, and I rode in the funeral limousine together. Adelaide and I were given this special privilege not because we were special but because we were Mama's eyes and ears. With Ruthie, you got three: Ruthie, Adelaide, and Charlotte. Sometimes only Adelaide. Sometimes only Charlotte. And in a pinch, Joe, but he required a note. With us, it was easier. It was "tell her this. . . ."

"It's an honor to the family that he died praying," Marian remarked as the limousine pulled away from the cemetery.

"A real honor," Nettie commented.

I spelled the words into Mama's hands. She shook her head with a solemn nod, "yes."

CHAPTER

23

A SMALL window to our worlds had opened since Zadie's death. Mama seemed more willing to talk of Papa's moods, and I, in turn, told her of my petty annoyances with Al. When Adelaide sat in our kitchen, our two boys off in Andy's room, playing with their trucks, we gossiped. We talked women talk.

Rosie had died of cancer the year before, freeing her mother of worries over Rosie's future. Sarah's appearances had dwindled to a few surprise visits. Mama's only true friends were her daughters. Everyone else, it seemed, was more interested in talking to Mama only when Papa was around. I suppose they felt that, if Mama didn't get their attempts at talking in her hand, they could turn to Papa and say, "tell her that. . . ."

It was tedious, bone aching to keep one's fingers going in that small palm. It could also be frustrating when Mama's eyes indicated that she didn't understand. What was needed was more precise, careful fingerspelling. Her friends sometimes didn't have the patience.

One night in our fourth year together, my father came home and stashed his lunch box and bowling ball in the hall closet, slamming the door as if he'd never use them again. I poked Mama in the ribs, my secret way of telling her he was upset. She nodded carefully in my direction to let me know she understood. We had talked about it just the previous afternoon. It made no sense to me that the Teamster's union was about to strike. Papa was doing better financially than he ever had, not counting his boxing and bootlegging days. Every week, he rolled out his wad of bills and peeled off his share of the expenses with a flourish. It was an expression of confidence and good times, something I'd never seen as a child.

"Why would he vote to strike?" I had asked my mother.

"Loyalty to the union," Mama had commented. "Your father is very loyal to those who take care of him. You know that. And it was his brother that got him the job. So if your uncle says Papa should vote for a strike, then Papa will do it."

I didn't expect it to happen so soon, and neither did Papa by the looks of him. He sank into the kitchen chair and drummed his fingers on the table.

"Strike?" I signed, as we sat down to dinner.

"Yes, well, that's the way it's supposed to be," he answered.

"It's what you wanted, Papa."

"True," he said making the sign. "But I won't be able to pay you my rent until it's over. I'll get strike pay, but it won't be much."

"It's not a problem, Papa."

"Pretty soon you'll have the new baby. I should give you more, not less."

"I'm not worried. I'm sure the strike will be over soon."

Papa spelled the news in Mama's hands. She patted him on the shoulder to reassure him and helped me serve dinner. Al reached for the A-1 sauce. "Union striking?" he asked, noticing my father's mood.

"Yes. Papa's worried about paying the rent. I told him it's not a problem."

"It isn't, but it bothers me that he has to go on strike for the Teamsters. They're a bunch of crooks, that's what they are. In the end, he'll get a pension that won't pay for a loaf of bread."

He poured A-1 sauce on his steak and proceeded to eat as if his words of wisdom needed no more explanation. Fancy engineer, I thought, who couldn't fathom working on a bottling line. I had accused him of this kind of snobbery before, every time he got into a snit about the Teamsters.

"Don't start up about the union again. My father's proud to be in it. I know it sounds silly when you think of the times he broke up strikes, but he's legitimate now. Like Mama says, he's loyal." I cut up my steak and ate it, annoyed that he would bring up his dislike of the union when my father sat discouraged, his shoulders hunched over his meal. Why couldn't he see it, this bow-tied, three-piece-suited man who wore dungarees only on Saturdays, this educated man with no sense of how his own moods colored his face for Papa to see? The electrical engineer frowned. Papa, seeing it, looked worried. I smiled to reassure him. "When do you think the strike will be over, Papa?"

"Did Al ask you to question me? What else did he say?"

"No, he didn't ask. I was asking. I was just wondering."

He grunted and busied himself with his steak. I put a smile on my face and cautioned Al to be careful. "You know he reads things into the way a person looks."

"Well, you oughta tell him how I feel about the union."

"If you think it's so important, you tell him."

"You know I'm not good at signing."

"Then write it down, if you must, but I'm not going to hurt his feelings, and I hope you give this some thought. It's a decent job, the best he's ever had. And I hope you control the anger on your face. How many times must I remind you!"

"Why do you keep things from him?" he asked, putting on his own smile to fool my father. "You treat him like a baby."

"Because," I countered, "I don't share your opinion of the Teamsters. I'm not going to put doubt in his mind."

"Pass me the salt," he requested, impatient with my logic.

"Sure." I offered it to Papa first—a peace offering—but he shook his head no. I handed it to Al.

"What's the matter with it?" he asked, examining the shaker. "It's got brown stuff in it."

I dabbed a bit on my finger and tasted it. "My God, it's got pepper in it."

"Well, forget it then. Can I have my coffee?"

"Sure." I poured his coffee. Papa seemed relaxed now, but distant. He kept his eyes on his plate as he ate. I poured his coffee, too. He preferred his black and strong, like mud sometimes. He liked me to heat it over and over again.

Al, detesting the taste of mud, took two teaspoons of sugar and stirred it in his cup. He took a swallow and spit it out. My father chuckled. I could imagine his thoughts. "Too strong for you, huh, engineer?"

"There's salt in this sugar!" Al fumed.

"That's ridiculous," I said.

"Then you taste it," he said, offering me a teaspoon.

It was bitter. Salt bitter. I turned to Andy and asked, "Did you . . . ?"

"Not me," he said, banging his toy against the side of his chair.

"Mama," I poked. "Did you fill the salt shaker and the sugar bowl?"

"No. Why?"

"Here, taste." I put the sugar in front of her.

She tasted it and *hmned* her laugh, her fingers discreetly covering her mouth.

"What's so funny?"

"Wait. I'll show you," she *hmned*, walking over to the refrigerator. She opened the door and pulled out my crystal cigarette lighter. "I felt it in here this morning, but I thought you put it in here for some reason."

"Andy!"

"Not me. Not me."

"He did it, Mama. I can tell by his lying face."

"He's a little devil, that's what he is," she laughed.

"It's not funny," Papa stormed. "You thought *she* did it!"

203

"What's the difference, Papa? So what if I thought she did? It would be an honest mistake. Sometimes she can't. . . ."

My timing was bad. There was tension in his face. The same old lines of vulnerability when he didn't have a job, the same old sense of paranoia when he felt stripped of his worth. "Oh, Papa, it's a funny joke. Forget it!"

But it was too late. He grabbed their coats from the hook on the kitchen door and handed Mama hers. Mama, not seeing or hearing what had happened, threw her hands up in the air, but something about the way she looked told me she understood. So what else was new? Hadn't he stormed away, angry before? She slipped her arms into her coat. Papa's last words before he slammed the front door were "I told you I'd make up the rent when I can!"

Al looked at Andy and frowned. "Not funny, Andy. Not funny at all. But I don't think it was so bad that Grandpa had to leave in a huff. It can't be Andy's antics that forced him out of here, is it?" he asked me. "What did you say to make him so angry?"

"It's not what I said! It's the look on your face. He thinks you asked me about the rent!"

"I never said a word."

"No, you looked it!"

"What do you want me to do? Freeze my face into a zombie's every time I have something to say? Why didn't you tell him it was the Teamsters I was upset about?"

"Who had the time? You can see he's not here anymore. Besides, I wouldn't tell him and when . . . *if* he comes back, I won't tell him!"

"Well, I tell it like it is. You cloud everything to make it fit your father's needs. You're wrong, you know."

"How can I change a whole lifetime of hurt? Of being left out of things? Why must you be so critical and show your displeasure? You think it's been easy for him?"

204

"I'm tired of being the heavy in this. Everything that happens here, he thinks is my fault."

"That's not true!"

"Yes, it's true! I see the way you spell your words, the way you both look at me when you do your signing. God knows what it is you say to each other." He picked up his coffee and left the room. I stared at the three empty chairs. Oh hell, not again. Not a what-did-he-say, what-did-he-mean confrontation. But there was nothing I could do about it now. They were gone, all three of them, without finishing their dessert, leaving me with dirty dishes and cups half filled with strong coffee. I picked up the salt shaker and sugar bowl, dumped them on the table, and smeared the contents through the bread crumbs.

"Mommy did it," Andy laughed.

"Oh, be quiet!" I grabbed my coat and left the house.

IT WAS freezing cold. I walked through the park along the river, shivering, looking for them. I knew they liked to walk along the river after dinner. They were as predictable in their routine as the calendar. Spring, summer, and fall, through the park, up the wide boulevard, and into the coffee shop at the corner. But the weather had turned unpredictably cold, and the winds off the lake smashed into me like a tidal wave. They would have been home—Papa, enjoying his muddy coffee, sitting in front of his TV. Where was I going to find them? How did I know they would come back this time? I thought of Al and Andy in the house, and I was torn with allegiance. How was I going to fix this?

I went into the first warm place I could find: Mr. Swenson's empty drugstore. Every sane person was home waiting for the rain, possibly the first snow of the year, to come dumping down. I sat at the counter and ordered a hot chocolate. Mr. Swenson set it in front of me and stirred in a double helping of whipping cream. "How's the expectant mother?" he smiled in greeting. "You should be home. It's gonna pour."

"I should be in a bar drowning my sorrows in a double vodka."

"I think you mean a double scotch."

"Is that what they call it? I've never had a scotch. I'm not a drinker. So here I am, moping over a hot chocolate."

"So pretend I'm the bartender, ready and willing to listen to your troubles."

"Just a family squabble. Happens all the time, I guess."

He shook his head, "Uh huh."

"My father's union's on strike."

"So I heard," he said, wiping the counter with a wet cloth.

"Has my father been here?"

"Yes. With your mother. He ordered his special brand of alcohol and witch hazel. Just like the old days. What a tough guy he was. Still is."

"Don't tell me you knew my father in the old days!"

"No, I didn't. But I heard plenty of stories about him. You'd be surprised how many people have heard of him."

"Yeah, everybody knows him." Except me, I thought. I don't know when to keep my mouth shut or when to smile.

"Shame about your mother," he said, leaning closer over the counter, his glasses fogging up from the steam of my chocolate. "Must be hard on your father."

If it hadn't been so cold outside, I would have bolted out the door. It was too painful hearing him talk like this, but I sat riveted to the stool. "It's hard on all of us, but I'm not complaining. I don't understand how it is to be a normal family. How do real families settle their quarrels?"

"They talk about it. They air things out. They settle it." And then he laughed as if what he said didn't make sense. "I mean they talk any way they can." He looked embarrassed, as if he had stepped into uncharted territory. "Don't worry. You're good people. It will all blow over by morning."

I left the store feeling foolish. I had poured out my troubles to a man I hardly knew. He made it so easy, like the perfect father character in a movie, wise, with his horn-rimmed glasses and gentle way of talking. Papa never sat next to me and listened to my troubles, but I'd never given him the chance. I'd never brought my troubles to this man who grunted and mangled his words with poor spelling. I suddenly felt ashamed of the memories. Al was right. I treated my father as if he didn't have the wisdom.

Hearing a rumble of thunder in the distance, I hurried home, darting my eyes up and down the street, looking for them. It was useless. For all I knew, they had rented a room in a motel. Or gone to Sarah's or Adelaide's to complain. The warmth from the hot chocolate had dissipated. I was cold again. I gave up and braced myself against the wind. I expected at least a phone call from Adelaide or Sarah's neighbor. Papa would do that to put my mind at ease.

I SHUT the front door and took off my coat. Al called from the bedroom. "They're home, so stop worrying. Come to bed."

"In a minute. I need to see if they're okay."

They were standing in the kitchen in the dark, with just the light of the hallway silhouetting their forms. I moved toward them, sliding toys with my foot to the sides of the walls, then stopped. They were talking. I was ashamed for spying but I couldn't tear my eyes away. Papa's fingers moved haltingly in deaf talk. "Maybe better we go Addle," he said, her fingers wrapped around his for his words.

"No. Silly idea. Addle have baby. Same thing. Toys everywhere. You feel better, Joe?"

"Hurt me see you black and blue all time. Should punish Andy."

"No. Not Andy fault. No worry, Joe. I strong fighter like you." She put her arms around him. He gave her a long kiss and stroked her back. I'd wondered if they were still doing that—kissing and hugging.

"Silly," she giggled, covering her mouth, "Somebody maybe see."

I wanted to turn away, embarrassed at Mama's sixth sense, but I leaned against the wall and watched the way he stroked her arm and the way she moved closer to him. Because they stood so close to each other, the talking stopped. Dreamy, quiet, where sound made no difference, and darkness was right for the moment. And then she moved a step away and put her fingers in front of her.

"Come bed," she said. "Strike over soon. You go back work. Everything all right. Tomorrow we visit Sarah. Have fun. Like vacation. Plenty time. I be with you."

I switched on the dining room light to let them know I was there. Papa turned and peered down the hall.

"Papa, I sorry. This all bad mix up. Al didn't say. Must not blame him. Baby didn't mean. . . ."

His eyes widened. It was a stupid thing to mention the baby. He would know I was spying. But he didn't let on. He put his fingers to his lips. "Shush, we forget, okay?"

"Okay."

I GOT into bed and curled myself against Al's body. "I guess I got carried away with my words. I'm sorry."

"No, no," he whispered. "I shouldn't be sticking my nose into their business. But sometimes I feel left out of this family. You move your hands around and say your words, and I wonder what it is you're talking about. Hell, it's not the signing you do with each other. It's the way you see and feel each other like you're in each other's heads. A shrink would say it's unhealthy."

"Maybe. But I don't know how to stop it. When I watch *your* family, I'm uncomfortable. You shout from the other room, and someone hears you. You stick your head in a game of cards with your father while your mother's talking from the kitchen. You're always in touch. It's different for us. It's the eyes and Papa's poke in my arm to tell me he's ready for talk. But we don't need to talk sometimes. Our eyes talk. Mama's body talks. I can tell by the way she holds her head or curls in the rocking chair how she feels. I'm not any more used to your family than you are to mine. Sometimes I can't stand the noise in your mother's house. It hurts my ears. I'm deaf, Al. Something you can never be."

We stopped talking but stayed curled up in bed. The rain came softly down, making quiet splotches on the window pane. It was smooth and gentle like the tick tock of our wind-up alarm. Al breathed in even, strong breaths. I thought he had fallen asleep, but he lifted himself up on his arm. "How about I take your dad to the ball game?"

"The season's over, silly, but it's nice of you to think of him."

"Then I'll take him for a long ride. We'll do something together."

"They have other plans. They're going to visit Sarah and Little Joe. They discussed it in the kitchen. Maybe next week, huh?"

"Okay. Next week."

I left out their talk about moving to Adelaide. I pretended it was just talk, and they would forget it in the morning.

CHAPTER

24

$\mathbf{T}$HE STRIKE lasted six weeks. During that time, Papa carried a placard when asked, leaving early in the morning without his lunch box and coming home as tired as if he'd spent a full day on the line. On his free days, they visited Sarah or went downtown. They spent time with Adelaide and came home with funny stories of her baby's antics. Mama spent hours at the kitchen table telling me how Adelaide cooked a new recipe for chicken and how she ran her household. Gossip. That was all.

Adelaide and I knew that most of the irritations Mama and Papa had with us or Al or Arthur were just musings about their errant daughters and their men. We never spoke about it to each other. If Papa discussed his latest unhappiness with Adelaide, I never knew it. After a while, when tempers had quieted, we could laugh about Andy's clever arrangement of pepper in salt and salt in sugar. Mama told Sarah, and Papa told Little Joe. My father poked Little Joe, "You know, I wouldn't be surprised if my grandson grew up to be a pharmacist. He'll mix my magic potion for me. Look how clever he was. Salt in the sugar!"

"Very clever," said Little Joe, and he shook his finger delightedly at Andy.

WINTER CAME, and they stayed home in the evenings. Andy tried to keep his trains, trucks, and his three-foot stuffed lamb where they belonged. Al kept his arched eyebrows to himself, and I smiled even harder, my cheeks in a permanent smile. But misunderstanding grew. Late nights of sitting on the sofa during the spring rains, wondering where they were. Wondering if drunken Mr. Tass, the president of the Hebrew Deaf Auxiliary, was driving them home in a storm. "Why do they let deaf people drive anyway?" I asked Papa one night. "Why not!?" he responded, angrily.

Afternoons in the backyard with Mama, who sat quietly, thinking her private thoughts when I was too tired or bored to lift my fingers in talk. Closed bedroom doors where their hands flew silently. Wondering what it was they said. Talking to Al in the kitchen while Papa ate his dinner, saying something to my father so he wouldn't read meanings into our looks.

Being interrupted with "What did you say to Al? What did Al say to you?" and my exasperation with having to retell the words. But I smiled and did it. And Papa smiled on his good days. On bad days, he was distant, our imagined talk festering in him. He had even kept his pant-leg spelling to a minimum for fear I'd see it. He raked the leaves in the early autumn, his cigar in the corner of his mouth, while Andy made neat piles behind him. He took Andy's hand afterward, and they walked to the store to buy candy corn and little pumpkins on which Papa carved faces that looked curiously like Indian heads.

The second baby came, sick with colic, crying all day and night. Mama walked her through the house, crooning her sounds to Ellen, patting her to comfort her, feeling useful for a change. Then the colic ended and Ellen turned into a happy, smiling infant. One day, when both the children were sound asleep and Al was out of town, Mama, her words carefully enunciated so there would be no misunderstanding, announced that they wanted to move.

"IT'S PAPA who wants it, isn't it?" I demanded.

"No," she said emphatically. "I want it. I want to cook for

Papa, have my own place to clean, to be with my friends in the old neighborhood."

"Is that true, Papa?"

He gulped the last of his muddy coffee and put his hands up in the air, palms up, and shrugged. I didn't know what that meant. I put my hands up in the air the same way and shrugged. If he'd asked me what I meant, I could not have told him. His hands went back in the pockets of his bathrobe. The talking was done. Panic rushed over me. I left them in the kitchen and called Adelaide. "What are we going to do?"

"We'll do nothing," she said. "We'll let them go. We do too much for them now. We never let them breathe."

"But she can't be alone. Papa will go crazy again. And what about me? I can't be in my safe house wondering if she turned on the stove and burned herself."

"I'm calling Social Services for the Blind. She'll have to learn to live like a blind person. She's got the guts to do it, Char. I know it."

She sounded hopeful. I wanted to believe her because I was too emotionally exhausted to care anymore. I hung up and lay in my bed, trying to imagine Mama alone in unfamiliar surroundings. I got up and walked into the kitchen to look for them. I wanted to talk some more, but they'd gone to their room and closed the door. The light under their doorway was out.

I went to the bathroom, pulled a wad of cotton out of the medicine cabinet, and stuck it in my ears. I walked back to my bedroom, pulled a black scarf out of the top drawer, and wrapped it around my eyes. I turned the lights off. Red images danced before me. I pulled the scarf tighter until the back of my head hurt. Deep, dark black surrounded me like some horrible Halloween witch. I walked through the house, tripped over a toy, guided my hands along the walls, trying to remember how far it was to the front door. I panicked when there was no more wall to touch and fell to the floor for safety, groping for the edge of the rug to mark my place. I slapped my hand hard on the floor and heard nothing. Not even the sound of my own crying.

A WEEK went by with no more talk from Mama. Sensing my pain, she kept her plans to herself. It was only through Adelaide that I knew where they'd gone to search for an apartment and what they said to her about their reasons for leaving. The answer was the same: Mama wanted to try living alone. Papa put his hands, palms up, to Adelaide. The meaning in his hands were not any clearer to her. The day finally came when Adelaide called to say they'd found a satisfactory place. Mama and Papa had shown it to Adelaide, and Adelaide had approved.

"It's not far from either of us," she assured me, "almost smack in the middle. We'll take turns checking in on her. I didn't tell Mama, but I called the Social Service people. Everything's on target. How are you feeling?"

"Better," I told her. "I've done something I've never done before," I hesitated.

"What?"

"Did you ever put a scarf around your eyes and pretend?"

"Yes," she sobbed.

"And did you ever put cotton in your ears and . . . ?"

"Yes, yes. So what do you want me to say? That it's going to be easy?" she cried. "Please stop it."

"I'm sorry. I didn't meant to upset you. Should we tell Papa you called Social Services?"

"Why don't we wait until they're settled in? Papa's got enough on his mind now. I'll bring it up to him when the time is right. But it doesn't matter what he says. We have to do this."

"We're mixing in again."

"This time we're right."

CHAPTER

25

S ETTLED IN the new place, Mama ran her hands over her new furniture again and again to familiarize herself with its fabric. She smoothed her hands over the new refrigerator and felt the knobs on her stove. Throughout the rooms she marked her way with the measurement of her feet and began to call this place home. Whatever she did in her house alone, she did it without harming herself, she assured me. But I was filled with doubt. I looked for telltale bruises on her body or panic in her eyes when I came to visit. But there was nothing of the sort.

She was cheerful, neatly dressed with a smear of company lipstick on her mouth, her hair pulled back and pinned in a simple hairdo, her hand ready for conversation. But her words were empty.

"Yes, Sarah came to visit," she said, gathering the crumbs from her half-eaten coffee cake into the palm of her hand. "Yes, I'm feeling fine," she said, as she dumped them into the trash can. "Yes, the stove works well," she said, sitting back in her dining chair. "And how are you, Sha?"

I was pleased to hear that Sarah had come. I had misjudged her and wondered if her renewed support came about because she could talk freely with Mama, away from my prying eyes. The kind of talk that I had with Shirley and Hannah, talk that only close friends would have.

"I'm fine, Mama. And what about Aunt Marian and Aunt Selma?"

"They came, too. When Papa was home." It had to be that way. What else could Marian and Selma have done alone with her except to drink tea and pat her on the hand?

The apartment was clean and orderly. Adelaide and Papa had picked the furniture, visiting one store after the other. Papa wanted a sofa, chairs, and tables that were reasonably priced. "After all," Papa told her, "how much longer are we going to live? Whatever we buy today will outlast us, I'm sure. Do you want a pattern, Ruthie?"

"I'd like burgundy, maybe like the flowered burgundy we had in the old house. Do they still have it, Joe?"

They searched the store. Adelaide finally convinced her that her preference was old-fashioned; nothing came close to her wishes. Mama acquiesced, and their choice was a modern beige affair with no arms to it. "We sat up and down like jack-in-the-boxes," Adelaide told me, "until we found a sofa and chair that fit Mama's body." For in the end, it was comfort Mama wanted, something that felt soft to her skin.

Behind her back, with Papa's approval, Adelaide and I held conferences with the bureaucrats at Social Services. Someone had to be found who could communicate with Mama through her hands, someone who knew sign language. I'd grown tired of the search, discouraged and untrusting of their promises, but Adelaide hung on, unwilling to give up. I left it to her.

One day, Adelaide called to say they had found the right person. Thrilled that her months of detective work had turned up something promising, her voice bubbled over with excitement. "Meet me at the front door of their apartment building, but don't go into the house," she cautioned.

"Why?" I asked, thinking this was a peculiar request.

"She wants to meet you, talk to you before she meets Mama."

"She could have called me."

"Don't get smart."

"All right. I'll be there."

I arranged for a babysitter and caught the ten o'clock bus. What was there to talk about? Hadn't Adelaide told her everything? I was beginning to feel this whole thing was a mistake. Mama already had enough to adjust to. Just getting her to accept her neighbor's offer to call me if necessary met with obstinacy. But I insisted, and the neighbor tacked my phone number on her wall. She knew that if Mama knocked on the door and waved a *C* against her cheek or said "Sha," she was to phone me. Adelaide, too. We'd found another Mrs. Goldberg, who listened for every bump coming from my parents' house. She assured all of us that she was watching over Mama, and I breathed easier.

It had been six months since they moved in. Now we were going to shove a new life in her face, and I wasn't sure how she would react. By the time I got off the bus on Division Street, I was convinced we'd been stupid to think Mama would even talk to this stranger.

Adelaide was standing inside the front door of the apartment building. Since I'd never spent more than a minute walking through the vestibule and up the stairs to Mama's apartment, I hadn't noticed how eerily reminiscent it was of our old place on Washtenaw Avenue. The front door had an oval of glass neatly spaced in its dark frame; the steps were the same shiny white marble. A bank of mailboxes took up the right wall, and a sliver of paper stuck in the second box had Papa's distinctive left-handed writing on it: Mr. and Mrs. Jos. Herzberg. Papa liked to abbreviate his name for the public. It was never "Joe," always "Jos."

Adelaide and I sat on the steps with our dresses neatly wrapped around our knees, too grown-up to splay our legs immodestly across the cool marble. We were waiting for a woman named Eleanor.

"This is what they sent me," Adelaide said. "Look it over."

She handed me a sheet of bond covered with raised dots. I rubbed my hands over it. "There are twenty-six sets of dots," I said. "Exactly the number of letters in the alphabet!"

"Now try rubbing your fingers over it with your eyes closed."

"No."

"Come on, Char. Do it."

"Shouldn't we be in the house? Shouldn't Mama know we're here?"

"Eleanor said to wait outside until she comes."

"Who is this Eleanor anyway? What do we know about her? I don't like the idea of a perfect stranger dealing with Mama."

"Social Services says she's an expert at teaching deaf-blind people. She's blind herself, you know."

"You never told me! That's amazing. How could she possibly hold down a job?"

"Sometimes, Char, I have trouble believing you. You're beginning to sound like those strangers who were always asking us if Mama and Papa could read and write or if Papa could hold down a job. Your prejudices are showing!"

"I didn't mean it that way."

"Well, then, your ignorance is showing."

"Okay, you're right. Mama's the only blind person I know. And I know she can't walk outside alone. So how does this Eleanor get around?"

"See for yourself," she said, staring through the doorway.

A splash of brightness bounced through the glass door and ricocheted off the metal mailboxes. A car, its metal hood ornament sparkling in the sunshine, parked in front of the building. A woman with dark glasses, smartly dressed in a checkered suit, got out of the back seat, moving her cane in front of her. I guessed her age to be about thirty-five. She bent over to say something to the driver, who started the engine and drove off. I moved quickly to the door to help her in, but Adelaide pulled the back of my dress. "Leave her alone."

Eleanor guided her cane right and left, scanning for obstacles. When the cane touched the door, she felt for the handle and let herself in. "Adelaide?"

"Hello, Eleanor. I'd like you to meet my sister, Charlotte."

"How do you do?" she offered her hand. "I'm sorry we have to meet like this. It would have been better, I suppose, to meet in a coffee shop where we could discuss things more comfortably, but Jim, that's my driver, hates coffee shops. Besides, it's one more place where I have to find my way. Truth is, I hate coffee shops, too. Too many waitresses at the end of my cane," she laughed. "Is there a place to sit?"

"On the steps," my sister offered. "Have a seat."

She sat between us, wrapping her skirt around her knees. I wondered if she, too, had sprawled across some marble steps as a child and how she came to be so perfect now, so immaculately clothed and made up. Adelaide was right. I was ignorant. So ignorant that I couldn't believe Eleanor would be so normal looking. My eyes took in her dress, her perfect white teeth, her stylishly manicured nails, and I wondered how many others besides her driver made her life seemingly perfect and without the stresses my mother endured. *My mother's* nails were not perfectly manicured. She filed them down to nothing and applied no nail polish; she swept her graying hair back behind her ears after washing it in the kitchen sink. Eleanor's perfection filled me with envy.

"Now tell me about your mother," she asked me. "Some things Adelaide has already told me, but I want to hear it from you. Do you remember how long she's been blind? And since she's lived these past few years with you, perhaps you can tell me how much she sees."

"I can only guess. Sometimes I think she didn't tell me the truth. You know, saying she could see a tree against the sun, maybe to make me feel better."

"I understand. Do you have a doctor's report?"

"She hasn't seen a doctor in years. What's the use? They all say the same thing. She can't be helped."

"I'll need a doctor's report."

218

"All right," Adelaide sighed. "I suppose we can get that for you."

Eleanor must have had a tape recorder hidden in her purse. She took no notes—she just stared at the front door. "Tell me about her first handicap."

"You mean her deafness? Well, she had typhoid fever in Russia."

Eleanor smiled. "Perhaps, but unlikely. Adelaide mentioned that her right hand is deformed."

"You didn't say 'deformed,' did you?" I signed to Adelaide over Eleanor's head.

"No, no, Eleanor, it's not deformed," Adelaide said. "It looks perfectly normal, but it's lifeless to the touch."

"Sorry, improper use of words." She smoothed her dress with her perfectly normal hands. "So she has no feeling."

"None."

"Well, that's not a problem. We only need one hand to read braille."

"What do you mean 'unlikely'?" I asked, changing the subject. "Are you saying my mother lied about having typhoid fever?"

Adelaide put her fingers to her mouth. "No," I mouthed. "I won't shut up. Just what is it you're saying, Eleanor?"

"I'm not saying your mother lied. If that's what her mother told her, that's what she believed. Sometimes what children hear from their parents isn't always the truth. It's easier to explain things to a child in simple ways. Pick a disease. What difference did it really make to them? And the hand. What did she tell you about the hand?"

"A horse ran over it. I think that's what she said. She hadn't seen or heard the horse and was lucky she didn't get killed! I remember that now! I must have been four. How old were you, Ad?"

"I really don't remember. Maybe it was you who told me the story. I can't say for sure."

"And your mother obliged *you* with a story," Eleanor smiled, "just as *her* mother did. What do you think, Charlotte?"

"I don't know what to think." But, deep in my heart, I wondered if the story were true. I remembered how Mama had smiled and darted her eyes around when telling it to me, as if it had been a fairy tale or a dream, as if she hadn't remembered it herself. "Maybe the story isn't true, Eleanor. I can't be sure."

"It's more likely that she was born with it. So much for family lore. I've been going over my conversations with Adelaide." As if anticipating my question, she said, "I tape-record everything. The symptoms of deafness and blindness fit a disease called Usher's Syndrome, which, I suspect, nobody understood in those early years. Your family probably never heard of it. Even the doctor who gave her the diagnosis of retinitis pigmentosa."

Stunned by her revelations, I got up and paced the vestibule. Impatient, I signed over Eleanor's head, "Did she tell you this before? Why didn't you tell me?"

Adelaide signed back to me. "I'm hearing this for the first time. I can't believe it." Putting her hands back in her lap, she asked Eleanor, "If that's the case, why didn't it happen all at once?"

"Deafness comes first, at birth or soon after," she said matter-of-factly, "then blindness, usually starting in the teen years. Your mother was lucky, I'd say. She married, had her family, and has you two to help her. Yes, I'd say she was very fortunate."

"But you can't be positive that it's Usher's Syndrome, can you?"

"No, I can't. And it's not something I think we should pursue today. Maybe in my office another day or perhaps during a visit to her doctor. It's really not my place to discuss it. I'm sorry. I suppose it was my own curiosity more than anything." She looked embarrassed for a moment and rubbed her hands against each other and stared straight ahead.

I watched my sister's eyes. They were vacant. She wouldn't

look at me. She stared out the door like Eleanor as if she, too, were blind. When she did turn to face me, her eyes were angry. I remembered I had told her the typhoid fever story.

Eleanor broke the silence. "Why don't we go in now? I'd like to meet your mother." She pulled herself up with the help of her cane, felt for the wall, and started up the steps. I got up, too, but my legs were weak. This new revelation had come as a punch in the stomach. This perfect stranger had transformed my mother in the course of five minutes. Given her a disease I'd never heard of and made me doubt my own memories. Stories at the kitchen table that didn't make sense anymore. I didn't want Mama to know. What point was there in it? I tugged at Adelaide's shoulder. I signed again, this time in quick deaf talk. "Mama doesn't need know. Keep ourselves. Maybe not true. Who she think she is? Smart Aleck, know everything person! Come here, talk like this, make worry!"

"Quiet," my sister signed. "What difference make?"

All the way up the steps, we signed and argued like children fighting over stuffed toys. "No, won't shut up."

Adelaide threw her hands in the air. "Want her leave? Want all my work down drain? Want not try?"

"Yes, want try."

"Then shut up!"

Eleanor stood at the front door, waiting for something to happen. Maybe it was the swoosh of air that wafted about her as we signed, maybe it was that sixth sense that blind people have; Mama had it. Eleanor smiled through her perfect white teeth and said, "Well, now that you've had your secret talk, shall we ring the bell?"

Blushing with embarrassment, we both reached for the bell.

Mama didn't come. The bell light was sometimes hard for her to see, especially if it was sunny in the house. She probably had the shades pulled up to let the warmth in. More to the point, she wasn't expecting anyone. Adelaide reached for her key and had just put it in the door when Mama finally opened it and stuck her hand out for identification. She was wearing a housedress splattered with red stains. If she had known company was coming, she would never have turned up at the door dressed that way. Ashamed at her disheveled appearance, I was tempted to apologize to Eleanor until I remembered that she could see nothing. Two blind people unaware of what each other looked like.

"Hello, Mama," Adelaide spelled.

"Something's wrong, isn't there? The baby?"

"No. All the babies are fine. I have someone with me, and Sha's here, too."

Mama spread her hand out. I took it. Puzzled, she waited for more.

"I'd like you to meet Eleanor," Adelaide said, as we walked in.

Eleanor followed my sister's hand and put hers into Mama's. Adelaide guided them both to the small table in the living room. My mother sat transfixed. This was the first person who wasn't deaf besides us who spoke in her hands. She wrapped them around Eleanor's, nodding to show she understood. "You're blind!" she exclaimed. "Oh my," she said in our direction. "Does she walk outside by herself?"

"I'll answer her," Eleanor said. "I have a driver who takes me to my appointments," she spelled and spoke at the same time.

Appointments! That tipped her off! Mama began to pull her hand away. "I don't understand why she's here. I didn't make any appointment!"

Eleanor kept Mama's hand tight in hers and spelled again. She kept her voice quiet this time, but the expression on Mama's face said that we had betrayed her. "I'm not going to learn braille, so you can leave. Thank you for coming, and good-bye!"

"Well, then can I visit you anyway?"

"What for?"

"I can teach you to cook and walk in the house without hurting yourself."

"I do well, thank you very much," she said, ladylike and polite. "I don't need your help!"

"I can teach you to weave, to make belts and potholders. Would you like that?"

"Weaving? You mean like sewing? I used to sew. I still do when my husband threads the needle for me." She rubbed her fingers along her lap—a dead giveaway to her thinking. Could this person teach her to stop pricking herself with the needle?

"There's a better way to thread your needle. You don't need your husband to do it."

Mama became quiet while she thought. She fussed with her housedress. "You should have told me she was coming. Look how I'm dressed." Then she laughed, realizing that Eleanor couldn't see her. "How long have you been blind?" she enunciated clearly.

"I had an infection when I was seventeen. It took its toll."

"I'm so sorry."

"Don't be. It's not the end of the world, Ruth. May I call you Ruth?"

"Yes."

"If you just want to talk, I'll come to hear you talk."

"Can you understand my voice? Sometimes people say they can, but I know they can't. I believe only my daughters can and maybe my sisters and my grandchildren. Have my daughters been translating my words to you?"

Eleanor spelled in her hand, "I understand you perfectly."

The discussion had taken over an hour of laborious hand-spelling. Sometimes they only held each other's hands; then each of them told the other about herself until my mother decided to trust Eleanor. "Would you like a cup of tea?"

"I'd love it," Eleanor signed.

Mama got up to put the kettle on. I turned to Adelaide and signed, "I think she's found herself a friend."

"Are you jealous?" my sister signed, smiling.

"A little."

"So am I."

We stifled our laughter so Eleanor wouldn't know we'd been sneaking talk. What we felt wasn't really funny—it was more a release of overwhelming emotion. Eleanor was going to make Mama different, different in a good way, but different. Our mother would change.

Mama came back with two cups, one for Eleanor and one for herself. She waved in our direction. "Can you help yourselves? You know where everything is."

From that moment on, Ruth and Eleanor were fast friends.

CHAPTER
26

FIRST THERE were potholders in a range of colors that Mama and Eleanor could only imagine. In the beginning, they were a garish mixture of colors—Eleanor's choice. As nicely as she was put together herself, her taste in potholders was sadly lacking. Papa recoiled when he saw them. Not wanting to offend Eleanor, Mama conferred with us on how to break it to her gently.

"Tell it to her straight," I offered. "It's a matter of coordination. Your kitchen is blue and white. Tell her you want blue and white. Tell her you'll even pay for the yarn if she doesn't have those colors."

Ultimately, blue and white checked or striped potholders clung to the side of the stove. Mama had done a fine job of weaving. After filling her own kitchen with potholders, she presented many to Adelaide and me, to Sarah, Aunt Marian, Aunt Selma, and the nice lady next door. Then there were belts for Al, Arthur, Papa, Little Joe, and the nice lady's husband. After those projects, she wove a lampshade of light wood, and Al constructed a base for the fixture. She displayed the lamp on her bedroom dresser. For my birthday, she glued seashells and bits of beads on a wooden box that I set on my makeup table.

She and Eleanor wrapped fine cloth around tiny plastic dolls that Mama presented to her granddaughters. "When Eleanor was a little girl, she made the same clothes for her dolls. It was before she was blind, so she remembers exactly how they look," she told the children. Eleanor was all she talked about lately. She even worried about her tripping up the stairs, so she checked her clock, the one whose glass face had been removed, and stood guard at the top of the steps at the appointed time.

Twice a week, Eleanor came to drink tea and talk and teach. When the weaving was done, Mama listened to Eleanor's life as if she'd been remembering one of her beloved novels. She told Eleanor about us and the grandchildren (there were four now since Adelaide had her second), and when I came to visit, she told me, filled with wonder over her new friend, how much she admired Eleanor.

Neither Adelaide nor I was invited to their meetings. We could tell only by Mama's prolific handiwork and the happiness she radiated that things were going well. But she still hadn't learned to read braille.

ADELAIDE CALLED one day to say she was pleased with Mama's progress. "I'm sure you are, too."

"I'm pleased she has a friend, Adelaide, but I've given up hoping she'll agree to braille. By the way, I researched this disease called Usher's. I checked the medical books in the downtown library. Eleanor may be right."

"Then why didn't anyone tell us?"

"I called Aunt Selma and told her what we heard. I figured she'd say she knew all along, but all she said was this woman was wrong to frighten us. I guess she really didn't know. I guess none of the aunts knew, but we can't be sure. We weren't always asked to come along to the doctors. Maybe they thought we were too young to hear it."

"I suppose we should tell Mama and Papa."

"Maybe they already know."

"Do you think?"

"If they don't know, shall we tell them that her life was predictable? What good would it do? This disease is incurable. There's nothing that will change it."

ONE DAY a year later, the phone rang. It was a message from Papa. "Come for dinner Saturday. Mama will make meat loaf. Addle and family are coming, too."

The table was already set with Mama's theater china. There was nothing Adelaide or I needed to do except help with the serving and clearing of the dishes. Papa seemed relaxed and happy.

"How's the work at the brewery?" Arthur asked, his fingers moving haltingly.

"Busy," Papa said. "I'm thinking of retiring next year, but they want me to stay a year longer."

"How are your finances?"

"My bank account is getting big," he laughed. He plugged his waiting cheek with Mail Pouch and waved the children to him. He pulled off a dollar for each of them, chuckling at their deaf "thank-you's." "Now we have a surprise."

Mama sat down in the center of all of us, her hands on a paper. She moved her fingers, her head bent, the top of her gray hair sparkling under the chandelier. It was a braille paper. A collective gasp of surprise rose from the dinner table. "Papa, why didn't you tell us?"

"Shush," he pointed to his lips. "She wanted to be sure. Now listen to her."

"Is everybody here?" Mama asked.

I shook her hand "yes."

"Are the children close by? This is for them."

I took her hand. "They're all here."

"Now listen," she said, spreading her fingers along the dots. "There was an old woman who lived in a shoe. She had so many children, she didn't know what to do." She raised her hand and put it in Papa's.

Papa asked, "Did she read it right? I made her practice every day."

"It's wonderful, Papa."

He spelled O-K in her hands, and she smiled to no one in particular. "Wait, let me find my place again." She rubbed along the lines. "She gave them some bread. . . ."

Adelaide looked at me with unabashed pride. She took Mama's hand and held it tight. Impatient to continue, Mama squeezed her hand and then let it go. The children listened intently. When it was over, they casually kissed her as if they'd been expecting their deaf and blind grandmother to read to them their whole lives, and now she had finally obliged them. It was, I'm sure, her proudest moment. In the years to come, she would wrap herself in her braille and read much more than nursery rhymes. She would read novels, current events magazines, and fashion journals. She would bombard me with recipes from her cookbooks and argue with Papa about world events. She would cry bittersweet tears, her arms wrapped around Eleanor when it was time they said good-bye. They would never meet again.

On that first night, when she moved her fingers haltingly, I noticed that everything in her house was perfect: handcrafted boxes with lids of fake gems and colored ribbons nestled in shelves and on the tables; fake flowers emerged from an old umbrella stand; artificial philodendra hung in pots from the ceiling.

"Easy to take care of," Mama smiled. "I'm not good with live plants. I drown them."

Even the furniture, which I thought was cheaply made, looked good. The sofa was the right height for reading her braille and good enough to last a long time. How could I know that they would outlast this furniture and buy another three rooms full that Papa assured Mama would outlast them? He was sixty-three. She was fifty-five. And how could anyone know that the best years of their lives were still to come?

PART

3

CHAPTER

27

T HEY CAME by train, first class, as they had done
on their honeymoon. She spread her braille on the
small table in their drawing room and read to pass the time. He
studied the railroad guide, informing her of their progress and
the reasons for their delays. They played solitaire, she with her
braille cards, he with his own. They had played gin rummy
together in the dining room at home, but she suspected he was
cheating, so they played alone, together. He guided her through
the heavy doors of each car until they reached the first-class
diner where they ate off fancy plates and poured coffee from silver pitchers. He was a sport, tipping the waiter and the porter
lavishly. After all, he could afford it, he told me. He had ten
thousand dollars in the bank, a Social Security check that paid
extra because Mama was blind, and a thirty-five-dollar-a-month
pension check from the Teamster's Union. Wasn't that wonderful? my father had asked Al. And Al, after years of muttering to
himself about the Teamsters, graciously replied, "Well, that's
terrific, Pa."

What was the point of scrimping and saving any more? He was
retired; now was the time to spend his rainy day money to come
to California to Andy's bar mitzvah and visit his old haunts. But
there was nothing left of the Los Angeles of his memories. The
gym on Spring Street was gone. The *Los Angeles Times* had no
articles on Dummy Jordan in its archives. Neither did the *Herald
Examiner*. For days he moped on my patio, munching incon-
solably on an orange picked from our tree.

"Nothing is the same," he complained as we searched for his past. "Los Angeles has changed. Main Street is different. Everything is different! The highways are too dangerous. I could never drive here."

"You *never* could drive, Papa," I reminded him.

"That's not so. I drove a '26 Olds once, but it wasn't mine, so I lost my touch. You know, when I was here back in. . . ." He counted the years on his fingers and poked imaginary milestones in the air until there got to be too many years, and he gave up. "Your Uncle Dave and I could have bought a piece of land out here back in those days for a thousand dollars. Well, Dave didn't want to buy it."

"Too bad, Papa. You would have been a millionaire today."

"Who needs a million dollars? I've got enough to have a good time, so let's have one, Ruthie," he poked her. "I'll show you the sights."

HE SHOWED her the things he remembered as well as the sights he'd never seen before. There were visits to Disneyland, where Mama marveled at all the twinkling lights and held Pluto's arm. And Tijuana, where the broken sidewalks and disintegrating curves told her of its poverty. And Las Vegas, where she perched on a stool, her lifeless hand in the till of the slot machine, the bottom of her coat dragging on the floor. Like a committed gambler, she pumped the lever with her good hand and counted her loot. "Sha," she whispered, when the till overflowed with quarters, "take the money and buy me a candy bar."

"Sure."

"But don't tell Papa."

"Why?"

She smirked. I realized then that she hadn't held change in her hand for years. Now she had the power to buy a candy bar. I took the money, bought two, and gave them to her. Offering me one, she gleefully unwrapped the other and indulged in a five-minute break before going back to the slots.

Papa looked up his old friends from Puddie's card room on Roosevelt Road. They wandered through the Stardust Casino, where they had now found a legitimate place to ply their skills. To his dismay, he found that "Red" Cohen, his card-playing buddy, was no longer red. He was as bald as a plucked chicken, and a sober realization spread over my father's face that he, too, was old. Swollen everywhere with arthritis, Papa was still imposing enough from the waist up, waving his arms in talk with enormous strength, but his legs hadn't kept up with the rest of him. He had to rely on a cane, holding it in his right hand for stability and relying on my mother with his left hand for support. If someone had dared to cut through them, she would have been stranded in darkness, and he would have had to totter with only the cane to hold him up. He was seventy-one.

She had just turned sixty-three. Her full hips were gone and her fine bosom flat, but her cheekbones were still high in her sunken face and her skin unusually smooth for a woman her age. Sarah remarked to Adelaide that her face had remained unlined because she saw none of the ravages of time on others.

ROSY-CHEEKED and dressed in her favorite color, blue, her gray hair falling softly around her face, Mama beamed as she sat in the first pew of our modern synagogue, her hands caressing Ellen and my younger son, Larry. Andy read a portion of the Torah, while Papa, the honored guest, sat behind him on a thronelike chair. He wore a yarmulke. After the service, he took Mama's hand and greeted our guests. With pencil and paper, he made small talk, then spelled their words in Mama's hand. She nodded politely.

Emboldened by friendly stares, the children fingerspelled and signed to each other. I smiled, remembering the goldfish days of my own childhood. If any of this bothered the children, there was never a hint of it. They had had a wonderful time, they told their grandparents. Next year they would show them the San Diego Zoo.

EVERY YEAR Mama and Papa came by train to spend the winter. Outraged at the thought of being tagged like school-children on a field trip, they tucked a slip of paper with Adelaide's and my phone numbers on it into the recesses of their clothing, assuring us that in an emergency, someone would dig deep enough to find it. Besides, Raymond, the porter, would take good care of them. They paper-and-penciled together. Raymond was a fine man.

One year my father's cane proved too thin to do its part, so Raymond brought them their meals on a fancy tray. Papa tipped him "big time." Then, because he couldn't rely on his knees to hold him up ("one day they're good, another day they're bad," he wrote me), they gave up their apartment and moved in with Adelaide. "Six months with Sha in Los Angeles," he told Little Joe, "then six months with Addle."

"HOW MANY tobacco animals on your bathroom wall?" I asked Adelaide when she phoned one day.

"I've counted five this time. When they leave next week, I'll wash the wall. For six months, it'll stay clean. How about you?"

"He spits it in the flower bed. My begonias are the best-look-ing ones on the street. Do they hate staying with you?" I asked Adelaide.

"They don't say a word. What do you hear when they come out west?"

"Nothing. I don't question them. I think they feel they've run out of options. They seem content, though. When they get off the train, it's still like they're on a vacation. At least for a while, until they read in the paper that the snow's gone in Chicago. Then Mama looks forward to being with *your* children."

"So we'll go on this way," Adelaide said, "until one of them gets fed up with the arrangement."

"Then what?"

"A home, maybe?"

"Never."

"You're right. Never."

CHAPTER

28

I T WAS a week after their arrival. They had unpacked, set up Mama's braille on the small table in their room, taken their walks to familiarize themselves again with our neighborhood, and picked our oranges to keep in their room. They said hello again to the dogs and cats and scooped up the kids' torn jeans and socks for their yearly mending. They visited the deaf temple in Van Nuys and said hello to their California friends. They had settled in for another winter. And then Papa started talking of retirement homes. Well, that's what I assumed he meant.

"But, Sha," Papa said. "This is not a home. This is an apartment building for the deaf."

"How do you know about it?" I asked.

"Your Aunt Flora is moving there. She's tired of the Chicago winters."

"She never told me. Not once did she write to me that there was such a place!"

"Then see for yourself. Flora's not the only one. Some of our Chicago friends are renting apartments there."

"Mama, what do you think?"

"She's the one who really wants it," Papa interrupted.

"Let her speak, Papa. You have this terrible habit of speaking for her and cutting up her food. I bet she could do it if you only gave her the chance."

He threw me a slightly wounded look. I don't know why I picked this time to challenge him. I suppose it was my own hurt.

Here he was, talking of leaving Adelaide and me and giving hardly a thought to our feelings.

"Ask her. Go ahead, ask her," he demanded.

I put my fingers in hers. She shook her head yes and then said, "This is nobody's fault. You and Addle have been wonderful. But now that Papa's using a walker, it's impossible to travel by train. It's time to stay in California full time. But to stay all year with you is too hard on everybody."

"Then take the plane."

She didn't answer.

"Why is it hard? We've managed before, Mama."

She laughed her polite cover-her-mouth laugh. "Three children, two dogs, two cats, and Larry's snake—my God, you have a houseful!" She tilted her head in Papa's direction, then turned away from him. "Is he watching me speak to you?"

"Yes, but, of course, he can't hear you, Mama."

"If what I hear about this place is true, I think it will be wonderful for both of us. You know, Papa's not getting any younger."

"I promised you. Never a home."

"This is not a home."

"All right, let's see it. But I don't think you've got your information right. I've never heard of an apartment building for the deaf. It has to be a nursing home, and it can't be just for deaf people. I refuse to let you even think of such a thing. Papa can still get around." In truth, he could barely manage. His walker had become a permanent extension of himself.

PILGRIM TOWER was an imposing thirteen-story building set on Vermont Avenue in the mid-Wilshire district. The small lawn in front was beautifully manicured, but I was still pessimistic about its promise. I couldn't believe the things Papa had said about government subsidies and that the Lutheran church had built it. Besides, what were Jews going to do in a

237

Lutheran development? We sat down in the manager's office. I had my list of questions. Opal Jones, the manager, was ready for me. Rotund and middle-aged, she filled the space between desk and back wall, leaving no room for anything else. She rattled off a list of amenities, the rental price, activities, the special TV signals, and the lights over the apartment doors. She explained all those things to me while she signed to my father in flawless sign language.

"You sign very well," I told her.

"My parents were deaf, too," she said.

"How did this place get started?"

"Pastor Jonas, who preached to the deaf, thought there should be a special housing project for the senior deaf—a place where they could be in their own environment, not stuck in a place where they couldn't communicate. I don't know if you've looked into retirement housing for them, but, believe me, it's hard to get admitted to one of the standard developments if you're deaf. They won't take you if you can't hear fire bells."

"No, I didn't know that," I said. "I've never investigated it. There was no reason for us to consider it. My father and mother manage very well!"

I wondered again what the hell they were going to do in a Lutheran home. What was Aunt Flora thinking of? At the end of their lives, they were going to be converted! I was convinced that, if they moved here, they'd be brainwashed. Well, not Mama. But Papa! No, Papa doesn't even believe in God. But Aunt Flora. What's gotten into her?

"We're Jewish, you know," I prompted Opal.

"This is a nonsectarian building," she responded. "In order to get government subsidies, we need to follow those rules."

"And what are the rules?"

"An applicant must be over sixty-five, deaf or otherwise handicapped, and have an income of less than . . ." she spoke and signed.

238

So far, the rules seemed tailor-made for Mama and Papa. "And blind?" I asked Opal.

"As long as they can take care of themselves, they can live here. They must be ambulatory. We have a small kitchen, but that's for parties and meetings. We don't cook for the tenants. They have their own kitchens. Understand, this is a standard apartment building, but we're set up for deaf communication. We can make appointments for them and take phone calls. My husband also signs. There is a van that will take them shopping and to their doctor if they need it. Otherwise, public transportation is very good in this area. There is also a doctor in the area who signs."

My father listened intently to her signing, nodding his understanding, and my mother waited for someone to tell her something. "Let's look at one of the apartments, Ruthie," Papa said, helping her out of her chair. Opal pulled a key from a bank of keys on the wall. "These are master keys. Just in case their alarm bell goes off, and we need to get in."

"Alarm bell?"

"Yes. There's one in the bathroom. If you're living alone, it's easy to lie on the floor for hours before someone finds you've slipped and fallen. Follow me."

"What are these?" I pointed to the signs hanging from doorways.

"We call them roosters. If they're still on the doorknobs after ten o'clock, we come into the apartment to see if the tenants are okay."

Just then a dozen doors opened, and a dozen hands emerged and removed the roosters. I looked at my watch. It was a quarter to ten.

"I assume you're interested in a one-bedroom?" she asked my father.

"Yes, why not? The rent is reasonable."

"The studio apartments are best suited for a single person, don't you think?"

"Yes, of course," Papa signed.

"I understand your sister, Flora, will be renting a one-bed-room."

Papa replied vehemently, "Well, if a single woman wants to waste her money, it's her business. My wife and I wouldn't consider anything less than a one-bedroom."

"Yes, of course," Opal agreed.

Mama trudged along the corridor, her arm in my father's as he lumbered along with his walker. In order to sign to Opal, he had to stop walking. Mama walked, then, as Papa stopped, she lurched to a halt like the caboose at the end of a train. Eventually, we reached apartment number 402.

I took my mother's arm, and we investigated the apartment together. A bedroom, small but big enough for twin beds. Papa had become too clumsy in bed, pushing Mama toward the edge. She had decided years ago that she was more comfortable in her own bed. We toured through the kitchen, the living room, a small bathroom, and one closet. A light on the ceiling was hooked up to the doorbell. The apartment was freshly painted, boasted new draperies, and had attractive carpeting.

"It seems very nice. Is there a place for my braille?" Mama asked.

"We'll get you a small desk and put it on this wall," Papa said, stopping to confer with her.

"What do you think, Sha?" Mama asked me.

"I think we need to talk about this some more."

As we left the apartment, Opal said, "We have two tenants who are half-sighted. I think your mother would find them good company."

So there were deaf-blind people around. How would my mother feel about that, I wondered. As we rode down the elevator, Opal said, "The Braille Institute is only a few miles away. Did you know they have a Deaf-Blind club?"

My heart stopped. I took my mother's hand and told her. Wonder spread over her face. My father seemed surprised.

"Can we go by bus?" he asked.

"Our van will take you. I believe they meet twice a week." We walked past the large recreation room with its card tables and chairs, a large television set with closed-captioning, and a pool table. I saw dozens of people signing and whooping their deaf noises. Papa asked for an application, promising Opal he would look it over, fill it out, and return it by mail. But my mother reminded him, "Sha wants to talk it over with us first."

"All right," Papa said, "we'll talk it over." He folded the application and put it in his pocket. He moved his walker to the door of the recreation room and watched the pool players. I could see his mouth chomping on his tobacco and his mind working, "Well, I could handle a game of pool . . . just rest my legs against the edge and shoot." One of the players saluted hello. He waved back and said good-bye to Opal. We drove home.

All the way home, I wanted to ask him who would do the shopping and how often he thought we could come to see him (the valley was a long drive from Vermont Avenue). Wouldn't they miss us? I wanted to know. Unable to take my eyes off the road to spell or watch him spell back, I bided my time until we were back home. I pulled my coat off hurriedly and asked.

"Didn't you hear Opal say the van will take us to the supermarket?" he reminded me.

"But can you manage with the walker?"

"All right," he conceded, "you can come every two weeks to do the shopping."

"Every week! And we'll take you to lunch or dinner."

"My treat!"

"All right, your treat. And if I don't like the doctor in the neighborhood, you'll go to the one near me."

"Of course."

"And you won't have Thanksgiving dinner in the rec room. You'll come to my house."

"Do they make Thanksgiving dinner at Pilgrim Tower?"

"Yes, there are people there who haven't any families."

"But we do," Mama smiled, "so we'll spend the holidays with the family like we always have. Nothing's changed, Sha. And please remember, it's not your fault or Addle's. It's nobody's fault. I like the plaçe."

I looked at Papa. He was smiling and holding her hand. I think it was the pool table that convinced him. But I knew the idea was right. It was so right, in fact, that it seemed that God had decided to give Papa another chance to believe in him. And the Deaf-Blind Club. My God, how is it that I'd never thought to investigate the opportunities for Mama at the Braille Institute? When I mentioned my oversight to Opal, she said, "It's understandable. You were a close family, working things out your own way."

I CALLED Adelaide and gave her the news.

"You mean they're never coming back?"

"Of course, they'll come back for visits. They'll take the train like they always do, although Mama's been complaining lately that it takes too long. They're considering flying."

"Don't change the subject," she said, tearfully. "I want to know all about this place."

She asked all the questions I had asked of Opal. And I answered her in the same way, remembering the bell lights and the alarm systems. I told her everything.

Papa and Mama sat at my kitchen table, Papa intently watching my movements, waiting for Adelaide's approval.

"I remember Aunt Flora telling me about this place," Adelaide recalled. "I didn't believe she'd go through with it, though."

"Well, she has. She'll be living on the thirteenth floor, and Papa and Mama will be on the fourth. Do you think it's far enough away from each other to keep another war from starting?"

Adelaide laughed. "Post a notice on the recreation room door. Only one Herzberg at a time."

"Ad, I'm sure they'll come to see you often. And you'll come here."

"Art and the kids and I will as soon as they've made the move. Tell them I think it's a fine idea, but, Char, I don't really know, but don't tell them that. Just tell them. . . ."

I told Papa that Adelaide had given her blessing. He smiled, spelled into Mama's hand, and they walked off to the patio.

"Well, I told them it's okay with you."

Adelaide's voice trembled, "It sounds too good to be true."

"What it sounds like, Adelaide, is that for the first time in our lives, we won't be their ears and eyes."

CHAPTER

29

WE CAME every week as I had promised and as Papa had agreed to. But soon they had no time for us. One Sunday the van was taking the group to Lawry's factory to see how spices were made. Another Sunday they were going to Lake Arrowhead. The following month was the Valentine's Day party in the rec room. At the Deaf-Blind club, Papa made himself useful, serving cake and coffee while Mama visited with the others. The club was an enormous tonic to Mama. She went back to working with crafts. This time she and her newfound friends discussed and compared their handiwork. Their meetings were filled with nonstop words flowing through their fingers.

There were endless games of pool and numerous meetings in the rec room at Pilgrim Tower. My parents spent countless hours talking to anyone and everyone in the elevators, the laundry room, and the small convenience store on the first floor. While Papa played pool and argued politics with the others over coffee, Mama passed the time with Ethel, whose eyes were failing, and Bertha, who was completely blind.

She kept an immaculate home as always, feeling for crumbs on the floor and lint on the carpets. She cooked, he served. She read her braille, he watched TV with the sound off. Once in a while, she wanted to gossip, so she waved a hand in his direction. He poked her side with the cane he kept (for that purpose solely, I believe) to say he was listening, but many times he was watching the ball game and only pretending to listen.

Every night she served danish and made her muddy coffee, which he poured. Every night she stood ready, towel in hand, to help him out of the tub. Animals blossomed on her bathroom wall. Instinctively, she ran a wet sponge over it every few days. He checked the lights and the gas under the coffee pot before they went to bed. And if they needed anything, all they had to do was open their door and walk downstairs to the manager's office.

THERE WAS one chore he couldn't handle, however. When we came every two weeks to visit them, he treated us to lunch, and we helped him with the grocery shopping. Papa pushed the grocery cart. Al picked up items from Papa's list, running back to the car where I sat with Mama, needing an explanation of Papa's misspelled words.

"What is a gelish?" he'd ask, and I'd interpret, "gefilte fish."

"What is an orange juicy?" he'd ask. I'd respond, "orange juice."

"And toilets? What the hell does he mean by toilets?"

"Does it say six toilets?"

"Yes."

"Well, he wants six rolls of toilet paper. It doesn't take a genius to figure that out, now does it?"

Shrugging his shoulders, he returned to the store. Inevitably, as soon as he got used to Papa's uniquely spelled grocery lists, Papa would find something else advertised on TV and write his wishes down, befuddling Al all over again. One year, when they had become so firmly rooted in Pilgrim Tower that I could not imagine them living anywhere else, Papa requested a bottle of "forty niner."

I looked at the word, poked my head through the window, and notified Al, "He wants a bottle of 409 cleaner."

"How the hell do you know?"

"I just know."

"Smart engineer," I smirked to Mama as Al walked back into the store.

"It's Papa who is a pest," she complained. "I swear, when he dies, I'll never marry again."

I shook with laughter. Who would marry her? Who would want a deaf and blind old woman? Mama saw nothing funny in her statement. She stared straight ahead, but the nerves in her cheek were twitching. Ashamed, I composed myself again. "What's wrong now?" I asked.

"Blood in his bowels."

"Hemorrhoids, that's all. Remember the doctor told us it was nothing to worry about?"

"He eats the wrong foods."

"Maybe. What else is wrong?"

"He never picks up anything he's dropped on the floor. Papers everywhere. Little pieces of paper."

"He can't get up again if he kneels down to pick them up. It's too hard for him."

"So *I* have to do it. I tell you I'm getting tired of it. I'm thinking of getting a cleaning woman."

"Can Aunt Flora help?"

"As soon as Flora walks in the door, the fighting starts."

"About what?"

"Do they have to have a reason?"

"That's too bad, Mama. It must be hard for you. I know you two are good friends. Do you get a chance to visit her alone in her apartment?"

"Of course not. Papa never lets me walk out of the apartment alone. He's afraid something will happen to me."

I hadn't realized that Papa was always holding on to her. I thought she'd be freer in the building. "Well, a cleaning woman is a good idea, Mama."

"You think so?"

"Why not?"

246

"Then I'll do it."

"Good for you."

"But do we have the money?"

"Doesn't Papa tell you?"

"Yes, but I don't believe him."

"Why not?"

"I think he's betting on the horses again."

"You mean he's going to the track?"

"No, of course not. But there are men in this building. . . ." Her words trailed off. "I know for a fact he places bets with them."

"Perfectly harmless."

"Why would you say that? I don't want to be broke again. Ever!"

"Mama, in case you don't know, Papa shows me his bank book. He's got plenty of money, so don't worry about it. Get your cleaning lady."

"I'll show him!"

"Good. Now don't forget to mark your braille calendar with a thumbtack on December 4. The party is all arranged. Any more guests you want me to invite?"

"Adelaide's coming, isn't she?"

"She wouldn't miss your fiftieth anniversary if she had pneumonia."

"She has pneumonia? You didn't tell me!"

"No, Mama, you missed some of my spelling." Oh lord, my fingers were tired.

"Did you remember to invite Frances Mannino, the director of the Deaf-Blind club?"

"Of course."

"I admire her so much. Do you remember Eleanor, the lady who taught me braille? Frances reminds me of her. Another blind woman who helps others." She smiled, and then she said, "Flora says the Beverly Hillcrest is a beautiful place."

"Yes, it is. And then we go to Hawaii. Are you excited about that?"

"I'm thrilled. But maybe it's too hard for Papa."

"Don't worry. We've arranged for a wheelchair. He can see the sights sitting down."

"Good idea."

"And, please, Mama, wear the dress we picked out at the May Company. And the slip I bought you."

"What slip?"

"My birthday present to you! You never remember our presents. Addle asked me if you liked the sweater she sent. I had to pretend I knew you had a new sweater. Where is it?"

"In my drawer somewhere. I keep forgetting if it's blue or black. I should ask Papa, but he's so busy all the time."

"Well, Addle's coming, so you'd better pull out the sweater. And my slip!"

"I'll try to remember," she laughed. "I have so many clothes, it's hard to keep up with them."

I FORGOT Mama's corsage. It was still in the refrigerator when Adelaide and I walked into the banquet room, but Mama didn't care. Two drinks of champagne, and she became a whirlwind. At seventy-seven, she was still beautiful, dressed in a blue print dress with a gold medallion on a chain around her neck. Adelaide had made her face up and teased her hair into the latest style. Mama kissed fifty guests as they arrived to honor her.

Papa thumped his walker to every table and shook everyone's hands. Then he returned to the head table and made an emotional speech. Mama waited her turn. She rose and addressed the unseen crowd, arms extended before her in a collective embrace. Then she moved fingers in talk.

"I don't think I've ever seen Mama so happy," Adelaide cried, "and I haven't the foggiest idea what she's saying to all those people. Her hands are moving too fast."

"She's probably calling Papa a bum."

248

I FISHED the corsage from the refrigerator the next morning and put it on Mama's shoulder. Our first stop was Honolulu. The wheelchair was a splendid idea, and we decided to get one for Mama, too. For a while, she sat comfortably as we wheeled them through the sights, but Mama eventually became morose.

"What's wrong?" we asked her. "Aren't you having a good time? Everybody's been so nice, giving you special tours, letting you touch things."

"Yes, they've been nice. I appreciate it," she said dourly.

"Then what's wrong?"

"I can't talk to Papa while I'm in this chair. I can't feel him. I need to feel him so we can talk."

"I'm sorry, Mama," Adelaide apologized. "We didn't realize."

For the rest of the trip, she hung on to his arm. It greatly complicated our movements, but she refused to be separated from him.

Our next stop was Maui. We had planned it for the end of the trip so they could rest. We reserved separate condominiums on the water's edge. Papa was incensed when we pulled up to the building. "What is this place? An apartment?"

"No, it's a hotel."

"How can it be a hotel?" he challenged, coming through the door. "There's no lobby or bell captain. There's no dining room. Where are we going to eat?" He turned to Mama to tell her of the disaster.

"You mean I have to cook?" she exclaimed.

"No," I laughed. "We'll go out to eat. We thought you'd be exhausted by now, so we picked a quiet place to relax."

They were not convinced. To make matters worse, Mama discovered the kitchen in their room. She gave me an "I thought so" look but unpacked anyway. I took the extra key to their room and went to my own room, dismayed by their disappointment. I rang Adelaide. Arthur answered, his voice groggy.

"What are we going to do about the folks? They seem unhappy," I asked him.

"Maybe they'll understand after a nice nap. I'm tired myself. I'm gonna take a snooze on the balcony with my face to the sun. Talk to your sister."

"What's up?" she asked into the receiver.

"They're upset."

"They're tired. I'm tired. One island was enough for me!" She thought for a while, then suggested, "How about a fancy dinner at a supper club this evening? Give the sport a chance to tip big time."

"Maybe Aunt Selma was right when she said it would be tricky to take them on a long trip. If we're tired, they must be in a coma!"

"Why would Aunt Selma say that?"

"Well, Papa *is* eighty-five!"

"So, if he dies in Hawaii, he will have seen Hawaii." She hung up the phone.

My sister was right. She understood Papa's need for glamour and adventure. He was a man who traveled first class when he had the money, who stayed in elegant hotels and slept in drawing rooms on a train. As a young man, with no money in his pocket, he had managed to find excitement in new places discovered while riding the boxcars. A quiet condo on the beach wasn't his style.

Feeling guilty, I returned to their room and suggested the fancy dinner to make up for my poor choice in lodgings.

Papa liked the idea. Excitedly, he told Mama. Her eyes sparkled. "Okay, we'll be ready at six," he said. "Knock hard on the door. We'll answer."

"No need. I've got an extra key. See you in a couple of hours."

AT SIX o'clock, my sister, Arthur, Al, and I, dressed up in our finery, let ourselves in to their room. Papa was sitting in a chair in his undershorts, a baseball cap on his head. He was fast asleep. Mama was nowhere to be found. Panic struck until Adelaide discovered her under the covers. She was snoring.

We broke into uncontrollable laughter at the sight. Adelaide found a chair and plopped into it, holding her sides.

"Well, no fancy dinner tonight. We'll never make it," said Arthur.

"Oh, let them sleep. We'll do the dinner tomorrow," I told them.

Al whispered, "I'll get some cold cuts and salads for them. We'll leave them a note."

"You don't have to whisper," I whispered.

"I keep forgetting."

We tiptoed out of the room anyway.

THE FOLLOWING morning, rested from their sleep and mildly embarrassed, they joined us for a breakfast of fresh pineapple, toast, and coffee. Papa was wearing a colorful Hawaiian shirt. Mama wore the muumuu Papa had bought her in Honolulu and a lei of frangipani around her neck. After the meal, we boarded a glass bottom boat. A pleasant and helpful tour guide put every living thing and some dead ones into Mama's hand. "Tell her this is a. . . ."

I told her, feeling squeamish at the sight of the marine creatures, but Mama touched them like a biologist. "Isn't that interesting?" she murmured politely. She told me to thank him for his kindness. We moved on to other sights.

As Papa thumped his walker, my mother's hand on his, they examined the banyan tree. He explained it all to her, reading from a brochure he had taken from our "hotel." After lunch at a beachside café, we rode up the coast, stopping to watch the surfers skim over giant waves. "How do they do that?" wondered Papa. "I was light on my feet in my day, but these boys amaze me. Ruthie, they take this board and. . . ."

"You're joking."

"No, Ruthie, ask the girls."

"Yes, Mama. They take this board and. . . ."

They settled back in their seats, and we drove off again. An hour later, their eyes closed in fatigue. Papa's baseball cap hid half his face, and Mama's head lolled on my father's shoulder.

"They're missing the waterfalls," I wailed.

"Oh, leave them alone," Adelaide said.

By the time we reached Hana, traveling on winding, badly paved roads, they had stirred alive again.

"Where are we?" Papa asked.

"Hana," I told him.

"Very pretty," he said, slightly embarrassed again.

"Smells lovely," my mother added.

"We don't have to go out tonight," I offered as we made our way back to Maui.

"Of course, we do," a chagrined Mama responded. "We're rested now. We'll see you at six."

WHEN I put my key into their lock at the designated time, we found them dressed up in their best clothes, sitting in their chairs, fast asleep like two store mannequins who'd fallen off their pedestals.

"Should we let them sleep?" I asked Adelaide.

"No. It's our last night here," she chuckled. "They'd be awfully unhappy if they missed the fancy stuff."

"You're right," I said. I poked Papa gently on the shoulder. He awoke, startled. "Is it time?"

"Yes, Papa."

"Okay. Ruthie, it's time," he said, shaking her fingers.

Mama changed from sleeping old lady to smiling flapper. She stood straight and tall as we rode down in the elevator. She strode into the elegant dining room with Papa as if she was expected. He settled her into her chair and held her hand while fire dancers pranced on the stage.

The dinner show continued with a baritone singing "Sweet Leilani." Papa watched politely, applauding when it was over. When dinner was served, Adelaide poured Mama a glass of wine, and I began cutting her chicken. Papa threw daggers at me with his eyes. "This is my job," his eyes said. "Back off!" I let go of the knife and fork.

While an unfunny comedian delivered his act, Papa and Mama carried on an intimate conversation. Their hands carefully shielded from us, they spoke of things unknown.

AN IMPROMPTU welcoming committee greeted us in the lobby of Pilgrim Tower. We waved hello.

"Wonderful time," Papa signed to all of them. "We'll tell you more tomorrow. I've got souvenirs for everyone!" He put his hands on his walker and thumped to the elevator. Mama walked in by herself.

Flora was in their apartment, waiting. She had made a fresh pot of coffee and was sitting next to the pile of braille magazines that she had kindly offered to retrieve from their mailbox. Bristling at the sight of her, my father chewed hard on his tobacco, then graciously thanked his sister.

"It was a good trip," Mama told Flora. "Addle and Sha are the best daughters a person could have."

I never recalled her saying that before.

Flora smiled.

ENDINGS

One

THREE YEARS later, Mama talked of going to the Panama Canal, that elusive place of her daydreams, but Papa wasn't up to it. He had developed congestive heart failure. The doctor said medication would help, and Papa, although thinner than he'd been in years, moved about unusually well for his age. I promised her that when Papa died, we'd take the trip alone, just the three of us—Mama, Adelaide, and I.

"Which reminds me, Sha," she said as we remained in the car while the men shopped for groceries. "I've been thinking about this wonderful place. You know, the home for the deaf and blind. I was thinking that's where I'd like to live when Papa dies."

"I don't know anything about it."

"You know. I told you. Frances Mannino mentioned it to me."

"It's not something I'd like to discuss with you now."

"But Papa's much older than I am. I think we should talk."

"We'll talk another time. Papa's coming back with Al. I have to help him put the groceries in the trunk."

I'd told her before that she needn't worry, that Adelaide and I would take care of her. But every time I said it, she shrugged her shoulders. I couldn't believe she still wanted her independence. But how could I have thought otherwise? Although she had become forgetful—new slips and blouses tucked away in her drawers, chagrined when they were exposed—she was still full of the sass and vinegar she had showed during my childhood. I felt

254

abandoned by her when she talked about going to live in a strange place. I knew it was not what Papa wanted.

Just months before, as Papa and I sat in Dr. Paul's waiting room on the day of his checkup, I acknowledged that I knew he would die one day and that we needed to sort things out for the future. It was the grownup and practical thing to do. But it was hard for me to say it. I still felt like the little girl who walked the neighborhood streets in awe of Papa's popularity, wanting to stand in front of Charlie Mandel's candy store and peek through his legs as he talked to his friends, wanting to hold his huge hand as we walked past the four o'clocks. While Mama sat next to me, her eyes closed, bored with the waiting, I said, "Papa, you know you never have to worry. Addle and I will always take care of her."

He stared at me for a long time. I remember thinking, "The silence is deafening in here."

"I have enough insurance to take care of my funeral and hers," he finally answered. "You don't have to worry about it."

"But, Papa, I want to ask you about this place. . . ."

Mama stirred in her chair. She opened her eyes, put her hand in mine, and asked, "Did Papa go in yet?"

"No, Mama, we're still waiting."

She settled her hands in her lap and closed her eyes again. He looked at her with warm eyes, then put a plug in his mouth and chewed carefully. "Mama will live with you for six months and with Addle for six months."

He moved his fingers quickly as if he'd been meaning to say it for a long time and finally found the opportunity. But then I realized he knew he never had to say it. It wasn't a question of dependency. It was his understanding of the right thing to do. I nodded my head in agreement. The doctor poked his head out the door. "Mr. Herzberg."

"The doctor's ready for you, Papa."

Papa got up and moved his walker steadily into the examining room.

IT WAS Thanksgiving of 1981. We sat in my dining room after dinner, the dishes washed and dried. Mama was still wiping the last of the silverware and putting them back in their slots in the silverware case. Her cheeks were flushed.

"Mama, are you feeling all right?"

"I'm fine. Just a little warm."

Four days later, at the age of eighty, she died from a massive heart attack. Adelaide came the day before and spelled her name in Mama's hand. We stood in Papa's living room and shivered as Papa made the most awful noise we'd ever heard come from his mouth—he moaned like a wounded animal. After the funeral, I helped him collect her things. An empty pill bottle stood on her dresser under the handwoven lamp she'd made in Chicago. It was her blood pressure medicine. By counting the days, I could see it had been empty for at least a month.

"Papa, didn't she ask you to refill this?"

"I didn't know it was empty," he said.

"Maybe she forgot."

"Maybe."

I packed her braille magazines to take to the Braille Institute. She hadn't done much reading in those last months. Her fingers were losing their sensitivity to the dots.

Two

WE BROUGHT him home every weekend so he could treat us to dinner and watch the ball game with Andy and Larry. When the ball game ended one day and the boys had left and Ellen was entertaining friends in the den, I asked Papa, "What was she like?"

"You mean when she young?"

"Yes, before I knew her. She was pretty, don't you think?"

"You saw her picture. Yes, she was pretty. She was sweet. A sweet girl. I feel half of me gone," he signed. "What is right word? Balance? Yes, my balance gone. Is that right word, Sha?"

"It's a very good word, Papa."

"Time to go home?"

"If you want."

"Yes, tired."

Because it was too hard for him to buckle the seat belt in the front seat, he sat in the back seat while I drove. I fingerspelled backward so we could talk. "Tell me more about Ruthie," I asked him.

I watched through the rear view mirror. He put his fingers to his lips. It was a simple sign that said, "I don't want to talk anymore."

Flora came to talk with him after she'd picked up the pieces of paper he dropped on the floor, but he didn't want to talk with her either.

Every morning when he awoke, he waved hello to Mama's picture on the wall. He told me that was why he wanted the older picture of her, the one where she was gray and thin. I'd suggested the picture of the youthful Ruthie, the one where she wore her flapper dress, but he barely remembered the young girl he had courted. I had a copy made of the flapper picture and sent it to Adelaide and kept the original for myself.

When I came one day and let myself in with my key, I saw him sitting in his rocker, talking to her. "I'm tired, Ruthie. Very tired."

I stood in front of him. "Hello," he said, palms up. "Why you here?"

"The doctor says your tests show something. He wants you in the hospital."

"Maybe that's why I tired."

"Maybe."

THE TELEVISION set was on a shelf, too high on the wall for Papa to watch it comfortably. He shifted his weight in the hospital bed trying to find a good position from which to see the color TV. Papa hated color TV, but the last game of the series was on. I had brought a coloring book with me, a silly diversion for a middle-aged woman, but I'd always loved to color. I displayed the pages for him now and then. "See how nice I color, Papa?"

"Very nice," he said.

I didn't say those words, and he didn't answer that way; I just showed the pictures to him, and he nodded in a half smile. He dozed on and off. I watched his fitful sleep, then went back to coloring. Sometimes he dozed too long and missed a couple of good plays. I prodded him. "Too bad. Looks like the Dodgers are going to lose." He smiled his half smile and dozed again.

He was scheduled for tests the next day. Whatever was wrong with him was serious. He knew it but didn't want to talk about it. And I knew it when he had spit his last tobacco juice in the toilet the day before and left his Mail Pouch on the coffee table.

The Phillies were celebrating their victory when he opened his eyes and sat up.

"They lost," I explained.

He seemed surprised, disappointed with the Dodgers, as if they had betrayed him. "It's all over," he said. "No more baseball." He fell asleep again.

My back was to the wall across the room; bright sunlight streamed in through the window. Feeling a warmth over my right shoulder, I turned to see if I were standing close to a wall heater, but there was nothing. Not even a splash of sunlight. I smiled and colored. "Mama's here," I thought. And then, because it seemed so ridiculous to think it, I moved away from the wall.

The family came to take me to dinner. It was my fifty-fourth birthday. Papa smiled. "Happy birthday. Don't worry about me."

I drank too much wine, giggling when the waitress brought me a little cake with a candle on it. I blew it out.

"We need to talk about Papa," I said as they drove me back to the hospital.

"We'll talk later. It's your birthday. Try to have a pleasant time with him."

He was sitting in a chair when I came into his room. "Did you have good birthday?" he signed.

"Yes, Papa. And don't forget *your* birthday in two weeks. We've planned a big party for your ninetieth. Addle will be here."

He looked confused. "Your birthday," he said.

"No, Papa, your birthday. Fifteen days after mine."

"Who wants to be ninety?" he grunted.

"Do you want to go back to bed?"

He nodded yes. I put the walker in front of him so he could walk back on his own, but he was too weak. We walked there together, my arms around him, and sat on the side of the bed. Then he slumped. The heavy weight I'd felt seconds before was gone. I propped his feet up on the bed and covered him with the blanket. I poked him. "Papa?"

THE FAMILY came back, and the nurse helped me gather his things. I took his watch and the belt buckle with his engraved initials, the one he kept on his belt from the time he boxed in Yuma. And the glasses he wore from the time he moved into Pilgrim Tower.

"Do you want the walker?" the nurse asked.

"No."

"Do you want the coloring book?"

"Leave it with him."

1983

ADELAIDE TELEPHONED. She wanted to know if it was time for her to send Mama's wedding ring to me.

"Has it been six months?" I asked her.

"It's your turn now," she said.

"Do you want me to send you the bride and groom, Ad? I've had them for a while."

"No, that's okay. You keep them."

"How about Papa's prayer book?"

"No, you gave me his belt buckle. Remember?"

"When am I going to see you?"

"In the winter," Adelaide promised. "The real reason for my phone call is because something wonderful happened today."

"Really? Let me guess. You're pregnant."

"Very funny."

"Then what?" I laughed.

"I was on the bus this morning and saw a deaf woman with a little girl. I knew she wasn't deaf. She couldn't have been more than seven or eight."

"So?"

"I couldn't help myself. I had to say something to her."

"The little girl or the mother?"

"I told the mother about Mama and Papa. She smiled sort of funny as if I was invading her privacy."

"And the girl? What did she think when you let loose with your fingers?"

"She didn't pay much attention to my signing. I guess she thought I was deaf. But when I finally spoke to her and told her about our childhood, she lit up like a sabbath candle."

"I wish I'd been there," I said.

"Yeah, me too," she answered.

ACKNOWLEDGMENTS

I WISH to acknowledge Theodore Berland, Paul Rubenstein, and Linda Feldman for their wisdom, friendship, and enthusiasm for this project. To my husband Al for his encouragement and computer expertise and to my editor, Ivey Pittle Wallace, for her patience and good humor.